# Dr. Robert S. de Ropp

biochemist, formerly a visiting investigator at the Rockefeller Institute, has carried out research in the fields of cancer, mental illness, and drugs which affect behavior. His books, which have influenced people of all generations, especially the young, include *The Master Game, Drugs and the Mind,* and *The New Prometheans.* In his role as the Gardener in *Church of the Earth,* he "looks over the lattice of his life" and finds that he has launched "three children, two houses, six kayaks, seven books, forty-five scientific papers, a fertile garden, and fifteen fruit trees." When he broke ground for the Temple of Church of the Earth, he felt that he was about to initiate a "new octave of development."

# CHURCH OF THE EARTH

## Books by Robert S. de Ropp

# CHURCH OF THE EARTH

## The Ecology of a Creative Community

### ROBERT S. DE ROPP

*A Merloyd Lawrence Book*
**Delacorte Press / Seymour Lawrence**

Manufactured in the United States of America

Designed by Jerry Tillett

First printing


Library of Congress Cataloging in Publication Data
De Ropp, Robert S.
    Church of the Earth.
    1. Church of the Earth.   I. Title.
HX656.C48D47     335'.9794'18     73-12238

ISBN: 0-440-01232-5

# CONTENTS

# PART ONE

## *Introduction*

Introduction

I

# The Two Streams

There are two streams in American culture. The first is a raging, eroding torrent, like the Colorado River in Grand Canyon, that gouges huge scars in the landscape and stirs up great quantities of mud. The second is so quiet that it is hardly noticed. It runs silent but it runs deep. It does not destroy the country through which it flows, but, like the older and quieter rivers, brings life-giving moisture to meadows and farms. It is a stream in harmony with life. The other is a torrent of destruction.

Those who look at the surface of American life see mainly the torrent. According to their type they are either appalled or filled with admiration by the sheer noise and force of this natural phenomenon. They see it working in all the great cities, madly erecting buildings that rise higher and higher, tearing down the old and serene, replacing it with acres of concrete and glittering glass, filling the air, in the process, with noise and fumes. They see it raging through the country, burying good earth under concrete highways, criss-crossing it with miles of electric wires, elbowing aside farms and orchards, spawning endless slurbs with parking lots and supermarkets, spreading noise and stink and pollution and rubbish. All this it does in the name of the two great idols, Progress and Efficiency, twin Molochs to whom the Americans sacrifice their souls. It is this torrent, by and large, that is labeled the American Way of Life or, by skeptics, the American Way of Death. And it is this style

3

of existence that countries labeled "undeveloped" seem eager to emulate, and Americans eager to export.

Those who know America better can detect the second stream flowing in the background, its murmur drowned out by the noise and fury of the torrent. The second stream represents the soul of America. Without it, American culture would be as lifeless as the steel and concrete of its cities. The second stream is created by *those who turn away*, who refuse to bow down to the idols Progress and Efficiency, whose life aims and life games are not formulated in terms of selling their souls, who refuse to toil endlessly to satisfy needless needs, to impress, to possess, to have power, to make a noise.

"Those who turn away (from the worship of idols)." This is the meaning of the word *Hunafa*, a group of seekers for truth of which the Prophet Muhammad was a member. It is the American equivalent of the *Hunafa* which forms the core of the Alternate Society. From the very beginning America has been blessed with those who turn away, with nonconformists who refuse to be molded into the accepted pattern. The spirit which expressed itself in Emerson's essay on self-reliance, and in Thoreau's self-imposed solitude at Walden Pond has shown itself repeatedly in communities based on plain living and high thinking. The theme recurs again and again. Simplify, simplify, simplify. Live unknown. Make your wants few. Shed this externalized clutter, these needless needs. They are merely a form of bondage and hinder man's journey. He has better things to do than load himself with mechanical junk like a pack horse. Man is designed to travel in steep places, his proper journey is inward not outward. How can he climb if he clutters his life with possessions?

This book describes one of the manifestations of the second stream, a creative community located in Sonoma County, California, incorporated as the Church of the Earth. It is not a large community and makes no claim to any importance. It does, however, exist and has, after a long period of trial and error, managed to attain a certain degree of stability and independence. The story of its development might be of interest to those concerned with the creation of similar communities.

# II

## The Three Pillars of Wisdom

"It is within your power," said the Gardener, "to build, right here in California, a little Eden. The climate is excellent, the soil fertile, the ocean with its fish is within reach. You can enjoy the best of everything, have music, dance, love, creative activities. You can build houses for yourselves, a school for your children, gardens, vineyards, orchards, workshops, laboratories. You don't even have to attain any great spiritual heights or develop very lofty states of consciousness. The only thing you *must* do is pull together instead of pulling in opposite directions, formulate your aims clearly and make the necessary efforts to attain them."

The little Eden, he explained, would be supported on three pillars, the garden, the temple, and the university. The garden would take care of man's physical needs, the temple of his spiritual needs, the university of his intellectual needs. Within such a matrix a man could develop harmoniously. He could attain the correct balance between his three separately spiritualized parts and enjoy that happy state which the Greeks called *ataraxia*.

It was natural for man to hanker for such a state. That inward calm, that harmony, that steadiness, were the basis of true happiness. The harassed inhabitants of the contemporary world, driven at an increasingly furious tempo in an atmosphere of clamor, pollution, and violence, particularly longed for this inner peace. It was a pearl of great price, perhaps *the* pearl of great price. But were they willing to pay for the pearl?

The answer was probably no. There were serpents in Eden, and experience had shown that the serpents, consisting mainly of man's inborn egotism, greed, and stupidity, generally wrecked the little Eden before it could be created. The Gardener, however, was a scientist and preferred experiment to theory. So the building of the little Eden would be an experiment in human relationships, designed to show whether humans of this age can relate to each other and to the biosphere to form a creative community based on a stable ecosystem.

It was clear, in designing the experiment, that they would have to put the garden first. The garden was the source of their bread and beans, a place in which they were forced to be realistic. In the temple they could easily fall prey to delusions, could think they had attained higher states of consciousness when in fact they were merely indulging in colorful daydreams. In the university they could lose themselves in philosophical speculations, endless theorizings, and futile debates. But in the garden they were forced to come down to earth, to spade the soil, shovel shit, sweat in the sun, or shiver in the cold. The garden was no place for theorists or talkative professors or for those who wished to speculate about the psyche. In the garden you either worked or went hungry. It never forgave. If you failed to dig the soil, sowed seed at the wrong time, forgot the manure, were too lazy to control the weeds, you did not get a crop. And if you didn't get a crop you would starve.

As with the garden so with the ocean, the second source of food. No one could fool with the ocean. It was vast, powerful, utterly indifferent, and entirely capable of swallowing people whole. Those who went out on the ocean in little boats needed to know what they were doing, to know tides and winds and waves, to have their eyes and ears open and their wits about them. And if they wanted fish they had to know where to fish, what bait to use, and how to land the catch. The ocean was an extension of the garden, the garden of the sea, and it was even more demanding and unforgiving.

The garden and ocean were much more than a source of food. They were gateways to knowledge, sources of new insights. From the garden it was possible to learn about levels of materiality, about the secret powers hidden in certain kinds of plants. There were flowers which could nourish the beholder through his impressions, through subtleties of colors and shapes, through varieties of perfumes. There were multitudes of aromatic herbs that, added to food, could endow the dullest dish with a peculiar magic. Then there were the power plants, feared or banned by a race of men too weak or stupid to know how to use them wisely, the devil's weed, the peyote, the hemp, the poppy, the sacred mushroom. There were fruits of varying degrees of delicacy. There were vines and grapes and the wonders of transformation when the grape juice frothed and bubbled and was transmuted into wine.

In the garden there would be, in addition to flowers and trees, a sundial and a fountain. The sundial would remind men of their dependence on the great luminary—that they were eaters of the sun and children of its body. It would demonstrate the rotation of spaceship Earth and bring to mind the influence of alternating periods of light and darkness on the growth of living things. It would speak of the mystery of time itself, that strange dimension of the great continuum that *cannot be reversed*. About the sundial would be engraved the words of Heraclitus linking the flow of time with the flow of water.

"No man can enter the same stream twice."

The fountain would also speak, teaching many lessons. Dwellers in desert areas have long regarded its message as sacred. *"The voice of water is the voice of God."* So in the courtyard of the mosque, there is a fountain that he who has ears to hear may listen to its voice. This reverence for water is fully justified, for water is the life blood of the biosphere. On its circulation, powered by the heat of the sun and the rotation of the planet, all things that grow on the land-mass depend for their existence. It is the hydrosphere, the copious storehouse of liquid water, that gives to the planet Earth its beautiful blue and white sheen when seen from space. Without water Earth would be a desert like Mars, which has either lost its hydrosphere or failed to develop one.

Those who understood the message of the outer garden could better appreciate the laws of the inner garden, the garden of the soul. In the inner garden also there took place a transformation of materials, a building up and breaking down. What was the inner garden of undeveloped man? A weed-infested mess producing nothing. Only in developed man did the garden bear fruit, in the form of certain high-energy substances that made possible a breakthrough into the locked rooms of the psyche. The fruit of the garden was higher consciousness and liberation from the personal ego. But that resulted from careful cultivation, from the elimination of weeds, which are all sorts of useless activities, dreams, fears, hates, anxieties, petty cares that rob the psyche of its creative force.

As with the garden so with the temple. It had two aspects, an outer and an inner. From time immemorial men had built temples. But the work of building the outer temple was meaningless unless accompanied by the building of the inner temple, which had to do with the attainment of a higher level of being.

So the building of the temple symbolized man's inner growth, and different parts of the temple symbolized various aspects of his being. The actual building of the temple was a practical aim for the members of the Church of the Earth. It demanded from them the best they had to offer in the way of skills and materials. It stood for the highest aim that man could attain, harmony with the cosmic forces around him. In the process of building the temple its builders could learn about themselves. The temple was a mirror in which those who wished to see could see. This is the characteristic of all holy places. In them, man can see the truth about himself. If he does not wish to know the truth about himself he should not enter temples.

The third pillar of the community, the university, was concerned with the development of knowledge in man. Harmonious development depended on a balanced growth of knowledge and being. Knowledge was concerned with relationships, with interactions. The mere absorbing of isolated facts did not give knowledge, yet knowledge of facts was necessary. You cannot relate phenomena if you do not know they exist.

This was the essence of the experiment. The commune would rest on three pillars, garden, temple, university. The members of the commune would have to build all three by their own labors. They could not go for help either to the government or to the larger community, they had to depend entirely on themselves. Nothing would count except results. By their results the value of their work would be judged.

# PART TWO

## *The Temple*

# III

## Building the Temple

He who has begotten and raised a child, built a house and a boat, grown his own food, planted an orchard, written a book, and tried to create in himself a soul may surely be said to have used his life well. Even Yama, Judge of the Dead, could hardly find fault with such a one.

The Gardener, standing on the slope facing the east, weighed himself, as it were, in the balance of Yama and looked back over the lattice of his life. The complex forces that had shaped his fate had brought him to this point. Three children launched on life, two houses, six kayaks, seven books, forty-five scientific papers, a fertile garden, fifteen fruit trees . . .

Now, spade in hand, he was about to initiate a new octave of development. He was about to break ground for the Temple of the Church of the Earth. To that point the forces had led him on that 26th day of March, 1972.

He wondered what powers to evoke as he lifted his spade. "In the name of the Father, the Son, and the Holy Ghost?" The formula passed through his mind, a leftover from a pious Christian youth. How many times, in the chapel of his English prep school, had he heard it sanctimoniously proclaimed? It was engraved in his soul. But now, gray and aging, he could find no magic in the phrase. It rattled dryly. His intellect rejected it. Far more meaningful was the concept of the *gunas*, the three forces of nature, the force affirming, the force denying, the force

equilibrating. Meaningful too was the verse from the *Bhagavad-Gita* which he now repeated:

> *All action results from the play of the three forces.*
> *Only he who is blinded by egoism thinks: I am the doer.*

He plunged the sharp edge of the spade into the breast of Mother Earth, cutting through the herbage, so green and fresh at that season in California. Perhaps he should offer the earth an apology, and the grass and the worms and other soil dwellers he was disturbing? But really, in this world of eat and be eaten, you could hardly move without disturbing something. The Gardener lifted the chunk of sweet-smelling topsoil and laid it carefully to one side. He instructed his fellow Whole-Earthers to keep the topsoil and subsoil separate. He continued digging.

The building of the Temple marked the end of a period of trial. Fate had so shaped events that the Whole-Earthers had

a home they could call their own, a piece of land with ample water, a barn, and a view. But though they had land on which to build, they ran into difficulties immediately. A struggle developed between the ideal and the practical, between principles and realities.

"We cannot really claim to have built the Temple unless we assemble all the materials ourselves, use stone or adobe brick, cut the rafters and floor joists from the tree, make our own floor boards, and so on." This from the Gardener.

The statement was received without much enthusiasm. Such methods of building, said the Zealot, who had been cast in the role of Master Builder, would never be approved by the swarm of bureaucrats in Santa Rosa whose blessing was needed before one could even erect a rabbit hutch. Nothing could be done without their okay, and the catalog of their commandments was far longer and more complex than that of Moses.

"Thou shalt not construct any dwelling on any foundation save that approved by the code. Thou shalt use 4x12s for the floor joists thereof and 4x10s for the rafters thereof, and the walls shall be 2x4s on sixteen-inch centers. Thou shalt not empty thy bowels in an old-fashioned outhouse or return thy wastes to the garden from which they came. Thou shalt do thy shitting on a properly designed flush toilet, consuming no less than four gallons of water per flush, connected to an approved septic tank and an officially approved drainage field. Thou shalt have heating facilities to maintain every room at a temperature of 70° F." And so on and so forth.

The Gardener sighed. His loathing for bureaucrats caused him to rebel instinctively against rules and regulations. Contemplating the jungle of red tape he wondered why he had supposed that the true Temple could be built in Sonoma County, California. Obviously, to get any freedom at all, the Whole-Earthers would have to flee into the wilderness, beyond the reach of bureaucrats and building codes. Equally obviously, if they did build in Sonoma County, they would have to submit to bureaucratic dictation. His battle with the bureaucrats had cost Lucky Louie of Morning Star a jail sentence and fifteen thousand dollars in fines. And what did he have to show for it? Nothing at all.

Moreover one had to admit that the zoning regulations and codes were necessary. They provided some protection against those rapacious developers, who seemed bent on turning California into a slurb.

But the code made progress difficult. It stood in the way of the use of bold designs. For years the Gardener had worked on the plans of his dream temple, incorporating in its structure the ninefold *naqsh* of the Sarmouni, and a dome-like roof supported by three interlacing triads. But his perusal of the building code made him hesitate. The central hall of his dream temple had a span of thirty-six feet. Any building with a span of more than twenty-five feet had to be engineered, so said the code. Which meant finding someone with appropriate qualifications to sign his name, in exchange for a large fee, on a document stating that the building was structurally sound.

The Gardener thought of the Gothic cathedrals, whose incredible spans and lofty arches testified to the bold spirit of medieval man. He thought particularly of Salisbury Cathedral, within sight of which he had spent part of his youth. What courage, what faith! That soaring spire had been superimposed on a structure never designed to support it. If you stood under certain of the pillars and looked up, you could see how they had bent under the added weight of the spire. And yet the cathedral had withstood the storms of seven hundred years. It had been constructed in the thirteenth century before the days of building codes. If the bureaucrats had been dominant in the Age of Faith, not one of the great cathedrals would have been built.

The span of Salisbury Cathedral was two hundred and twenty-nine feet. Must he now crawl to the bureaucrats for permission to erect a modest dome thirty-six feet in diameter? But, apart from his distrust of the bureaucrats, the Gardener was haunted by fear of failure. The Whole-Earthers, as builders, were rank amateurs. Even the Zealot, who at least knew a ripsaw from a crosscut, was only an apprentice carpenter. The Gardener, who had built two houses himself, was only too familiar with the sort of errors that amateur builders could make. Even putting up a simple building with all corners right angles and no awkward angles in the roof was difficult enough. Once one departed from the right angle one's problems multiplied.

It was fine for Buckminster Fuller to sing the praises of the geodesic dome, an aesthetically pleasing and structurally sound design. But amateur builders who tried dome building ran into problems unless they bought the struts ready-made. It was quite hard enough to cut a 2x4 square. When one had to cut really complex angles, the chances of error became overwhelming. And the errors multiplied like rabbits. One wrong cut threw out everything else. Even when you corrected all mistakes and assembled the skeleton of your dome, you had troubles to come. The lumber was never really seasoned. It shrank and warped. The dome leaked. The leaks swelled the wood. The dome leaked still more. It was heavy karma.

As for doing things the hard way, gathering rocks, building in fieldstone, that was a lofty ideal but hardly practical. One would need an army of workers simply to gather the stuff, let alone put it together. The Whole-Earthers did not have an army, nor did they have eternity in which to build. They needed a place to practice and a roof over their heads.

"Life," said the Gardener, quoting Sartre, "is a bourgeois compromise."

It was not so in the Age of Faith but the Age of Faith had ended. The Gardener excused his compromising by assuring himself that they were not building the real Temple.

"This will not be our permanent home," he told the Whole-Earthers. "We are too near the man-swarm. We will build here something practical and resellable and then move out of reach of the bureaucrats. There we will build the true Temple as it should be built."

The practical, resellable structure gradually emerged, two dwellings, a garden enclosed, a common room for exercising and meeting. No mention of a temple, which might arouse some strange reactions in the hearts of the bureaucrats.

"Keep it simple," said the Gardener.

Simple it was. Working on the plans, they discovered that there were only so many ways in which a living room, kitchen, bath, three bedrooms could be arranged on one floor. A mass of details had to be borne in mind. How much space did one allow for a bed, a sink, a cook stove, a refrigerator? Where do you fit in the fireplace? Where do you store the wood, park the car, hang up the wash? These were standard, three-bedroom bourgeois houses with all conveniences. Hopefully they would be heated by solar heat, would use water pumped by wind power, would house cars in the carports powered by methane generated from chicken shit. All this, however, lay in the future. The two dwelling houses that flanked the Temple were standard dwellings designed to use electricity generated by the P.G.&E. The P.G.&E. was very much in evidence. Its enormous pylons marched right across the ranch. Its power poles were everywhere. The former owner of the ranch had fought the monster in vain. It had ended by planting a huge pylon in the middle of his orchard.

"Though we live quite literally under the shadow of the P.G.&E., we will not become its slaves. We will not use power tools in constructing the building."

This from the Gardener.

Howls of protest arose from the Zealot and the Mechanical Genius. It was useless for the Gardener to assert that he had built two houses and never used power tools on either. The Zealot belonged to the carpenters' union. To him, power tools were as necessary as his right arm.

"But power tools offer no challenge, no room for skill. They operate by an entirely different triad. What can you learn about the working of your moving center if all you do is flip a switch? Also, they're dangerous."

The Zealot gave not a fig for the danger. Power tools helped a man to stay alert. Only fools lost their fingers.

"We have plenty of fools around here. Maybe you haven't noticed?"

The battle raged, ding, dong. In the end there was a compromise again.

"These are two dull bourgeois little houses without a shadow of distinction, like a million others. They are boxes,

mere boxes. Use any method you wish. But no power tools may
be used on the Temple itself. It will be built by hand with love
and, I hope, awareness."

There were still more compromises. Should all the concrete for the Temple foundation be mixed by hand? The Temple measured forty-six by thirty-one feet and required in
addition fifty-five concrete slabs for the 4x4s which would support the floor joists. In one hour a big cement truck could
vomit out of its huge gut enough cement to fill the forms, which
would then be truly monolithic, a single stone. To mix enough
concrete by hand would take many days and the concrete
would not bond so well, and, when one figured it out, it was
actually more expensive to buy the sand, gravel, and cement
and mix it oneself than to call in the concrete-spewing leviathan with its huge load of ready-mix.

Then there was the matter of nails.

"No iron was used in the construction of the Temple at
Jerusalem. It was said 'Iron is used to shorten man's life but
the Temple is built to lengthen man's life.'" This from the
Gardener, quoting Josephus (more or less). But the Temple at
Jerusalem was built of huge blocks of stone, whereas the Temple on Sonoma Mountain was being built of wood. How did
one hold wood together without nails? One used dowels and
glue, the old method popular in New England in Colonial
times. Dowels and glue made very strong joints, but every dowel
had to have its hole carefully drilled by hand with brace and
bit. And would the building inspector approve of such archaic
methods of construction?

Compromise, compromise.

The concrete-spewing leviathan rolled in, with much hissing of pneumatic brakes. The Whole-Earthers were caught
short-handed by the flood of concrete. It slopped over the forms,
trapped air pockets, flowed where it was not meant to flow. The
Zealot sweated. His apprenticeship had not prepared him for

the crisis. The wretched stuff was starting to harden and he hadn't put the anchor bolts in place. He hammered in the bolts with desperate haste, not too careful about the angles. A sloppy job, all things considered.

Fortunately he had decided to pour the foundation in two sections and certainly didn't make the same mistake twice. The call was: "All hands on deck!" and all hands it was. Ice Maiden and Reverend Mother wielded trowels and smoothed the footings. The Mechanical Genius, the Designer, the Patron, and the Gamblin' Man rammed the concrete down into the forms. The Gardener smoothed the top and removed the excess. The Zealot skipped around supervising everything and managed to get his anchor bolts in on time and more or less vertical. Then came a second gush of cement to fill the holes for the piers. On every soupy holeful a concrete pier had to be set and carefully leveled. But the piers, 55 of them, kept moving in mysterious ways and losing their true positions and the task of correcting them in the hardening concrete became more and more difficult. Despite all the efforts of the builders, some of them ended out of true.

By the time the floor joists were in place, supported every six feet by a 4x4, the lower part of the Temple looked like a jungle. There could be no doubt that Ken Kern was right, reflected the Gardener. That enterprising true Whole-Earther had made it very clear in his *Owner Built Home* that houses were being grotesquely overbuilt simply to comply with an outdated building code. But the post-and-beam method certainly simplified construction. Instead of finicky 2x10s, one used massive 4x12s, on forty-eight-inch centers. The troublesome bridging was eliminated and in place of the usual subflooring one nailed heavy 2x8-inch tongue and groove to the floor joists.

O that tongue and groove!

"If this is what they call utility grade," said the Gardener, "I'd like to know how they define utility."

He hit the sloppy stuff with his hammer in disgust. Some of the planks were obviously rotten, and all were moisture-saturated.

"How in the world is anyone expected to construct a tight subfloor with this garbage?"

The Zealot, an optimist, stated an opinion. If they drew it up good and tight and put in plenty of nails, the floor would be solid enough. So they drew it up tight with clamps and nailed it heavily, none of which altered the fact that the wood was water-soaked. The open deck, 1,200 square feet of it, lay in the full glare of the California sun. The boards, so carefully and tightly laid, soon become separated by gaping cracks. In places you could see between them. The tongue had been pulled completely out of the groove.

The Gardener ruefully contemplated the floor.

"If we were honest workmen," he declared, "we would pull up the whole rotten thing and lay it again."

But he had to admit that such an operation might leave the last state of that floor worse than the first. There were three 16-penny nails holding each board to each joist. By the time they were removed, the boards would be reduced to wood pulp.

"I've seen other subfloors that looked a lot worse than this," said the Zealot.

The Gardener growled and muttered something about the *kalijuga*. Sloppy workmanship, rotten materials, dishonesty, carelessness, laziness, greed for money . . . Modern man, the *kalijuga* dwarf, was a shrunken misshapen creature whose technical achievements merely hastened his spiritual decay.

"Of course," the Gardener admitted, "we could have got seasoned wood by buying all the lumber and storing it in the barn for a year to dry out before we started building. But how could we get it into the barn when they deliver it in these huge bundles which no one can handle without a fork lift?"

There was nothing to be done except replace that part of

the floor that had actually cracked open in the process of drying. Obviously what had happened to the floor would happen to the whole building. It would shrink and warp and crack as the wood dried. The massive beams that were to hold up the roof were checking badly in the sun. And the Zealot was murmuring like the Children of Israel against Moses. He objected to cutting a two-foot bevel in the 4x12s by hand. Wanted to use a Skilsaw. The fleshpots of Egypt . . .

"We cannot," said the Gardener, "keep sacrificing principle to expediency. We agreed, no power tools. Let's stick with it. If you never have to do anything harder than rip a two-foot cut in a 4x12 you'll be lucky."

The ripsaws were duly set and sharpened, and the cuts were made. There were thirty of them, fifteen rafters, two ends each. The Whole-Earthers learned a lot about the feel of a ripsaw. Next there was an earnest debate about how they would lift fifteen 26-foot 4x12s each weighing about five hun-

dred pounds onto a wall that was fourteen feet above the floor. Block and tackle? House jacks? Straight muscle power? There was talk of the pyramids of Egypt, the megaliths of Stonehenge. In the end they simply used muscle power, lifting one end at a time, using a series of three platforms. The job that had seemed so formidable turned out fairly simple. No one was ruptured. No heads were broken, though several Whole-Earthers donned hard hats in anticipation. The big beams were leveled, spaced, and locked in position with metal straps.

"When I was building out east," observed the Gardener, "an old experienced carpenter told me never sheath the roof until I'd put on the wall siding."

He went on to explain how a high wind could get under the roof of an unsheathed structure and take it off like a hat.

"It just so happened," said he, "that when I was building

in Rockland County, New York, we had a hurricane. I had the boards laid out on the deck but not nailed. They were 1x8 tongue-and-groove. That wind picked them up and threw them around like feathers. No harm done. But another fellow had three houses in a row with the roofs blown off. All because he closed in the roof before putting on the siding."

But the Zealot wanted to put the roof on before the siding. That, said he, was the way things were done in California. The Gardener countered that the Californians were rotten builders. The Zealot replied that there were no hurricanes in the state.

"At least," said the Gardener, yielding, "you might put in a little diagonal bracing. This structure shakes like Jell-O everytime you walk on the roof."

Diagonal bracing was installed. Once again the hillside echoed with hammers as 1,380 square feet of 2x8-inch tongue-and-groove was nailed to the rafters. At least the tongue-and-groove was of reasonable quality, kiln-dried and free from obvious rot. It had to be sound because it showed. The simple shed roof, 4x12 rafters on four-foot centers, 2x8 tongue-and-groove with inch-thick insulation and three-ply tar and gravel was the simplest form of roofing and the cheapest. No ceiling rafters, no ceiling, no attic space, nothing but a deck between oneself and the sky, suitable for a mild climate in which snow fell rarely and did not linger.

By early August the roof was closed in. One could stand in the big room and absorb some impressions.

"As a vehicle for *baraka*," said the Gardener, "it will never rival the Blue Mosque. But at least we put it together with our own hands even though the material was bought from a lumber yard. The practice we've gained will come in handy when we come to build the true Temple."

As every builder knows, the closing of a roof marks a definite interval in the octave of building. The Zealot, complaining of nervous strain, departed with the Reverend Mother to fish for trout in the Sierras. The Patron departed to tour the Middle and Far East, the building activity paused. A heatwave came and went, and the dry California hills slowly bleached in the sun. In the basement, like an industrious mole, the Mechanical Genius busied himself with yards of electric cable, drilling holes through the plate, nailing outlets to the studs. Hopefully they would use oil lamps or candles for the illumination of the Temple, but wiring was installed anyway, while the walls were still uncovered. Hopefully again, they would devise ways of generating their own electricity from sun power, thereby freeing themselves from bondage to the P.G.&E. There was much to be hoped for.

Finally, in August, the bare skeleton of the walls was decently clad in 4x8 panels of redwood. Much cutting and fitting would be required. The siding had to fit around every roof beam, not to mention doors and windows. And again there was the demand for power tools.

"Of course," said the Zealot, "one *could* use a handsaw for all this, but the glue in the laminate would blunt it in no time, and it costs two dollars to have a saw set and sharpened."

Compromise again. If you use modern materials you must use modern tools. The Gardener, who was learning to view operations with an air of increasing detachment, left the Zealot in peace to use his screaming Skilsaw on the plywood. The building with its aluminum windows and sliding doors, its plastic skylights and projecting redwood trim was beginning to look more like a rustic branch of the Bank of America than a Temple of the Church of the Earth. But, after all, what did it matter? Modern world, modern tools, modern materials, modern human beings . . .

It did one little good to hanker after the past. The soaring spires of the Gothic cathedrals, the domes and minarets of the great mosques all spoke of a different age and a different hu-

manity. The building the Whole-Earthers had made, of pre-fabricated materials hastily nailed together, was a true expression of the spirit of modern man, impatient and hasty, always on the go, madly rushing from nowhere to nowhere. A more leisurely age with visions of eternity could spend forty years building a temple. But modern man wanted results in a hurry. And *California man*, living amidst the dangers of earthquakes, forest fires, floods, freeways, and rampant pollution, wanted them faster than anyone. And if the Temple of the Church of the Earth had ended by looking like a branch of the Bank of America, was not this a sign of the time and the place?

The worst compromise of all, the ultimate insult, occurred in early September, with the installation of the sewage system. Like any Whole-Earther, the Gardener was well aware of the role of shit in the overall economy of the biosphere. Food came from the soil, passed through the animal body, returned to the soil in the form of urine and feces, was transmuted again, and again transformed into food. So the right way to live involved returning one's waste products to that portion of the soil from which the food had come. In this way one avoided robbing the soil.

It soon became apparent that no such cycle could be followed in Sonoma County, California. The Gardener had struggled in vain to develop some system of sewage disposal that would allow the return of waste to the garden, satisfy the bureaucrats, and not involve tearing up the ground. Nothing was accepted. To dispose of the modest flow of feces and urine from two small houses the bureaucrats demanded a fifteen-hundred-gallon concrete septic tank, four hundred feet of drainage tile in trenches six feet deep with four feet of gravel below the tile.

It was absolutely impossible for the Whole-Earthers to dig by hand these monstrous earthworks. Instead they were forced to hire a firm that made installing septic tanks its business. With backhoes and other items of heavy equipment these specialists managed to convert the piece of pasture behind the Temple into a fair replica of a World War I battlefield. Huge wounds were torn in the breast of Mother Earth, topsoil and subsoil were all jumbled together. The mess was unbelievable.

"And it was only as a favor they let us put it here at all," said the Zealot. "There's nothing but clay around here, and they couldn't get a good perk test."

The Gardener made a comment about goddamn bureaucrats getting above themselves.

"These people are going insane. They think they run the earth."

"They sure do," said the Zealot and went on to relate how a man he knew had bought a twelve-acre piece and wanted to build a house on it.

"Wouldn't let him build anywhere. Couldn't get a good perk test. And he paid plenty for that land. Now he's stuck with it."

"If I was him, I'd put up a tipi and shit in a hole in the ground just to spite them. The rascals are getting completely above themselves. Certainly one doesn't want people shitting everywhere and anywhere as they do over at Morning Star. But there are ways of circulating shit without spreading disease. It's a pretty sorry state of affairs when a man can't put up a house on his own land because some Jack in Office refuses a permit for a septic tank. Soon they'll be demanding that we train the livestock to use the toilet. Can't have those cows and sheep and horses shitting all over the place. It's not hygienic."

The Gardener realized he was wasting his sarcasms. No barb was sharp enough to penetrate the bureaucratic hide. He looked at the piles of dirt, the ravaged pasture, the huge concrete septic tank, and the hundreds of feet of drainage pipe.

"And just how much," he inquired, "are we going to have to pay for this devastation?"

"About two thousand dollars," said the Zealot.

"Jesus Christ!" said the Gardener.

He turned away in disgust. Two thousand dollars to dispose of a little excrement in a manner that assured its going where it would do the least good! The busy host of bureaucrats and petty officers, those accursed parasites of the Affluent Society whose salaries kept taxes sky-high, were entangling free citizens in an ever-increasing network of petty regulations. Why, for two thousand dollars one could build a comfortable cabin in the woods complete with well-designed, hygienic outhouse that would enable one to compost one's shit properly and return it to one's garden.

"How far would one have to go," he asked the Zealot, "to escape from these bureaucrats and live as one wishes? Is any part of California free from these pests? Mendocino? Humboldt County? I know Ken Kern escaped them by fleeing to the Sierras, but I want to be near the ocean. Where can one hide from the bureaucrats?"

The Zealot had no idea. He had grown up with bureaucrats and accepted them as people accept certain diseases. The

Gardener lapsed into meditation, contemplating the army of bureaucrats that swarm at every level from county to federal. They were, as he saw them, one more manifestation of the evils of the *kalijuga*, symptoms of a society in decay, slowly strangling in its own red tape. Obviously if one wanted to build the true Temple and form a commune of true Whole-Earthers, one would have to retreat much farther into the wilds. It certainly could not be done in Sonoma County, near the city of Santa Rosa, itself spreading like a cancer and doing its best to become a second San Jose.

He viewed the ravaged pasture again but this time on a different time scale, against a background of huge geological forces, slipping, sliding, grinding against one another, the uneasy substrate of an ephemeral culture. On this time scale it really mattered little whether they spent two thousand dollars having a septic tank installed because of the whims of the bureaucrats. The whole scene, the Temple, the septic tank, the ravaged pasture, the piles of black pipe took on an unreal quality, like a backdrop on a stage.

California culture was a shallow, shaky affair built on a network of earthquake faults and sustained by huge floods of gasoline. It would be swept away almost as quickly as it had formed. The floods of gasoline would dry up, the huge agribusinesses would grind to a halt, the cities would wither and their inhabitants starve, and the swarming bureaucrats would have to find other means of livelihood. The culture would go with the wind, nor would it leave great temples to proclaim its achievements, only a tangled net of empty freeways, acres of abandoned parking lots, and millions of lost golf balls.

# IV

## *The Bee Tree*

Near to the Temple stood a bee tree. It was a large and ancient live oak, hollow within, a narrow crack down its south side. Through this crack the bees came and went and, for the most part, attended to their affairs without bothering the builders. Now and then they became aggressive, and a few of them attacked the humans who had invaded their territory. Their attacks provoked a lively reaction. The Whole-Earthers lost all awareness of their fellowship with the insects, danced and whirled, frantically slapping and swiping with saws, hammers, hands, anything. They hit themselves on the heads, tore at their hair, leaped and cavorted in a most diverting manner. Anyone watching from a distance might have supposed they were celebrating a strange dervish ritual—the dance of the bees.

To the Gardener, who had kept bees, been stung frequently, and learned to accept the experience philosophically (one pulled out the sting and went on with what one was doing), these antics seemed overdone.

"You must be about five thousand times larger than these ingenious insects, yet you let them blow your cool."

The remark was received without favor by the builders, who added to their fear of being stung the horrors of imaginary accidents.

"Suppose I was up on the roof," said the Mechanical Genius. "Fourteen feet up, and one of those things attacked me."

"If you were upon the roof and one of them attacked you, you might try attaining the fourth state of consciousness."

"How would that help if I got stung?"

"You would be objective about it—not me, just my body. And at least you would only get stung. You wouldn't risk breaking your neck by doing a bee dance on the roof and falling off."

The Zealot, in the role of the Master Carpenter, declared that the bees should go. The Gardener protested.

"The bees were there first. We are the ones who should go."

But the Zealot rejected the bees' point of view and stuck to his own, as zealots will. He called the Farm Bureau and from them he got the name of a Bee Man.

"He's some old man who knows how to get bees out of bee trees. He's the only one in the county. I'm supposed to meet him in front of the Safeway at six o'clock tomorrow morning."

The Zealot, still breathing wrath against the bees, departed in his battered Triumph in the first light to meet the Bee Man in front of the Safeway. But the Bee Man didn't show and the Zealot cooled down, and for the next week or so the bees left the builders alone. The Zealot, who loved to speculate, decided they had attacked in the first place because it was full moon. It *was* full moon at the time and the bees *had* attacked. Therefore the bees had attacked because the moon was full. The Zealot had studied philosophy in college before he joined the carpenters' union.

"If you want to change the situation, get the bees out of the tree and into a hive," said the Gardener. "You don't need a Bee Man to do it. There is a recipe in the *Last Whole Earth Catalog* on page sixty-three."

And so there was. "How to Adopt a Colony of Bees" by David Collins, M.D., San Diego, California:

*This magical method may be used for removing bees and*
*their honey from an attic without the use of pesticides or*
*other violence or for adopting a colony from a bee tree.*

Just what the doctor ordered! One simply blocked up the
exit (in the dawn's early light, presumably, before the bees had
emerged) and left a single exit ¾ inch in diameter. Over this
exit one placed a bee escape which would let the bees get out
of the tree but prevent them from getting back in. Right in
front of the bee tree one placed a nice comfortable beehive, its
landing strip enticingly smeared with honey. The bees would
come out of their old home in the tree and, being unable to
return, form a large swarm in the hive in a few days. Then one
provided them with a new center for their collective existence
by suspending a newly purchased queen bee in her little cage
in their midst. The bees would adopt the new queen, eat out
the plug of sugar sealing her cage, liberate her, and start a new
colony. At that point the bee tree could be opened up and the
bees would go back, take all the honey out, and put it in the
new hive. One could then transport the hive to a safe distance,
and bees and men would live happily ever after.

"That," said the Gardener, "is what I call an intelligent
approach."

No doubt the approach was intelligent but experience
showed that there was a gap between theory and practice. The
task of transferring the bees to a hive was undertaken by Sailor's
Yarn.

"If you look under the roof of the old ashram," said the
Gardener, "you will find there a beehive and some frames. I
lost my bees in that very wet spring we had in '64 and I have
never gotten around to restarting the project. You should dis-
infect the hive and repaint it and put comb foundation in the
frames. You can get comb foundation from Sears and a new

queen and the bee escape from Kelly's. Let me know if you want help."

Weeks passed. It became apparent that this octave of development was low in active force.

"I've been procrastinating," said Sailor's Yarn. "Procrastination is a weakness of mine."

"Stop indulging," said the Gardener. "Weakness indulged equals more weakness. Have that beehive ready by next weekend or the project will be taken from you and given to another."

This stimulated Sailor's Yarn into activity. He scrubbed out the beehive, gave it a fresh coat of paint, inserted the comb foundation into the frames, purchased a bee escape and some plaster of Paris. Next weekend he and the Gardener donned bee veils. It was a miserable morning with a cold wind blowing in the fog from the Pacific. The condensed fog dripped from the live oaks and so shrouded the new building that, though it was only a few yards off, it was barely visible. The two men in their veils moved about the oak tree as if engaged in some weird Druidic ritual. First they nailed boards over the more obvious cracks, then stuffed wet newspaper between the boards and the tree. The hammering produced an angry hum within and a few bees emerged into the cold damp air to see what was happening. There was no mass attack, however, and the bee men proceeded to the next step.

This involved blending plaster and water to make a nice smooth paste and working the paste into all the remaining cracks. The job proved more extensive than they had supposed, for close inspection revealed that there were several exits from the bee tree. As soon as one had been closed, the bees started emerging from another. Soon the plaster ran out. The bee men stuffed wet paper into all the cracks they could see and adjourned the operation until they could get more plaster.

The plastering was finally completed, the bee escape was nailed over the last remaining hole. The freshly painted, well-

equipped hive was attached to the tree, its alighting board smeared with honey. A quart jar of liquid bee food was placed by the entrance. Everything possible was done to interest the bees in their new home.

Weeks passed. The bees showed no signs of entering the hive. In the struggle that ensued, intelligence (human) was challenged by instinct (insectal). Were the bees more clever than the humans who were so flagrantly interfering with their way of life? The bees kept finding their way back into the bee tree. They found unsuspected holes, they even managed to get in through the bee escape. The quart of bee food that had been intended to give them a good start in the new hive was transported instead into the bee tree.

"Perhaps," said Sailor's Yarn, "they'll be more cooperative when I put the new queen into the hive."

He had received the queen the previous day, neatly packaged in a little cage. But the queen never became established. The Gardener, inquiring, received astonishing news.

"The ants ate the queen."

"The ants? What ants?"

"The ants in our kitchen."

"Have you ants in your kitchen?"

"Always. They live there. But who would suppose that ants would eat a queen bee?"

The Gardener contemplated vistas of depravity in the insect world. He thought of the preying mantis, the female of which routinely devours her mate during the act of copulation. Perhaps the Manichees had been right, the material world was the creation of the devil.

"Well, order another queen and keep her out of reach of these fiendish ants."

"And I'll have to order another bee escape. The one I got is no good. They keep getting back in."

A new bee escape was installed. The last remaining holes were closed with plaster. Still the bees refused to enter the hive. They clustered over the bee escape, a disconsolate, frustrated mob. They began once again attacking the Whole-Earthers, but the latter had learned to endure their assaults without doing a bee dance, which was just as well as they were now working on the roof. The Zealot, attaching trim twenty feet above ground, remained perfectly still while being dive-bombed by a bee. When the bee became entangled in his head, he spoke calmly and with dignity.

"Would you mind removing this bee from my hair?"

The Gardener removed it.

"These bees are real gurus. They teach the noble art of nonreaction and detachment."

The tar and gravel crew had not learned this lesson. They arrived on a cool windy day to put the final touches to the roof.

The bees felt particularly frustrated. Perhaps the smell of boiling tar aroused their aggressive instincts. In any case they routed the tar and gravelers halfway through the job. The crew, abashed by its defeat, promised to return on the following day, hoping that the bees would be less aggressive.

By this time it was August. Apples were ripening, the Naked Ladies were in the bloom, and the Whole-Earthers were starting to harvest corn and tomatoes. Operation Bee Tree had been started in May. It seemed they would be lucky if they could end it by Christmas.

"Either the bees are exceptionally clever or we are phenomenally stupid," said the Gardener. "They are as hard to negotiate with as the North Vietnamese. It's a good thing for them that we are patient or we'd seal up the bee tree and leave them to die. But that would be contrary to the spirit of the Church of the Earth."

Sailor's Yarn, however, felt encouraged. The new bee escape seemed to be working and at least two pounds of bees had now settled in the hive. All they now needed was a new life center and organizer, for a swarm of bees is a single organism. Every worker, every drone, is a product of one mother, the queen bee. The worker bees are sterile females with a lifetime of six weeks during the busy season. Like short-lived cells in the body, they must constantly be replaced or the colony will perish. As all replacements can come only from the queen, this one bee is the biological center of the hive. She copulates once only, during the nuptial flight when one out of the numerous drones mates with her high in the air and perishes in the process, his entire sexual apparatus dragged out of his body by the ardor of the queen. Such is the sex life of the bee.

Sailor's Yarn had given the bees a new queen to replace the one that had been devoured by ants. Reluctantly, but following instructions, he had destroyed the queen's attendants, the group of worker bees that had arrived with her. This mas-

sacre was necessary, for the attendants would attack the bees
from the bee tree as soon as they were introduced into the hive.
So the attendants were killed, each beheaded with a needle, the
new queen was suspended in the hive in her little cage. She
was protected by a plug of sugar, for the workers might kill her
if she emerged before they became accustomed to her smell.
Sailor's Yarn removed the hive from the bee tree and took it a
mile away to the other ranch, set it down by a live oak near the
lake, and left the bees to gather honey from flowers of the late
summer.

This still left bees in the bee tree. They were frustrated and
angry, stung the Designer on the top of his head and the
Mechanical Genius between the eyes.

"I'm supposed to kill off the rest of them," said Sailor's
Yarn, who was beginning to see himself as a veritable Herod
massacring the innocents. "I don't like doing it, but I suppose
I'll have to."

"Set your mind at rest," said the Gardener. "The bees
massacre each other. See how they slaughter the drones. Nature
swarms with robbers and murderers and generally seems to favor
them. We still have a sulfur candle we used to use for sulfuring
the wine barrels. Light it and stick it in the bee tree some
foggy morning early. That will finish off the rest of the bees in
the tree. Then you can bring back the hive and the bees will
take the honey out of the tree and put it in the hive. Or so the
book says."

The bees, however, appeared immune to sulfur dioxide.

"I've burned three sulfur candles in that tree," said Sailor's
Yarn, "and they're still alive."

"How do you know they're still alive?"

"When I put my ear to the tree I can hear them hum."

The Gardener suggested that such heroic insects deserved
to survive.

"Open up the tree and let them carry on with their lives. If they sting people now and again, so what? They are as much part of the biosphere as we are and a lot less dangerous. Let the bees live."

# V

## The Natural Priesthood

Fellow Whole-Earthers!

The days of the paid professional priest are ending. Though there have been good men and great men among the priests, we may, on the whole, feel thankful to see them go. Their role in the life of mankind has always been of questionable value. They have, at various times and in various cultures, fostered the most absurd superstitions and been guilty of the most revolting crimes. A thick volume could be filled with the story of their misdeeds. One can think of the frenzied priests of Cybele castrating themselves in honor of the goddess, of the priests of Moloch sacrificing children to their idol, of the Aztec priests tearing out their victims' hearts, of the Christian Inquisitors torturing and burning alive in the name of a god of love. The catalog of atrocities is endless. No wonder the Roman author exclaimed in disgust: *Tantum religio potuit suadere malorum!* (So great is the evil religion has aroused.)

So when we see the priests gradually disappearing from the scene we may well breathe a sigh of relief. In an age of science the paid priest is outmoded.

There is, however, still a *natural priesthood.* It has always existed and probably always will. It has nothing to do with organized religion and none of its members is paid for his services. It consists of players of the Master Game who know the truth about man's predicament. Members of this natural priesthood are bound by the law called "one-hand-washes-the-other."

This law compels them to attempt to communicate the truth about man to others. They do this in various ways, depending on their type.

We here, in the Church of the Earth, have chosen a special matrix within which to play the Master Game. A priest of the Church of the Earth chooses of his own free will to struggle for independence and self-reliance. This means that he places himself directly under the laws of the biosphere and relies as little as possible on the Affluent Society. To say that he tries to live the Simple Life does not express his position accurately. Placing yourself directly under the laws of the biosphere does not make your life simpler. On the contrary, it involves constant effort and the exercise of a great deal of skill and foresight. A priest of the Church of the Earth cannot afford to be lazy or a fool. He has accepted as a religious obligation the task of growing or gathering the food he eats. He buys only a few things that he cannot produce, salt, sugar, maybe tea and coffee if he likes, but these are luxuries and can be dispensed with.

At this point you may say, so what? There is nothing new about this pattern of living. The pioneers all lived in this way. And the old mountaineers so well described in *The Foxfire Book*, the Aunt Aries and Hillard Greens, still live in this way. And although their spirit of self-reliance is admirable, no honest observer could deny that the mountaineers were ignorant, superstitious, and prone to violence, massacring each other in ludicrous feuds like the Hatfields and McCoys. There was a dark as well as a bright side to the life of those self-reliant mountaineers.

Well, so there was, and I'd be a fool to deny it. The mountaineers were self-reliant because they had to be. And they were poor because they had to be. And they made their own furniture and built their own cabins because they had to. And their children are leaving the mountains because they don't have to go on doing these things, and can find an easier life elsewhere and are tired of being held up to ridicule by the creators of Dogpatch and the Beverly Hillbillies.

But the priest of the Church of the Earth does not live off the land because he has to. He does it by choice, and makes it a part of his religion, as an orthodox Jew refuses to eat pork or a Moslem prays five times a day in the direction of Mecca.

Let us be clear about what we mean by religion. A religion is a system of beliefs. The beliefs may be utterly nonsensical or even criminally insane (like the belief of the Aztecs that the gods had to be placated with a continuous supply of human victims or the belief of our witch-hunting forbears that men and women could have sexual intercourse with demons and deserved to be burned alive for this imaginary indulgence). There is no guarantee that religious beliefs will reflect the sunny, cheerful side of man's psyche. They can and frequently do reflect his gloomiest, cruelest, most degenerate tendencies. The Judeo-Christian guilt cult with its emphasis on sin and damnation is a fine example. Man is free to believe in anything he chooses. He can build a religion of light or a religion of darkness, a religion of truths or a religion of absurdities. Or he can reject religion entirely and get along perfectly well without it. Man does not have to be religious.

The fact remains that many people are. They hunger for a religion. They need it in the same way that a traveler needs a map. They need to know where they came from, where they are, where they are going, and what position they occupy in the scheme of things. And, if they are not totally at the mercy of credulity and suggestibility, they want to know the truth and not be deluded by a bundle of myths and fairy stories elaborated by paid priests for their personal profit.

So the Church of the Earth offers them the truth. Here you were, here you are, this is where you are going, and this is the place you occupy in the scheme of things. You are a part, a tiny part, of a cosmic process. Every mouthful of food you eat, every breath of air you inhale, and almost all of your impressions are generated by this sacred triad, sun–earth–biosphere. You are part of a huge, complex mass of struggling beings living under the law of eat-and-be-eaten. You are at the end of the food chain, a member of the dominant species, the killer of killers, the arch-glutton, the prime polluter, the bully of the biosphere. You are aboard a runaway mechanism heading for a crash. You can't stop the mechanism, but you can get off. It is not too late.

So what else does the Church of the Earth have to say to its members? It says: Wake up, open your eyes, hear, smell, feel, taste, touch, become alive. You cannot afford to pass your life in sleep. All around you, ceaselessly at work, are the forces which generate and sustain your life. How can you afford to be blind to these great forces, to wander through life in a dream like the Fool in the Tarot, so asleep that he does not even know that he's losing his pants? The cosmic drama is displayed before you every hour of every day. An endless series of transformations, seeds to plants, flowers to fruits, plants to animals, refuse to soil, takes place before your eyes. Every plant, every animal, the clouds, the sun, the ocean, can tell you stories about itself if you will only listen. By learning to see, by learning to hear, by stopping dreams, and by awakening you become what man is supposed to be, the eyes and ears of the god, or if you prefer, a part of the consciousness of the cosmos.

This aim, this struggle to awaken, is the basis of the true religious impulse. All the other manifestations of religion, the dogmas and rituals, the myths and fairy stories, the threats of damnation and the dreams of heaven are merely aspects of the world's oldest con game, invented by paid priests to separate fools from their money. As for our Church of the Earth, we have no paid priests. We have teachers who know certain things, and their motto is plain.

*I cannot teach that which I do not know.*

What do they know, these teachers of the Church of the Earth? Some know how to plant and raise crops and harvest and preserve food. Some know how to build houses, work in metal, in wood, spin, weave, make pots, make wine, make bread. Some are fishermen and gather the harvest of the sea, taking only as much as they need. Some are foragers, familiar with wild food plants, some cooperate with bees and share the honey, some raise hens and collect the eggs.

All these teachers make it part of their religion to live as directly as possible under the laws of the biosphere. Everyone spends some time in the garden. We have no desire to train a group of narrow specialists. The more things you can do, the better, but you must aim to do at least one thing well and add other skills to this. In this way we train a harmonious, balanced individual.

And what of the inner work, the work toward consciousness? I assure you there is no distinction between inner and outer. It is true that we practice certain special exercises designed to bring about centering and induce a taste of the fourth state of consciousness. But don't put your faith in these exercises alone. They will give results only if you learn to apply the same methods to everything you do. The directing of attention, the practice of simple awareness, the struggle with wandering thoughts, these are the basis of the inner work. There is nothing secret about it. There is no mystery. The work depends on the struggle between intentional doing and accidental happening, between directing attention and letting it wander, between being aware and being lost in dreams. This inner work is the basis of all true religious practice whether it be Moslem, Hindu, Christian, Buddhist, Taoist. One who engages in this work is a truly religious person. Such a one is a member of the natural priesthood and has discovered the secret of the harmonious life.

# VI

## Scum of the Earth

Fellow Whole-Earthers!

You have heard the phrase "scum of the earth" used in a derogatory sense. Do not be misled. Scum has its place.

Next time we go fishing, look around. On one of those days when the surf boils around the rocks, note how the white flocks of scum accumulate. The wind takes them and plays with them. It lifts them clear of the water into the air. They are fragmented into tiny droplets, become totally airborne, dwellers in a new element. The water evaporates, leaving microcrystals of salt. These are borne higher and higher by the air currents. It is just on these crystals that the water droplets condense to form the rain on which all land-born organisms depend.

So scum is a vital link in the chain of the biosphere, the link between the atmosphere and the hydrosphere. Man, by a law governing the interchange of cosmic concentrations, is also the link between higher and lower.

*To angels he gave reason, to the beasts lust,*
*To the sons of Adam he gave both lust and reason.*
*So he whose reason prevails over his lust is higher than the angels.*
*And he whose lust prevails over his reason is lower than the beasts.*
*Angels and beasts are at rest from war and combat.*
*Man is engaged in painful struggle with two adversaries.*

RUMI: *The Mathnawi*, R. A. Nicholson, translator (London: Cambridge University Press, 1926).

Seeing that he was placed in the middle, he has power to go up or down just as scum can dissolve back into the ocean or, borne aloft, become a part of the air, falling back to earth with the life-giving rain. Therefore, be the scum of the earth, for the scum of the earth is the salt of the earth. Which does not mean wandering around unwashed, unkempt, tangled in beards and beads. The "hippie" is as much a show-off as his "square" equivalent, shaved and shorn and waving his little flag. The true member of the Church of the Earth makes no show. He does not try to appear different from his fellows. He goes his own way. He is part of the great experiment and knows it. We are God's guinea pigs, partly by fate, partly by choice.

> God said, Do thou grant his earnest request.
> Enlarge his faculties in accordance with his free will.
> Free will is the very salt of piety.
> Without it, heaven itself were a matter of compulsion.
> Put a sword in his hand! Remove his impotence!
> Let us see if he turns out a warrior or a robber.

Here our dear Rumi reveals the secret. The operative words are "let us see." Albert Einstein (a genuine *mahatma*, in the guise of a theoretical physicist) said, "God does not play dice with the universe." Let us treasure this saying. We are not inhabitants of a monstrous gambling casino, a sort of cosmic Las Vegas or Monte Carlo, all dancing girls and roulette wheels with the odds weighted in favor of the house. God does not play dice! Of course, if you prefer to think he does, there is nothing to stop you. A rabble of downcasts who like to think of themselves as *avant garde* dump on us their spiritual garbage in plays, books, and artworks balanced on the edge of imbecility. Swallow it if you wish. Much good may it do you. You may feed your soul on garbage or ambrosia. Man is judged by his appetites.

*He would fain fill his belly with the husks which the
swine did eat.*

That was while the Prodigal Son was still a *Stranger in a
Strange Land.* But man's appetites can change—and when his
appetites change, so does his destiny, for man goes where his
food is, both the lower food and the higher.

*And when he came to himself, he said, How many hired
servants of my father have bread enough and to spare, and
I perish with hunger! I will arise and go to my father.*

Note well the words—"when he came to himself." Before
that, he had been an eater of husks, a swine among swine. The
so-called *avant garde* feed us on swill and we swallow it as long
as our appetites are depraved. They reduce the great experiment to a dialog between two derelicts in garbage cans in a
street marked NO EXIT. It is meaningless, meaningless, meaningless. A senseless crap game. And not even played by God.
God's dead.

Well, so he is as far as that old "gaseous vertebrate" is concerned. The "god without" is dead. But the god within is not
dead unless we kill him. And when we kill the god within we
are dead indeed.

*The Greeks understood the mysterious power of the
hidden side of things. They bequeathed to us one of the
most beautiful words in our language—the word "enthusiasm"—en theos—an Inner God. . . . Happy is he who bears
within himself a god, an ideal of beauty, and obeys it; ideal
of art, of science, of patriotism, of the virtues symbolized in
the Gospel. These are the living sources of great thoughts
and great acts.*

Who do you think wrote that? A priest? A philosopher? No.
It was Louis Pasteur, another mahatma who appeared among

us in the guise of a scientist. Happy is he who bears within himself a god. Has enthusiasm, that is. Has a game worth playing.

But we have no enthusiasm. We don't have a god within. We are bored, depressed, alienated, full of destructive impulses. We hate the world we have made but despair of finding a better one. Something went wrong with our evolution. Koestler has said so, and anyone can see he is right. Our brains are top-heavy, unstable, a god in the top brain, a naked savage below. Our powers of speech do us more harm than good. We aspire to be saints and act far worse than beasts. We are paranoid, crazy, plagued by gigantic delusions. Fighters of phantoms. Look at our twentieth century. Huge wars fought for idiotic reasons, massacres, purges, riots, revolutions, liquidations. And this, dear Brethren, calls itself the Age of Science.

Science! A technological Juggernaut proceeding full speed ahead with no one at the steering wheel, a Juggernaut that poisons earth and ocean and does it in the name of progress. No one in control! The brakes won't operate. We'd like to get off—but how and where can we go?

Where go? Go back and start over, back to our father's house like the Prodigal Son. Join the Church of the Earth and enjoy your life. Guilt is useless. Shame over the past is useless. If you want to snivel and grovel and weep over your sins, do it someplace else. For twenty miserable centuries Western man has been groveling before a vengeful god that was only a shadow of his guilt. Terrified of some fantastic hell, dreaming of some equally ridiculous heaven, with all this nonsense fermenting in his head, how could he ever hear the song of the earth, the song of life and the song of the sun that gives life?

Go back and start over. Learn the lesson of the shit heap. What do you learn from shoveling shit, from making compost? That earth transforms filth into fruit. Look at the soil in our garden. Once it was thin and miserable. Now it is rich and fertile. Why? Because the earth feeds on wastes, the natural wastes that came from animal bodies, not the undegradable dross produced by an insane technology. We have the earth in ourselves and in that earth our own filth can be transmuted. Learn the lesson of the compost heap. A well-made compost heap steams like a tea kettle. It smells good too. No matter what shit you put in it, cow shit, horse shit, chicken shit, pig shit, man shit, it cooks and converts it and kills disease germs in the process.

Have you never been moved to marvel over this wonder? A well-made compost heap is hot enough to cook an egg. This is a natural sterilizer, and a source of astonishment to the biologist. How can these remarkable beings (we call them thermophilic bacteria) possibly live and thrive at a temperature hot enough to curdle their proteins? Leave the biologists to puzzle over this. Learn rather the lesson of the compost heap. That from shit and refuse, by the genesis of heat and its own special alchemy, it creates the substrate that enriches the earth and gives the green plants friable mulch to grow in. Have compost heaps in yourselves, throw in the filth of your psyche, your grovelings, guilts, anxieties, envys, hatreds. Transform them by heat into food for higher beings. Cultivate your own garden. Grow roses or cabbages, but at least grow something.

Join the Church of the Earth. But how does one join it? Get up early, pick up a hoe, raise some crops? That's not a bad start. It's part of the program. But joining the Church of the Earth involves more than that.

He is a member of the Church of the Earth who no longer listens to the song of his ego but hears instead the song of the great triad, which is the song of life, the Song of Songs. And what is the triad? It consists of a star (the sun), a planet (the earth), and a film of self-reproducing organized matter (the biosphere). The biosphere mantles the planet. It lies between atmosphere and lithosphere. It feeds on the body of the sun, quite literally, for sunlight is substantial. And this transformation of the sun's body into matter that moves, loves, hates, thinks, and strives toward the expansion of consciousness gives an answer to the question—*What's it all about?*

*Through the biosphere on this planet and on life-possessing planets in other solar systems the universe strives to attain consciousness of itself.*

And man, poor messed-up, half-baked, disharmonized man, represents the best that this solar system has so far been able to accomplish. Though nine planetary companions circle our star, it seems reasonably certain that only one has a biosphere. And that is the beautiful blue and white spaceship Earth, home of *Homo sapiens.* We may have doubts about the *sapiens* but still it appears that the great creative thrust, the thrust toward Omega point, passes through him at this moment. Other vehicles may arise in the future. The dolphins, those big-brained sea mammals, may develop consciousness far exceeding ours without the forms of nastiness that have resulted from our unbalanced brain system. But for the present, man is this solar system's contribution to the thrust toward cosmic awareness that may be regarded as the *raison d'être* of the universal drama. He who tells you otherwise merely serves the devil, the spirit who denies.

> THE DEVIL. *You conclude, then, that Life was driving at clumsiness and ugliness?*
>
> DON JUAN. *No, perverse devil that you are, a thousand times no. Life was driving at brains—at its darling object: an organ by which it can attain not only self-consciousness but self-understanding.*
>
> BERNARD SHAW, *Man and Superman*

What next? What now?
The pieces fall into place. The jumbled story starts to make

sense. Nature, which name we give to an evolutionary force that some consider blind, has generated in this biosphere a form capable of taking over the conscious control of its own evolution. But the evolutionary force has also built into this being a potent destructive mechanism, a chronic paranoia, a mechanism for the genesis of delusions, centering around the greatest delusion of all, that man has a separate ego, and is somehow apart from nature that produced him. Which causes this silly, strutting turkey cock to talk about "conquering nature." The arch-preposterous! The arch-absurd! The babblings of a lunatic!

Fellow Whole-Earthers! If you want to become real dues-paying members of our Church of the Earth, purge your minds of all this "conquering nature" nonsense. You can no more conquer nature than you can stop the rotation of the earth. You are part of nature, an integral element of the biosphere on which you depend for every breath you take, every morsel of food you eat, and for almost all your impressions. We are infinitesimally small cogs in a very large machine, a great chain of chemical reactions constantly transforming substances, fueled by the outpoured energy of a star. Because we are very numerous, very greedy, and very clever at devising gadgets, we can, to some extent, damage the balance of this machine with consequences that may be disastrous for ourselves. Probably, after we have followed in the footsteps of the dinosaurs, the biosphere will balance itself again. We shall hardly upset the ecology as much as one Ice Age. In thinking we can depopulate the earth, we exaggerate our powers of destruction. The biosphere will destroy us before we destroy it.

# VII

## The Three Sacred Qualities

Fellow Whole-Earthers!

What is demanded of those who would take part in the Great Work?

Practicality, determination, discrimination—the three sacred qualities.

Practicality means knowing that two and two will never add up to five, that if you don't sow anything you won't reap anything. It means knowing what sort of effort and what sort of materials are needed to produce a desired result. You want a durable house? Then don't build it from straw. You want it to withstand a flood? Build on a rock. Which means hard work. You have to dig till you reach bedrock.

Determination means getting up after you've been knocked down, starting again after all that you've built has collapsed. No one builds the spiritual house without its collapsing at least once. Inspiration is lost, courage wavers, will weakens. To take up the tools in spite of this and start again—this is determination.

Discrimination means knowing who is who, both in oneself and among teachers and guides. You want to climb the steep path to the top of the mountain? Make sure the guide you go with knows the way. This golden California swarms with false guides. They breed here like flies on a dung hill. They prey on those who lack discrimination. A seeker shows his level by the guide he chooses.

How shall he know the false guides?

Some are out for money—they charge large sums. Some love fame. They travel around wreathed in flowers. They have disciples by the thousands. Some claim mysterious powers—call themselves avatars—mahatmas—maharishis—claim to be reincarnations of King David or Akhenaten. They move surrounded by starry-eyed followers—mostly middle-aged women. Some are natural hypnotists. They have what is loosely called animal magnetism. Rasputin types. Their powers are often genuine, but they do not know how to use them. This makes them dangerous. You can learn a lot from such types, but you have to be clever.

"He who sups with the devil needs a long spoon."

Some really knew something once but have turned themselves into entertainers. They go the rounds of the various mystical circuses endlessly talking and putting on performances. There are people who do little else but attend these circuses. It provides a convenient substitute for real inner work. If they had discrimination they would not do this.

How recognize a true guide?

This is not easy, but there are indications.

The true guide never tries to attract followers, never permits worship of personality, stands in the background. Rumi says: "Don't look at me, take what is in my hand" and "Love the water, not the jug." Jesus says: "By their fruits shall ye know them. Do men gather grapes off thorns or figs off thistles?"

If you want a model, look at Leo in *The Journey to the East*. He is neither pompous, money-loving, nor overbearing. He does not boast of his high powers or run around giving seminars at mystical circuses. He is, to all outward appearances, simply a servant. "He who would be greatest let him be as a servant among you."

The guide does not particularly wish to be a guide. Certainly he has no desire to inflate his ego by absorbing the adulation of starry-eyed devotees. He can show the way, but you yourself must tread it. As soon as possible, he will let you proceed on your own. His aim is not to dominate you but to have you find the guide in yourself. This calls for discrimination and knowledge of the different selves.

*The being of man is a jungle.*
*Be full of caution of this being if you are of that breath.*
*In the being of man are a thousand wolves and hogs.*
*In the being of man is the righteous and unrighteous, the fair and the foul.*
*Now a wolf appears, and now a moonlike beauty with the face of Joseph.*
*Every moment a new species appears in the bosom;*
*Sometimes a demon, sometimes an angel, sometimes a wild beast.*

RUMI: *The Mathnawi*

Think of your being as a conveyance; horse, carriage, and driver. In waking sleep (the third state) there is only confusion. The driver is drunk, the horse unruly, the carriage in poor repair. Anyone can climb into the carriage, command the driver, have him go where he will. What sleeping man calls "I" is a dozen different beings, each with a different aim, a different set of desires. So the carriage goes one way in the morning and the opposite way in the afternoon. Can you wonder that the journey seems meaningless?

The journey takes on true meaning only when the Master enters the carriage, for the Master knows the way—the aim of the journey. But the Master will not trust himself to the ramshackle conveyance. It must be put in good order. The driver must be sober, the horse trained to obey, the carriage repaired. All this takes time. And discrimination.

He who has the Master in the carriage needs no teacher. But the Master does not come until the carriage is freed of all the illusory egos that formerly told the driver to go here or go there. The little selves must die or disappear before the Master takes over.

What then is the beginning? It is simple. Accept the truth about the third state—accept multiplicity. There is, in fact, no I. There is a multitude. He who knows this ceases even to think of himself as I. He speaks of "it," or "this." Meanwhile he observes how different I's come and go—actors in his personal theater. Something new develops in him. One who observes. In one part of his being, this man is becoming objective toward himself. In one part of his being, he has ceased to lie. Insofar as he has ceased to lie, he is becoming liberated. The Observer combines objectivity with discrimination. The Observer knows who is who in the jungle. The Observer is the forerunner of the Master.

Strengthening of the Observer is the first step in the inner work. You think this a small thing? It isn't. The Observer, to begin with, is quite weak and some of the other I's are strong. They fight against the Observer, try to shut him up in a closet or push him downstairs into the cellar and lock the door. How do they fight him? By lies, for they live on lies and like lies. For this reason they hate the Observer because he is the spirit of truth in man, objective conscience, the Holy Ghost. The Holy Ghost is the power whereby man can distinguish in himself the true from the false. When a man blasphemes against the Holy Ghost he destroys his power to separate truth from falsehood. If he does it often, he loses this power altogether. With it he loses all capacity for inner growth.

*He who blasphemes against the Holy Ghost shall not be forgiven.*

What hope is there for the beginner on the Way, surrounded as he is by hostile I's, in a muddled culture that has lost its traditional wisdom and become enslaved to false values? There are two ways open to him—the way of the recluse and the way of participation. The recluse simplifies his problems by withdrawing from a sick society. He becomes a hermit, lives on his own, reduces his needs to a minimum. This way is more popular in the East than in the West. You need to be a brave man to follow it. The solitary path is full of false turns and slippery places. Which does not mean it is not a good way. If he has courage as well as knowledge, the solitary may go far.

> Down to Gehenna or up to the Throne
> He travels furthest who travels alone.

But the recluse is always in danger of throwing out the baby with the bath water. In the course of simplifying his life he may lose much that is of value, many rich impressions, many valuable experiences. He puts himself in what psychologists call an impoverished environment. In trying to screen himself from the wrong kind of stimulation he may starve himself, deprive himself of the impressions he most badly needs.

Moreover, alone as he is, there is no one to whom he can turn for help or guidance. If he makes an error on the way, he must detect it and correct it himself. If he sinks into a depression, loses sight of his aim, there is no one to help him to regain that aim. So he who treads the way of the recluse needs plenty of courage and determination.

Safer, therefore, to join a group. Like mountaineers on a steep ascent, they are roped together. One falls, the others can rescue him. But a group is only as strong as its weakest member, as a chain is only as strong as its weakest link. And the guide who leads the group must know the way. If he falls off, what happens to the others?

It is easy enough to talk about forming a group—the country swarms with little groups, communes of one sort or another. But how long do they last? Look at the history of our Church of the Earth. How many have joined us and left? How many have betrayed the Work and, with it, themselves? All of us have within us the little Judas, ready to sell his Lord, to sacrifice high aims for low. If this is the age of anything, it is the age of the traitor. No relationship is sacred. Husbands betray wives and wives husbands. Both betray their children. People betray their teachers and their higher aims. Time was when men would let themselves be burned alive for their beliefs. To us such dedication seems incomprehensible.

If you betray the Work, leave after you have started, particularly if you leave after you have begun to develop, then it will be very difficult for you to begin again. Man is a seed. He has in himself latent powers. Out of millions of seeds only a few develop. This is the law of seeds. But once a seed has germinated, it must go on growing. It cannot go back to being a seed. So man, once he starts to grow, must continue or lose his possibility. Therefore he who considers entering the Way does well to ask himself whether he has determination enough to continue.

> For which of you, intending to build a tower, sitteth not down first, and counteth the cost, whether he have sufficient to finish it?
>
> Lest haply, after he hath laid the foundation, and is not able to finish it, all that behold it begin to mock him,
>
> Saying, this man began to build, and was not able to finish.
>
> LUKE 14:28–30

But there is more involved than this. He who gets from the Work must give to the Work, otherwise he is a freeloader and a thief. If he gets and gives nothing back, the moment soon comes when he won't get any more. He who gets must give, and only he who gives can continue to get.

> For unto whomsoever much is given, of him shall be much required: and to whom men have committed much, of him they will ask the more.
>
> LUKE 12:48

# PART THREE

## *The Ocean*

# VIII

## Boat Building

It all started with an advertisement for kayaks. The illustrated brochure, in brilliant color and written in a style which verged on the manic, was not of the kind to inspire the Gardener. He preferred moderation in advertising. The soft sell.

There was, however, one item that took his fancy. "Champion Ben Logan reports HOW and WHY." And there was Mr. Logan, a powerful mesomorph, up to his waist in the water with a mako shark in his arms which must have weighed as much as he did. Caught it from a kayak off Cocoa Beach, Florida. And tarpon. He had caught a tarpon six feet 4 inches long which weighed ninety-three pounds and towed Champion Logan plus kayak for four hours.

That, in the Gardener's opinion, was a sporting way to catch fish. He had nothing but contempt for the powerboat set, strapped in their padded barber's chairs with enormous reels, in fancy boats equipped with every mechanical aid. But to catch a six-foot tarpon from a fifteen-foot kayak without barber's chair or any other equipment than one's own muscles— this was quite another story. It required a fisherman cast in the heroic mold; it called to mind the epic struggle of *The Old Man and the Sea*. It was a confrontation in the full sense of the word, man versus fish in a small boat with no one to aid the fisherman if he got into difficulties.

Periodic physical stress was essential for man's development. One had to find some sort of physical challenge which would flood the system with adrenaline from time to time and demand from the body an output of great effort. For thousands of years men had lived dangerously, their minds alerted, their bodies toughened by the constant effort to get food by hunting or fishing. Man was a machine designed to travel rough roads. He needed the stimulation of physical effort. Without it he deteriorated. He turned into a degenerate city dweller, a creature poisoned by the exhalations of its own swarm, a flabby fat cat tied to his TV, incapable of endurance.

But effort had to be meaningful. There were plenty of ways of scaring oneself half to death, or exerting oneself to the point of total exhaustion which made no sense at all. You had to make effort for a reason. Food gathering was an eminently reasonable activity. For the Gardener, as a means of combining the profitable with the strenuous, kayak fishing became the activity of choice.

He built his first kayak from a commercial kit, a wooden frame covered with a layer of heavy plastic cloth. In it he fished on the surface of the Pacific. There were hair-raising moments. He knew absolutely nothing about the surf, that jealous guardian of the door to the ocean. He was rolled several times, broke a stringer and one of the kayak's ribs, and nearly broke a leg, lost all his gear twice.

It soon became evident that the wood frame was too fragile, the cockpit was too small, the boat was too heavy for easy carrying. A new kayak was needed, and he would have to build it himself, as nothing suitable was available commercially. The plan was to build the lightest kayak possible, big enough to carry two people if need be, strong enough to stand a pounding in surf, broad enough to be stable on the open ocean. It had to be smooth inside without projecting ribs in which one's feet could get caught, preventing quick exit if one was rolled.

No one in the group had any idea how to build a boat. They groped and struggled to make a plug for a mold from a

mixture of wood, clay, plaster, and formica. The Gardener, leading the enterprise, spent endless chilly winter hours in the barn where the mold was being made. The roof of the barn leaked. The ancient structure swayed and creaked in the wind. Air temperatures were so low that the resin refused to set, the plaster refused to dry. He had troubles.

It was, troubles notwithstanding, a fine archetypal sort of activity. He made spiritual contact with a shadowy host of boat builders, Eskimos, Indians, Neolithic fishermen who had ventured onto the ocean in fragile vessels made of skins on wooden frames. He was tempted to use the skin and wooden frame himself. As materials he hated the resin and fiberglass. They poisoned one with fumes and put little glass splinters in one's skin. The peroxide catalyst was dangerous. The resin was damaging to the hands, but if one used rubber gloves one became so clumsy, with the treaclelike resin sticking to the gloves which were thick and awkward enough anyway, that in the end one stripped them off in exasperation.

How much damage should one be willing to accept in order to enjoy the wonders of modern technology?

But the fact remained that, for a combination of lightness and strength, it was impossible to beat the fiberglass resin. Much as he disliked working with the material, he nonetheless felt that there was no alternative. So he continued to labor on the plug, intending to use it as a base for a female mold, from the womb of which would be born a whole fleet of sleek vessels. He even convinced himself that the enterprise had commercial possibilities, that the ocean kayak might become as popular as the surfboard, to be used by skin divers as an alternative to the paddle board. This would provide the Whole-Earthers with the home industry they so badly needed to pay the bills they received from the Affluent Society.

So he worked on the plug. Two 4 by 8-feet sheets of half-inch plywood formed the base. To it were nailed a series of wooden forms representing sections of the hull. They were placed one foot apart and connected with strips of veneer. That part of the enterprise went smoothly enough. But to get the sleek smooth curves he wanted in the finished project he had to coat the veener strip with something that could be molded. Plaster seemed like the obvious material. It was cheap, easy to work, could be sanded smooth. But it soon became apparent that the plaster had weaknesses. Applied wet, it caused the veneer to swell. As the veneer dried, the plaster cracked and fell off. If one patched it with fresh plaster more cracks appeared. Before the plug could be used, the plaster had to be perfectly dry. How does one dry out plaster in a cold, damp barn? A battery of infrared lamps? He tried them. The plaster dried unevenly and cracked worse than ever. In the end he was forced to fill the cracks with a mixture of resin and fire clay.

And the curves. How could one shape the hull so that the

curve on one side perfectly matched the curve on the other? Endless carving and sanding of the plaster gave a hull which was still not perfectly symmetrical. The Gardener gave up seeking perfection. He wanted a kayak prototype by spring for sea trials. How could one be sure that the design would prove suitable? They were working in the dark, did not even know how thick to make the walls of the vessel or whether the dimensions they had chosen would give stability in the great Pacific swells.

He left the hull and concentrated on the top. Because of the cockpit this proved even more awkward to build. It took weeks and weeks. Finally the great moment arrived. Both top and bottom were draped in resin and fiberglass. Spring had come. The weather was warmer. The resin and fiberglass set. As he prepared to remove the molds from the plug, the Gardener assumed that most of his troubles were over.

Wrong again! It was absolutely impossible to remove them. Despite lavish dressings of PVC mold-release the molds clung to the plug with monogamous devotion. He had no alternative but to rip the plugs off by tearing them apart piece by piece. The plaster clung to the resin and had to be chipped out. The inner surfaces of the molds were full of little cavities like worm holes and had to be laboriously refinished with plastic putty that kept shrinking and falling out.

Well, at least he had the molds and could proceed to make the prototype. The process seemed simple enough. One applied a gel coat to the mold to give the smooth finish, put in the fiberglass, impregnated it with catalyzed resin, and presto, there was the boat. Again too simple. The gel coat came away from the mold, the new resin dissolved the gel coat, the fiberglass refused to lie down smoothly. It seemed such an easy material to work with but actually was very tricky. And the joining of the top of the kayak to the bottom proved difficult also.

But they did have their prototype. It was the Coal Man,

always eager for thrills, who assumed the role of test pilot and took the boat out. The surf off Duncan's Landing was judged about right for sea tests. The boat had plenty of free board. With only one layer of cloth and one of mat it was very light. Flexible too. The hull moved gently up and down as the wave pressure varied. The Coal Man skipped around on the surf, courting a wipe-out. Carried away by his enthusiasm, he made for the south end of the beach where quite big breakers were rolling. He came in on one of them, too far ahead of the curl. The kayak dug its nose into the gravel and the boat was pitch-poled, end over end.

"I crouched in a fetal position," said the Coal Man, suiting the action to the words. "I threw my arm over my head. If I hadn't done that I'd have broken my neck."

The kayak survived. It seemed, in fact, to be a very strong

boat despite its lightness and large cockpit. And the molds which the Gardener had created with such labor did spawn a modest brood, though the operation never became commercial. Despite an accumulation of know-how the Whole-Earthers never turned out a kayak without making at least one major mistake, the job always took far longer than they expected. Commercial production was out of the question.

Three years later, with one kayak wrecked and the second patched and scarred after several rough encounters with the ocean, the Gardener was smitten again with the boat-building urge. He now knew enough about kayak fishing on the ocean to envisage the perfect boat. The first kayak he had made was unnecessarily big (fifteen feet long). The cockpit was too large. (It could accommodate two people but was never called upon to do so.) The flat bottom of the hull caused too much drag.

Unless one wanted to take out one's girl friend, paddle to Hawaii, or sleep on board, one could do much better with a twelve-foot boat broad in the beam (three feet) with a properly shaped hull to cut the water and a smaller cockpit.

He went so far as to draw the dream boat with several fancy modifications and a sliding seat which would make rowing possible (a far less tiring mode of progress than paddling). He even made a model out of paper and cardboard. But the memory of all those hours spent on shaping the plug damped his enthusiasm and the perfect dream boat remained only a dream.

# IX

## *Old Gray Guru*

They lived on the western edge of the American continent. The ocean regularly sent them reminders of its presence. Maybe for a week in summer the sky would be a clear California blue, the days hot, the air dry, and the fire risk extraordinary. But always the old gray Pacific reminded dwellers in the Coastal Range that it was there, just a few crests and ridges away. So the heat would pass, the cool white fog-layer enter the valleys. The members of the Church of the Earth, up early to greet the sun, would see below them, like a layer of milk, the condensed breath of the sea. Sometimes it would rise and cover everything with wispy fingers, dripping from the dark redwoods, from the leaves of the corn, shrouding, cooling, wetting, a message from the sea—a welcome message.

Who can forget the ocean, from which we came, the ocean we carry in our blood, our inland sea?

The answer is that many forget. City man, man of the man-swarm, forgets everything—except his miserable ego which he carries around him like a polluted rag. Even members of the Church of the Earth had a tendency to forget. Most of them would not willingly traverse the fifty or so miles that separated them from the ocean. It was a source of astonishment and sorrow to the Gardener, who considered himself, for a time, to be the leader of the group and who felt for the ocean that essence-love which some feel for their gods, wives, or mistresses.

It was the Gardener who proposed that the Whole-Earthers

draw their food from the sea as well as the land. They would brave the Pacific in kayaks, depart through the surf from any convenient beach, fish, skin-dive, commune with seals and whales and any other life forms that happened to be around. For Mother Earth has two tits, the wet and the dry. And who would despise the wet tit, the ever-generous ocean?

That the Gardener nearly drowned himself, had one kayak smashed by the breakers, emerged bruised with his ears full of gravel only added to his enthusiasm. There was a guru you could respect! No bullshitting the ocean. It didn't listen. Make a mistake, come in on the wrong side of a breaker or go out from too far up the beach, and wham! Those Pacific breakers slapped you down like a swatter. They were not to be fooled with. You could be sideswiped, rolled, pitchpoled, swamped, wiped out. You could lose all your gear. You could break a leg or some ribs. You could probably lose your life. So what! The Gardener learned some lessons he didn't forget. There were some forms of surf you didn't fool with, some beaches you didn't go out from, some winds you didn't trust (northwesters especially). An old fisherman of the Aran Isles had summed up the situation (to Synge, the playwright, collecting material for *Riders to the Sea*):

> *A man who is not afraid of the sea will soon be drownded for he will be going out on a day he shouldn't. But we do be afraid of the sea, and we do only be drownded now and again.*

Actually, if one took sensible precautions, one was as safe in a kayak as in any other vessel. Safer in fact. The canvas spray cover could be neatly closed. The vessel was low in the water, offered little resistance to wind, was broad of beam, steady, almost uncapsizable. It rode the waves like a duck, noiseless for the most part, but now and then slapping the water as it crested short swells. In a kayak one was part of the ocean, could feel its life through one's bottom, could glide without the noise and stink of an outboard motor into any number of secret coves and inaccessible places. One became a sort of sea beast, recognized as such by the seals and sea lions that disported themselves along the California coast and were always curious. Poking up their heads from the kelp they would examine the silent craft before returning to the serious business of fish hunting. Sometimes porpoises rolled along in pairs, exhaling rhythmically, smooth, black, streamlined shapes. Once two gray whales surfaced near him (on their way to Scammons Lagoon for the yearly breeding spree). They seemed as big as submarines, encrusted with barnacles. When they blew, a cloud of steam formed and lingered in the December air.

What tales the sea tells! What insights it offers!

> *The sea is like music; it has all the dreams of the soul within itself and sounds them over. The beauty and grandeur of the sea consists in our being forced down into the fruitful bottom lands of our own psyches, where we confront and re-create ourselves in the animation of the "mournful waste land of the sea."*

C. G. JUNG, *Memories, Dreams, Reflections.*

How was it that the others failed to hear the tales of the sea, failed to avail themselves of this opportunity? They were afraid perhaps. "O Lord, your sea is so vast and my ship is so small." Or perhaps not fond of fish.

The Gardener ate fish like a seal. It was his main source of protein. He ate it fried, baked, cold in salads mixed with mayonnaise. He shunned red meat, coarse product of the butcher shop. There was something revolting about devouring the bodies of one's fellow mammals. But one need have no qualms about eating fish. The fish ate each other incessantly, vora-

ciously. They even devoured their own offspring. The medium
fish ate the baby fish, the big fish ate the medium fish. When
they reached a certain size nothing else would eat them. Except
human fishermen. The fisherman was at the end of the food
chain, along with the sea lions. But even a sea lion would
hardly dare to devour a twenty-pound lingcod.

That twenty-pound lingcod had been the pride of the Professor, only other member of the Church of the Earth who
really had sea-love. The Professor who had seemed such a hope-
less fisherman that he couldn't drop a line overboard without
getting snagged—the Professor who had been rolled the first day
out, lost his glasses, his paddle, his seat, his lunch, been totally
immersed, bruised, and battered, his beard dripping seawater—
but that man was full of surprises. More than all the other
Whole-Earthers he had the quality of determination.

Practicality, discrimination, determination—the three sacred qualities. The Professor was determined.

So he became a good fisherman. Which suggests you can do almost anything if you really want to. And the twenty-pound lingcod which he snared off Russian Gulch, beating its brains out while it did its best to knock the bottom out of the kayak, was his biggest catch to date. He wanted it baked whole, visible proof of his prowess, but no oven would accommodate the monster. So it was filleted and served cold with mayonnaise on a hot, hot evening in August—a day to remember. Twenty pounds is a lot of lingcod.

So the Gardener went to the ocean with the Professor once a week if the weather permitted. They caught on the average fifty pounds of fish per trip—good fresh rockfish, tested mercury-free. And the Whole-Earthers said—Do please stop bringing us all this fucking fish. We're sick of it and there's no more room in the freezer.

That's gratitude.

They went anyway. Perhaps they could give away the fish to the starving poor. But there aren't any starving poor in Santa Rosa, California. They're all on welfare and doing very nicely. Probably they eat steak.

The Gardener and the Professor left early, five in the morning. Which meant getting out of bed at 4:15 A.M. On those days there was always a listening on awakening, a listening to the trees, for the voice of the trees is the voice of the wind and, where ocean trips were concerned, the voice of the wind was decisive. The wind talked in several voices. A steady rustle meant the trip was off. But the gusty up-and-down drafts of dawn turbulence were only signs of the approach of light. In the summer months the warm air would rise from the valley and lie like a blanket at the thousand-foot level, a thermal layer floating on the cool air below. Then, as earth rolled into sun-shine, vortices of wind would stir between hill and valley, blustery drafts, rattling the leaves on the live oaks. Such a wind would not be felt on the ocean.

The Gardener struggled into his clothes—five layers plus his fishing jacket. It was almost always cold on the ocean. He checked his equipment. A spare set of clothes (in case he was rolled over), lunch, bait, fishing pole, hooks, sinkers. The kayaks had been lashed to the car-top the night before. The stars were bright, a thinning moon hung in the west. The first sign of light showed over the mountains to the east. Faintly visible in the valley was a white sea of mist. The ocean would be fog-bound.

He faced the east, visualizing spaceship Earth as it rolled on its axis under distant stars. The man-swarms crawled on its face, unaware of its motion, unaware of sun, of stars, of galaxies, turning blind in the circle of their egos, "eyeless in Gaza, at the mill with slaves." Day had already come to New York, to Chicago, to Denver. The edge of light was racing from east to west across California. Already it illumined the Sierras. But the coastal ranges lay in twilight and there was darkness on the face of the sea.

Not a word was spoken. The Professor was up and ready to go. The kayaks reclined on top of his Saab, thin white ghosts, fifteen feet long, light as eggshells. ("You mean you go out on the ocean in one of those!"—"Sure we go out. Safest small craft there is."—"Hm . . . Well, it's your life.") Headlights scattered the darkness. The Saab nosed its way down the mountain, passed from the clear zone into the fog. Redwoods dripped moisture. Santa Rosa was shrouded, its citizens clinging to the ultimate hour of sleep—the sleeping dream before the waking dream. Along the Russian River the fog lifted a little, turning into a low cloud ceiling. All the river resorts were asleep, Montecito, Rio Nido. Guerneville, its streets silent, had one aged man sweeping litter from the gutters. The clock on Rexall's drugstore said five forty-five.

The dimly seen river was misty and mirror-smooth. It was hard to remember its winter aspect, a raging, frothing, cabin-destroying, rampaging monster. It flooded Guerneville. It started landslides at Monte Rio. It set off letters to the paper signed *Disgusted.* (*My cabin for sale—cheap. This is the third year running I have found it up to the windows in mud. When is someone going to do something about these annual floods?*) That was California. If it wasn't floods, it was fire. If it wasn't fire, it was earthquakes. Not to mention smog. But in summer the river was tame and silky smooth. Its water was green as soup, turning to blue as it approached the ocean.

Beyond Guerneville the road twisted and turned, held tight between river and mountain slopes. Shadowy redwoods arched over it. At one point it turned right back on itself so that travel was due east instead of west. Then, near Jenner, the river widened into a lake-like expanse, with cows on either side and seabirds above. Here they could sense the ocean, the enormous presence, the vast Pacific. Even before they saw it, its power was perceptible, a gigantic magnet.

At Jenner, below the River's End Café, the ocean met the river in a roiling, roaring, surf-splashing spectacular. During storms this clash of river and ocean released huge energies as all those discovered who planned to mine the Russian River gravels! One outfit tried. The ocean ripped apart everything, tore up the pipes that were to conduct the gravel to ocean barges, smashed all the installations. The rusting ruins of the venture were still scattered on the beaches.

Past Russian Gulch the Saab climbed, looping and turning up the steep grade. Day had dawned. The fog swirled and drifted past the sheep who balanced on the sheer slopes by the side of the road. Then, at the top, was a miracle! The fog thinned and vanished. The whole sky was suddenly revealed, rosy pink in the sunrise. And there below, mile after mile, lay a snowy cloud-fleece, an ocean over an ocean. It lapped into the valleys like milk in a bowl. The rounded hills rose out of this milky stuff, tawny as lions, or somber with crowding redwoods of deepest green. All the way from Fort Ross to Point Reyes the headlands projected into the ocean of cloud, pink-tinted by the dawn. The road dipped and curved, clinging to the cliffs, plunging into the fog, then again rising above it.

Fort Ross lay silent under the cloud cover, its stockade and blockhouses clustered like misplaced relics around California Route 1 which breached the stockade and rendered the fort defenseless. Just like the Californians to drive a highway through a historical monument! (In fairness to the Californians, we should mention that this error has now been corrected.) No flag hung from the flagpole. The place was deserted as if ashamed. The ghosts of the Russians who had built it had long ago left, driven out by the noise, the disrespect, the vandalism and violation. The two-domed wooden chapel, one of the treasured relics of California's brief past, had been totally burned, presumably by an arsonist, in 1970. The roof of the museum and part of the stockade had been burned, presumably by the same arsonist, in 1971. That was California, richest and most populous state of the Union, too stingy to protect its few historical monuments from the onslaughts of its too numerous lunatics.

Said the Gardener, nodding toward the ruins, "It's a sign of the times. The population of this state is going collectively insane."

*O generation of vipers, who has warned you to flee from the wrath to come.*

Now, balanced on the extreme western edge of the continent, the Saab followed the steep road down to the beach. Two salmon boats were anchored in the bay, ready to go, their engines turning, polluting the sea air with oil stink. Under the gray cloud-cover the sea extended, visible all the way to the horizon. Across it, in crude formation, flew four brown pelicans, doomed, according to the ecologists, to become shortly extinct, victims of DDT which prevented the eggs from hatching. The beach was empty. Surf pounded, frothed, receded. The kayaks were unlashed, loaded with gear, and carried to the beach.

The Gardener struggled into his wet suit bottom, old and ripped beyond repair. He wore it for warmth and protection against the fish, for rockfish, lingcod especially, have spines on their dorsal fins, needle sharp, capable of inflicting painful wounds. And as, in a kayak, one must land the fish in one's lap, a good layer of neoprene makes a handy protection. On the beach he stood for a while, the sand cold and wet under his bare feet, watching the waves. They came in, telling stories of some distant storm, a series of brutal breakers that crashed noisily and swirled up the beach, followed by a quiet spell with waves scarcely a foot high. You had to time it right. Get hit by a big one under the curl and you'd be swamped for sure, probably be turned over and pulled down by the under-tow.

There was always a thrill in the takeoff, the moment of truth. He watched the ocean, waiting for the big ones to pass. There were seven in all, arriving like express trains. Then he led the kayak into the water, keeping it lined up, facing the waves. Pick the moment, the right moment. Don't start from too high on the beach. A wave broke, swirled up and returned. He had those few seconds as it rose to step in, pull the spray cover over him, grab the paddle and move out fast. The next wave had formed already and rose ahead of him. He barely made it through the curl. Water poured over the spray cover which fitted badly. His fishing jacket was wet. There was water in the kayak. Keep going anyway. The worst thing to do when hit by the curl is to hesitate.

Beyond the breaker-line he paused, tossed the water off the spray cover, sponged out the kayak. It was just like the Pacific to throw a big one at you when you didn't expect it. The Professor was also having trouble, had been swept back up the beach, forced to bale out. He launched again in the quiet spell and made it smoothly. There were large and deep swells running from the northwest. The salmon boats, now taking off for the fishing grounds, dipped at intervals into the valleys between the swells, only their poles appearing above the water.

The kayaks also vanished among the swells, in the mountains and valleys of water that rolled around them. They rose, fell, rose again, lifted and dropped, nosing under from time to time, the water flowing back to the crest of the cockpit. Coming over the crest they hit the valley with a slap, quartering the waves, sometimes slithering sideways. It was not smooth paddling, but despite the superficial turbulence there was vast peace on the ocean. The long deep swells moved easily with a powerful rhythm, growing still deeper as they approached the rocks of the south reef, bursting high in the air in explosions of spray that drenched the rocks in water.

In the face of that power the men in the kayaks were nothing, no more significant than feathers floating on the water. Nothing, nothing, nothing. And they knew it. And rejoiced. To be put face to face with one's own nothingness was the ultimate in therapeutic experiences. As the silence flowed into the psyche the garbage flowed out, washed away by the vastness of the sea, by its power and its glory. It was the ultimate in yoga, a combination of physical effort and inner silence, a blending with air and ocean and the cosmic forces that moved them both. The fishermen were specks on the water's face. All around them the great interchange went on regardless, had been in process for centuries, millennia, millions of years. The moon and sun pulled on the watery mass, huge volumes of water ebbed and flowed. From the depths in the sea floor new matter rose through the skin of the earth, the continents drifted, mountains lifted, gigantic strains were released in horrendous earthquakes. Man's entire existence on earth shrank to an instant.

The ocean itself was awash with eggs and sperm, the ancient mother of all living, indifferent, patient, enduring. There were life forms everywhere. The giant kelp with stems as thick as ships' cables swayed in the great swells. There were blue-gray mussels on the rock, orange starfish exposed by the low tide, seaweeds like miniature palm trees, seaweeds with fronds green or pink, purple layers of edible dulse. In the water were plant plankton, animal plankton, baby fish, octopi, medium fish, bigger fish. There were seals, sea gulls, porpoises. There were Coho salmon migrating to their river spawning grounds. Down below there were abalone and snow-white sea anemones capable of grabbing the bait on a triple hook and holding with such force that a fifty-pound line would break before they would release it. Among the nooks and crevices of the reef, among kelp and purple echinoderms and white or red sea anemones the fish lived furtive, dangerous, savage lives, hiding among the weeds, pouncing, evading, devouring.

The two fishermen cautiously approached the south reef. It loomed ahead, jagged rock slabs projecting into the ocean, their distorted strata tilted almost perpendicular. The big swells, rolling in from the northeast, hit with the momentum of freight trains. All the water was in motion with swell and back wash, choppy, turbulent, unpredictable, dangerous. The kayaks bounced on the chop. Water slopped over the spray covers. Now and then a little entered the cockpit. It was a day to keep clear of the rocks and stay away from the kelp. Too rough for easy fishing. A bumpy trip, but stimulating.

The fishermen stopped paddling and checked the time—7:30 A.M. Two and a half hours to travel from their homes to the fishing grounds. Someday they would need to get a place nearer the coast.

Now began the serious business. The double paddles were

stowed against ring bolts by the cockpit. The fishing poles were extricated, armed with red and yellow feathered jig-rigs terminating in ten-ounce jigs with triple hooks. The hooks were baited with octopus or hunks of fish guts and the jigs cautiously released till they contacted the rocks below. The jig was raised and lowered in rhythmic motion, cautiously. Because of the powerful movement of the swells it was almost impossible to avoid hang-ups. Sooner or later the triple hook would snag on something, a clump of seaweed, a rock, a sea anemone. Hang-ups were the curse of reef fishing.

The curse and the challenge. It was only the constant threat of hang-ups that prevented the fisherman from falling into a doze. All the powers of the ocean converged upon him to weave a hypnotic spell. He was rocked and cradled by the great swells. The roar of surf on the reef became a soothing lullaby. Then there was the bell buoy far out at sea, tolling monotonously like a sea-borne church. All these exerted a certain soothing effect, lulling the fisherman until suddenly his jig refused to rise, compelling him to awaken, to struggle and jiggle and try every means to free the object, and finally, if all else failed, to pull violently on the line hoping to break the fifty-pound test nylon.

Such hang-ups, of course, could happen even when the fisherman was fully alert. They were bound to happen if he let his attention wander. This made the whole performance an exercise in awareness, using the jig on the end of its nylon line to tap cautiously on the sea floor, feeling the way like a blind man with his cane, ever ready for entanglements. Such awareness, such knowledge of what goes on below, differentiates the skilled fisherman from the novice. A good rock fisherman is rarely skunked by the ocean. He knows where the fish are. He knows what bait to use, knows the tides, the currents, and just how to fish the kelp beds without getting snagged. He even knows, before reeling it in, what kind of fish he has on the hook.

There were, according to ichthyologists, some fifty species of rockfish on the California coast. Of these the Gardener and the Professor had made the acquaintance of seven. There were the black and the blue, the vermillion and the orange, the olive and brown and China. Of these the blacks and blues, so alike as to be almost indistinguishable, were by far the most numerous. They congregated in swarms in certain parts of the reef and would rush impetuously upon the colored lures, imparting to the rod a peculiar jiggle which told the fisherman at once that he was fishing in a school of black rockfish. Often all three lures on the jig-rig would be taken and three fish would end up flapping on the floor of the kayak. And all their friends would come up alongside to see them hauled in, gregarious to the last. Peculiar also were their eating habits. Though quite uninterested in the tastiest bait, they were irresistibly attracted to jig-rigs which were nothing more than hooks concealed in tufts of red and yellow wool. What they actually lived on was hard to tell. In their stomachs one found nothing but a jellylike fluid.

There was no mystery about the diet of the orange rockfish. These were most common after the blacks and their stomachs were generally full of baby octopus. So to catch them one removed the octopus from the stomach of one and used it as bait for the next. By far the coarsest feeder was the cabezon, a creature endowed with amazing digestive powers. More than once the Gardener had recovered from the stomachs of these monsters entire crabs and whole abalone, swallowed shell and all. As for the lingcod, they preferred strips of fish meat, especially greenling sea trout. Or they would go for bare jigs, attracted by the flash of the metal.

That day there was the usual swarm of black rockfish, small and numerous, hardly worth hauling in. The State of

California had seen fit to impose a fifteen-fish limit on the species, an absurd restriction in view of their enormous numbers. So the fishermen moved into deeper waters, away from the rocks in search of bigger fish.

For almost an hour nothing happened. The tide started to come in. Suddenly, like a herd of cattle that all start feeding at once, the big fish started biting. The rod bent. Several yards of line were pulled from the reel. The Gardener hastily tightened the star drag and horsed the fish off the bottom. A big lingcod by the feel. You couldn't fool around with that sort of fish. The sporty types who take pride in landing forty-pounders on twelve-pound test line would never land a lingcod. Those fish didn't understand the rules of the game. Give them one little run and they would dart into a crevice in the rocks, spread their pectoral fins, and refuse to budge. Even with fifty-pound line one could rarely move them once they hid.

So you could not play with big lingcod. The fight was on at once, a struggle to get the fish off the bottom and keep it off the bottom. As the fish tired and was drawn in alongside, the leopardlike spots of the lingcod became visible in the water. The big mouth gaped, showing rows of savage teeth. It was a fair-sized fish, maybe fifteen pounds. The Gardener struck with the gaff. There was a violent commotion, a shower of seawater. With a powerful heave he landed the fish in his lap, a beautiful sea-green beast with brown spots, three feet long, reptilian, savage, streamlined and exceedingly violent. The Gardener reached for the bang stick as the fish threshed about, reflecting that he had brought it in too fast, should have played it longer. He was on the point of stunning it with a blow to the brain when, with a flip of its tail, it freed itself from the gaff and plunged over the side.

Well. . . . Round one to the fish. In kayak fishing you could never be sure of a catch until you had bashed the beast's brains in and stowed it under the spray cover. The fishing, however, continued lively. He landed in succession five orange rockfish each about four pounds, followed by two more ling-cod. Then came a surprising and confused tugging at the line, the sort that makes a fisherman wonder what kind of monster he has hooked. The monster turned out to be a ten-pound lingcod plus a five-pound cabezon which had attacked one of the colored lures. He gaffed the lingcod, managed to haul in the cabezon on the hook, an ugly fish, huge mouth, flat toadlike head with a warty excrescence in its midst. And, as usual, a whole crab in its stomach.

No sooner was the line back in the water than one of the greenling sea trout made off with the lure and sneaked into a rock crevice before it could be hauled in. It took fifteen minutes of pulling and coaxing to extricate the creature. The greenlings, commonly called sea trout, are not related to trout in any way. They are pretty fish, daintily spotted, and the male differs in shape and coloring from the female.

Meanwhile the cloud cover had rolled back and the sun had come out. The ocean, formerly gray and melancholy, became blue and amiable. On its surface an armada of small Portuguese Man-of-War drifted past the kayaks with sails and purple bodies, their long stinging tentacles dangling in the water. Large blue and white jellyfish floated as if drawn out by the sun. The surface of the ocean was broken as swarms of small fish, probably surf fish or herring, exploded into the air, pre-sumably being chased by something below. They emerged like fountains of silver, creating wild excitement among the seabirds that suddenly congregated overhead. Pelicans, sea gulls, cor-morants all dived into the fish swarm. The air was filled with squawking and splashing. The birds were so glutted they could hardly rise from the sea.

The time had come to return. Already, the afternoon wind was disturbing the sea, and whitecaps were forming. The northwest wind rapidly freshened, forcing the fishermen to exert themselves to the utmost. It was astonishing how quickly that afternoon wind could develop. It took them an hour to paddle the mile back to Fort Ross, with the spray blown back into their faces as they crouched over the paddle. With relief they finally pulled into the sheltered water under the protecting cliffs and turned the kayaks toward the beach. Skin divers in black wet suits with sleek red and white paddle boards were splashing in the surf. The two fishermen paused beyond the breaker line to stow away their gear, putting the fish in gunny sacks. It was always possible to get sideswiped and rolled in the breakers, in which case the sea could take everything, even one's hat.

They turned toward the breaker line, looking nervously over their shoulders. One really needed eyes in the back of one's head to watch the breakers sneaking up behind one. Coming in was a matter of precise timing, of balancing just behind the crest of the wave. Go too far forward and the nose of the kayak would dig in and the whole boat be hurled end over end, a disturbing experience. Come in too far back and one would be swept back in the wave recoil, hit by the next breaker and rolled over. But a well-judged landing was pretty and very enjoyable, with the wave breaking just ahead of the kayak and sending it speeding up the beach.

Actually neither fisherman had much trouble. The surf, in the mysterious way Pacific turf has, had quieted down during the morning. They landed smoothly among the skin divers, hauled the kayaks up the beach, emptied their sacks of fish into the fish box, and drove home. They had, in the course of the morning, landed four lingcod, seven orange rockfish, two greenlings, one china cod, two cabezon, and eighteen black rockfish. The total weight, carefully recorded for the fishing book, was seventy pounds of fish, which gave thirty-six pounds of fillets for the freezer, a saucepan full of chowder from the heads and back bones, and a pile of tidbits for the cats. Plus sun, wind, fresh air, exercise, and a host of rich impressions.

Blessed is the ocean, mother of us all!

# X

## *Aquaculture*

They started early, five in the morning, a journey of exploration. Once again it was the Professor's Saab that bore the brunt of exercise. It traveled down Sonoma Mountain under the stars, to pass through sleepy Glen Ellen and hit the road toward Napa as the early light was showing in the east. Between Napa and Route 505 were rolling hills of barley. Then Route 5 turned north, with the coastal range to the west and the plain to the east as the sun rose higher and the heat began.

Beer cans, beer bottles, assorted garbage . . . mediocre houses that seemed unsure of their hold on life . . . across the valley, giant towers marching mile after mile bringing electricity from the mountains to dwellers in the plain . . . Around little towns such as Williams, monstrous machines that were either outdated or awaiting repair stood around like herds of dinosaurs.

The machines existed to harvest rice. The Gardener, who associated rice paddies with Asia, regarded the paddies with astonishment. They were neatly laid out between banks of bulrushes, perfectly level and part flooded, deep green in places, dry and bare in others. And in their midst, by the railroad tracks, arose huge storage towers, all presumably stuffed with rice, of the Rice Growers Cooperative.

The rice fields ended, the long climb into the mountains began. Lake Shasta, enormous and man-made, stretched its fingers back into the drowned valleys, bearing on its placid surface the floating summer cabins, the noisy outboards reeking of half-burned oil and the water skiers disturbing the mountain calm with shrieks. The road continued to rise, an enormous road still being widened by gigantic machines. Who but the Americans would have carved this great gash through the mountains? What did it imply, this mania for road building that made Rome's greatest efforts seem like toys? Would they ever rest, these maniacal road builders, before the whole country was buried under rivers of concrete, concrete roads, concrete parking lots, concrete foundations? But the land was still enormous and even the six-lane highway was dwarfed by the mountains. And then on the horizon rose Mount Shasta, snow-covered even in September and peaked by its own private cloud, which it wore like a banner. Near the foot of the mountain stood the Zen Mission, presided over by Kennett Roshi, an Englishwoman and certified Zen master.

Mount Shasta was full of strange spirits.

Oregon proved slightly tidier than California. In Eugene, where they spent the night, the dust and dryness gave way to damp and greenery. In the morning it rained. A deluge. The kayaks on top of the car sloshed with water and had to be emptied at intervals. It poured as they passed through Portland but cleared as they entered Seattle. They ate lunch in a semi-rustic side street on the outskirts of the city, that ended in a ravine partly filled with beer cans. Huge planes from the Boeing works rose in series, making their way aloft amid clouds of pollutants and an output of sound sufficient to deafen the dead. The houses seemed poor and shrunken, as if beaten down by the incessant din. On one of them a notice proclaimed: *Raided by the FBI*. A shaggy dog contemplated the travelers, thought about them for several minutes, decided to register a protest, barked ceaselessly but without conviction. A woman, baby in arms, eyed them from a doorway, a hard glint in her eye. Were they spies of the FBI disguised as kayak-carrying vacationers?

Said the Gardener, "The natives don't seem friendly."

The remark was drowned in a roar from one of Boeing's products.

"I think," said the Professor, "we'd better finish our lunch someplace else."

They sought peace but found none. Seattle seemed less a city than an endless urban sprawl, as if some drunken deity had vomited it onto the edge of Puget Sound. The sky was broken and stormy. It rained, it cleared, it rained again. The city was gray, wet, and largely unemployed. It exuded gloom.

The School of Fisheries at the University of Washington was more cheerful. Here, at least, was creative science and an escape from the din of Boeing. A talk with the apostle of aquaculture, Dr. Lauren P. Donaldson, did much to restore their faith in the human race. Aquaculture, the sister of agriculture, was a neglected science which mankind could not afford to neglect much longer. Governments poured millions into research that men might efficiently farm the land. Why not also teach them to farm the sea? At the moment men did not farm the sea, they merely robbed it. They scooped up its products in great nets wastefully, carelessly. They made no attempt to replace what they took out. So the fisheries declined. The great whales were hunted to extinction. Man, the arch predator, at his destructive worst, was turning even the ocean into a desert.

It was time for a change and Dr. Donaldson was the advocate of that change, a voice crying in the wilderness perhaps, but not entirely unheard. "The difficulty," said he, sweeping a hand across a large wall map, "is the concept of International Fishing Rights. This makes aquaculture impractical in the Northern Hemisphere, particularly where salmon are concerned. What's the use of raising fish for someone else to catch?"

The problem was obvious. In special breeding tanks an

aquaculturist could raise his own salmon as a cattle breeder could raise his own calves. They were raising such fish at the School of Fisheries, doing it, moreover, with a skill that rivaled the best efforts of plant and animal breeders. By crossing male steelhead trout (a relative of the salmon) with the fast-growing female rainbow trout they had produced an incredible hybrid that attained the weight of seven pounds in two years. The steelhead can go out and forage in the wide ocean ("the big pasture") and return to their home rivers to spawn. But while in the big pasture they run the risk of being captured by Russian or Japanese fishing factories that haul in everything they can reach independent of its origin.

Certainly, when it came to aquaculture, few nations could equal the Japanese. With 80 million people on mountainous islands they *had* to farm the sea. It was a question of survival. So they had used the Donaldson hybrids to restore their depleted salmon fisheries. Soon they would discover that the International Fishing Rights, which left them free to fish where they liked, would work against them. Their own prize salmon would be caught by Russians, Koreans, Chinese. There would then be an international conference and something more sensible would be worked out. It was a matter of time. When Russians, Japanese, Americans, Canadians all recognized the advantages of sea farming, new international agreements would become possible.

Dr. Donaldson was prepared to be patient. His efforts had not gone unappreciated. On the wall of his office hung a fanciful carving of a salmon, a gift from Japan—"To Professor Donaldson for helping to prevent World War III."

Meanwhile both steelhead and salmon had learned to regard the Washington School of Fisheries as home. They poured by the thousands into the raceway and pool at spawning time. There they were grabbed by the students and stripped of their eggs. The eggs were fertilized with selected sperm and placed in plastic trays where they absorbed their yolk sacs. The baby fish, transferred to troughs of circulating seawater, were sorted and branded (by cold, not heat, the "branding iron" being dipped in liquid nitrogen). They were raised to fingerling size on special foods and released into the ocean to fend for themselves.

Man's intervention made improvements in the natural process of fish reproduction which was wasteful in the extreme. In the wild a salmon might produce four thousand eggs of which perhaps 99 percent would perish. Of the forty survivors 90 percent would perish in the ocean, devoured by other fish, by birds, by seals. So, out of four thousand eggs, only four fish would return to the rivers. All legislation regarding salmon fishing was based on these four fish. "Two for the creek, two for the can." Which meant that 50 percent of the salmon run had to go free simply to maintain the population.

But in hatcheries all this was changed. The 99 percent mortality of eggs could be reduced to 20 percent. The 90 percent destruction of smolts could also be reduced by releasing them to face a hostile world after they had grown large enough to fend for themselves. It was a real farming operation. In long troughs of circulating seawater the baby salmon or steelhead hybrids ate their special food and grew safe from their enemies before being marked and released into the "big pasture." In the ocean off Tasmania and in the fiords of Norway this sea farming had been taken a step further. Floating enclosures prevented the fish from straying, just as fences on land confined the farmer's cattle.

But you could not set floating enclosures off the coast of California. The ocean was public. One had to hunt for one's fish all over the ocean, which was not only wide but also deep. So the trollers went out with their long poles extended, trailing herring as bait at all sorts of depths. It seemed something of a miracle that any of them caught anything. The good fishermen operated by instinct, knowing where the salmon were even in a blinding fog that wiped out all landmarks. So they caught fish. The dabblers, the amateurs, the beginners just wandered around. If they caught anything it was by luck.

It would be much more intelligent to farm the sea. In California this development lay in the future as far as the salmon was concerned. Sea farming in California was possible only for those who could keep one foot on land and one on the ocean. Which meant one might raise oysters or even abalone, convenient creatures that could be trusted to stay in one place. So the travelers set off in search of Lummi Indians on whose reservation this form of sea farming was being practiced with assistance from the State of Washington and the U.S. Department of Commerce.

Said the Gardener, "It's nice to know that someone is doing something for the Indians."

The Indians, in fact, were doing a good deal for themselves. They had always been fishermen. In former times their medicine men could see, in a trance, the whereabouts of the salmon. Thus guided, the fishermen, with only a dugout canoe, a wooden hook, and a line of twisted nettle fiber, could catch the wily fish. That called for real skill.

Now the projecting breakwater extending far over the tidal flats was the site of massive circular concrete basins where fish were to be raised and farmed in seven hundred and fifty enclosed acres of Puget Sound. On Lummi Island, to which they crossed by ferry, they found the oyster hatchery in operation. The oysters, male and female, were induced to spawn by "temperature shock" simply by exposing them to warm water. In large glass vessels under batteries of fluorescent lamps the food of the tiny oysters was grown nearby. Golden-colored single-celled algae swarmed in the bottles oxygenated by streams of air. These were fed to the oyster larvae which, in the early stages, were not like oysters at all but swam around like small dragons. Later they settled down, attaching themselves to strings of scallop shells suspended in the circulating seawater of their tanks. The oyster spat grew to the size of half an inch on their shells and could then be thinned and suspended in the ocean itself from rafts or floats.

Oysters could indeed be grown on the bed of the ocean, planted like onions in rows, weeded and thinned at intervals. But such bottom-growing oysters were apt to be buried in silt, devoured by starfish and sting rays unless protected by under-water fences. The suspended oyster, however, could grow free of danger of silt and benefit from the free flow of ocean water from which they extracted their food, mostly plankton. Once planted out, they grew rapidly, becoming as big as a human hand in eighteen to twenty-four months.

When it came to oyster farming no one could equal the Japanese (fifty-two thousand pounds per acre in Hiroshima Bay versus one tenth of that yield in U.S. oyster farms).

The explorers left Lummi Island debating whether to add sea farming to land farming. Should they, perhaps, rent the Tom Point oyster ground on Tomales Bay, put up a greenhouse, pump in seawater, raise oysters scientifically on cultured uni-cellular algae? Should they try their hand at culturing abalone? The Japanese had done it. But it took an abalone five years to reach legal size, and what was so special about abalone anyway?

It was only after their return that they discovered the most exotic of all the aquaculture projects only an hour's drive from home. The Bodega Bay Marine Lab of the University of Cali-fornia was situated on a delightful cove near the Hole in the Head. The Hole in the Head represented an abortive effort by the P.G.&E. to build an atomic reactor at the mouth of Bodega Bay. As the reactor would lie directly over the San Andreas fault, much opposition had been voiced by local in-habitants who saw themselves engulfed in radioactive wastes when the Great Earthquake came. They argued that, though it was humanly impossible to control the great earthquake, they could at least try to control P.G.&E. A Homeric struggle ensued, a real David and Goliath encounter. The P.G.&E. had one set of experts who proclaimed that no earthquake could damage the reactor, the conservationists had another set who said the exact opposite. The battle raged. Just as the outcome seemed to favor the P.G.&E., Mother Earth took a hand and destroyed the town of Anchorage, Alaska. That was too much, even for the P.G.&E. They abandoned the project, leaving the hole they had blasted for the foundation on Bodega Head, surrounded by an elaborate fence to keep out trespassers.

The Marine Lab close by was built in the grim gray monolithic style favored by the University of California. Within it an assortment of sea beasts lived pampered lives in tanks of circulating seawater. The exotic aquaculture project centered around the culture of the Maine lobster, a species so heavily overfished that it was in danger of extinction. While the price of lobster dinners soared, the lobster fishermen went out of business. There simply weren't any more lobsters.

Under these circumstances it certainly made sense to try to culture the Maine lobster. Female lobsters already fertilized were flown to the laboratory from Martha's Vineyard in Massachusetts. The larvae, about the size of earwigs, clung to the mother's swimmerettes, from which they were transferred to fiberglass pots. There, in water at a temperature of 72° F., they fed on brine shrimp and passed through four larval stages. The lobster's problem, like that of all arthropods, was to grow without getting eaten. There were drawbacks to having one's skeleton on the outside rather than within. The chief of these was that one had to step out of one's skeleton every time one wanted to grow. While out of its skeleton the lobster was naked and defenseless, a prey to anything that came along. Particularly they were a prey of other lobsters, for there is nothing a lobster likes better than to feast off its own kind.

These cannibalistic tendencies made lobster rearing difficult. Nothing would prevent the creatures from eating each other except keeping them physically separated. So there they were, at various stages of growth, each in a little apartment under a perpetual fountain of running seawater, a bare apartment, its only furniture a short length of P.V.C. pipe to give the lobster something to hide in when it had shed its skin and was naked. Lobsters in such condition feel the need to hide.

In their private apartments the lobsters grew rapidly. They had been selected specifically for fast growth. A lobster that took six to eight years to attain one pound weight in the ocean could reach the same weight in a year and ten months in his apartment. There was no prospect, it seemed, of turning the lobsters loose in the big pasture to let them fatten on natural food. It had been tried, with one result only. No one ever saw the lobsters again.

The picture, therefore, was one of artificial culture from start to finish. The lobsters would be raised like broilers, in circulating seawater at 72° F., each in its private apartment. Its food would be carefully regulated to give maximum growth rates. The circulating seawater would be scientifically monitored, its pH adjusted, its impurities removed. Indeed, the would-be lobster grower did not even need to locate by the ocean. A quite adequate seawater substitute could be made synthetically, and the evidence suggested that the lobster did not know the difference. One could raise lobsters in Chicago.

To this story the Gardener listened with mixed feelings. The scientist in him, who liked to get his teeth into any technical problem, found plenty to play with. There were lots of nice practical problems involved in the project, genetic, nutritional, engineering, economic. The Whole-Earther in him was repelled. Was there any virtue in repeating in aquaculture those fantastically artificial conditions that prevailed in the broiler industry? A lobster factory would be no better than a chicken factory, nonecological, totally against nature. On the whole, he decided, he would prefer to go fishing for his seafood. What was so special about lobster anyway?

# XI

## *The Salmon Hunter*

Blue sky and freshening wind, the tail end of a warm spell. Thin clouds were blowing in from the direction of the ocean which was making its presence felt again after a series of sweating days with temperatures in the nineties. That Sunday in May marked the beginning of a new venture, the launching or rather relaunching of the salmon boat *Marina*. All the Whole-Earthers with maritime leanings went off to see the event. They piled together into the Blue Whale, an ostentatious vehicle of the Lincoln Continental genus that the Gamblin' Man, who also functioned as a traveling salesman, had purchased to impress his customers. The Blue Whale was full of buttons designed to demonstrate the superiority of American technical know-how. There were buttons to raise the windows and lower the windows, cool the air, heat the air. The buttons jammed regularly.

The way lay west, not this time by the green soupy water of the Russian River but farther south through Petaluma. Petaluma had once been the egg capital of the world, resounding with the cacklings of thousands of chickens. These cacklings were now silent. Acres of abandoned chicken houses, gray and rotting, attested to the fact that taxes had steadily risen, egg prices steadily fallen. The small dairy farms were failing for the same reason. The developers had swooped on the farm land like carrion crows and were busily plastering it with boxlike dwellings.

Beyond the ex-egg capital of the world lay stark, bare hills, so stark that the very ribs of the earth showed through in the form of jagged upthrusts of rock. One could feel at such places the workings of enormous forces, for the tumult of rocks was caused by the collision of huge masses, where the plate of the Pacific met with and plunged beneath the coast of California, crumpling and upthrusting the land.

On the hill above Jensen's Oyster Bar the great expanse of Tomales Bay became suddenly visible. Californians who knew nothing of the sea-floor spreading and the collision of the plates of the lithosphere were sometimes vaguely aware of the force which had ripped open Tomales Bay. It lay right above the rift of the San Andreas fault, that sleeping dragon bound one day to awaken, bringing down in ruins a thousand developments, all built of ticky-tacky and all looking the same. Through the San Francisco suburbs the Pacific plate was creeping forward at the rate of two and a half inches a year. According to the geologist the slippage along the fault was thirteen feet in arrears. Somehow the fault had become stuck since the 1906 earthquake. The whole of San Francisco as well as a goodly section of the California coast was balanced on top of a coiled spring that at any time might suddenly be released, hurling buildings, bridges, aqueducts, everything, thirteen feet in one direction or another. And in the course of a few moments, geologically speaking, the whole strip of land now called Point Reyes Peninsula would be split away from the mainland and become a large island. The free Pacific would roll in the gap between island and mainland.

Meanwhile there was Jensen's Oyster Bar and the oyster beds that supplied it, carefully fenced to keep out marauding sting rays, starfish, and other foes of the oyster. And along Route 1 moved a steady procession of campers, with aluminum boats on their roofs, the rearguard of an army of abalone pickers who had been on the rocks that morning at 6 A.M. The year's major minus tide (−2 feet) had brought the abalone fanciers out in force to enjoy the rare experience of picking this giant sea snail off the rocks instead of diving for it in wet suit and snorkel.

The Blue Whale paused to guzzle a bellyful of super gasoline, turned its nose south, and cruised on toward Marshall (pop. 50). The object of the cruise, the Marshall Boat Yard, showed against the horizon as a jumble of masts leaning at improbable angles. On a strip of sandy soil between the road and the bay lay boats of all shapes and sizes in varying states of decay and resurrection. Formerly, before Californians became aware of air pollution, the irreparable hulks had been burned. Now such burnings were illegal so they were dragged higher and higher up the yard where they rotted slowly among the weeds or were hacked apart for their few remaining sound timbers.

The *Marina*, though born in Sausalito in 1927, was still far from such a fate. She had belonged to a logger at Fort Bragg who logged in the winter and fished for salmon in summer. But the logger's wife preferred to keep her husband on dry land, so the *Marina* had lain idle at Fort Bragg through two fishing seasons and accumulated her share of rotten wood in the process. The Salmon Hunter's previous boat had been a sixteen-foot fiberglass midget in the mosquito fleet with a motor so unreliable that he who went out in the boat could never be sure of returning. By contrast the *Marina*, thirty-three and a half feet from stem to stern, equipped with Loran, an eighty horsepower Ford four-cylinder diesel engine, and a hold capable of storing eight thousand dollars worth of salmon, was positively palatial. The only drawback was that the stem was rotten. The stem, in a wooden boat, is that portion of the bow that meets waves head-on and holds the planks together in the front of the boat. It is quite a vital part of the equipment.

The Salmon Hunter bought the *Marina*. The Gardener,

who loved boats and bold fishermen, made the Salmon Hunter an honorary member of the Church of the Earth (marine section) and advanced part of the purchase price. The process of buying the boat proved incredibly complicated. The Coast Guard, it seemed, had an interest in the vessel. It was "documented," which meant that its services could be drawn upon by the government of the United States in its hour of need. That need would have to be dire indeed for the government to require an old tub like the *Marina*, but the Coast Guard took the matter seriously and practically strangled itself in its own red tape, requiring acres of documents signed and sealed before the new owner could sail the boat from Fort Bragg to the Marshall Boat Yard. No insurance company would cover a boat the bow of which was held together mainly by paint, so the Salmon Hunter, with the Coal Man as mate, sailed the *Marina* uninsured to the boat yard through an ocean which was far from friendly.

The old bucket sloshed and wallowed in the lumpy water, radio communication was lost, several friendly boats set forth from Noyo to see if the *Marina* was going under. She was not. The paint held. She was hoisted out of the water at Marshall, dragged up the yard and left alongside the Coal Man's boat which was in far worse shape than the *Marina*, having been rammed by a fishing boat in Bodega Bay. No one had time to work on the boat at the boat yard, so the Salmon Hunter, with help from the Coal Man, hacked out the rotten wood from the stem and partly removed seventeen ribs from the ice hold. The Gardener, visiting the scene after this major surgery, found a hole in the stem big enough to put his fist in.

Now all that was changed. Self-reliance was the Salmon Hunter's strength. He spent the winter making guitars. He employed the same skill on the boat. As oak was almost unobtainable commercially, he found his own, going back to the woods to do so. He sawed it, shaped it, and planed it until the stem looked like new, sistered the rotten ribs, knocking out concrete ballast to reach the rot. By mid-May the boat was ready for relaunching, just in time for the start of the salmon season, delayed two weeks by an argument over prices.

So there was the *Marina*, on chocks, hauled close to the dock, all the Salmon Hunter's friends buzzing around the boat applying anti-fouling compound to the hull. She sat on her chocks plain as an old shoe, broad in the beam as a middle-aged hausfrau. There were no pretensions about her, no elegance, no grace, a beamy double-ender, tough and stable, an honest work boat, three gurdies a side, her freshly cut eucalyptus poles lying ready. As if to emphasize the contrast, she sat right next to a sailing trimaran, the last word in grace, all curves and swoops, like a seabird with wings extended.

Sailor's Yarn, ex-merchant mariner, looked contemptuously at the lovely trimaran. He allowed it was a beautiful boat and would sail swiftly in the sheltered waters of the bay. But anyone who took such a boat on the ocean was asking for trouble.

"Stands to reason," said he, "with those three hulls working against each other, sooner or later she'll fall apart."

Meanwhile the Salmon Hunter's wife restored the boat's name to the *Marina* which had been painted over. No time for a fancy job. She stuck on masking tape, enough to get by the Coast Guard who disliked finding unnamed boats in coastal waters. MARINA S.F. said the masking tape. All was ready at last.

There was no sign of a launching ramp near the *Marina*. The boat, it appeared, was not large enough to warrant such services. Instead, when the grand moment arrived, she was picked up bodily. Two slings from a lofty derrick were placed beneath her hull, fore and aft. An aged diesel engine was unveiled, and set in motion. The engine spluttered, emitted a cloud of smoke and a powerful smell of oil. The steel cable tightened, and the *Marina*, with the Salmon Hunter aboard,

rose in the air and described a graceful arc above the dock. She hovered above the water while the donkey engine coughed. Almost imperceptibly she was lowered, her side fouling the dock. The Salmon Hunter sprang ashore, fended off the boat with a long pole. All the Salmon Hunter's friends and anyone else who happened to feel like exercise helped push the dangling vessel away from the dock side. The operator of the donkey engine looked on with Jovian calm. The friction of the steel cable on the drum generated oily smoke and showers of sparks, but the *Marina* entered the water so gently that it was almost impossible to tell when she ceased to be airborne. Finally the cable slackened, the slings were removed, and the *Marina* floated free in her natural element.

The Salmon Hunter was now ready for business. Few forms of fishing make more demands on the fisherman than trolling for salmon. In that great expanse of water off the California

coast the swiftly migrating fish may be almost anywhere. Only the albacore is more elusive. To find the salmon a man needs some special sense. To catch them when found he needs skills that no textbook can define. There were high liners in the salmon fleet who seemed to know just where to look, who could drag in fish as fast as they could haul in the lines. But others, following them, might never land a fish. Even the noise made by the boat could be critical. A slight leak of electricity from the generating system into the water could ruin the fishing. Slightly tainted bait could also spoil it. One was, after all, dealing with a superbly discriminating creature, a migrating King salmon capable, by smell alone, of distinguishing the river in which it had been spawned from all other streams along the coast.

Of course if one used a net it was much easier to catch salmon, and not very much in the way of art was involved. The seiners in Puget Sound simply lowered a net and swept up the fish as if with a vacuum cleaner. But the trollers used oversized fishing poles with lines and hooks. They had to troll at just the right speed, with lines at just the right depth. Moreover the fisherman had to be a mechanic and a weatherman. The marine engine that powered his boat was vital to his survival. Engine failure on a stormy seat could result in a wreck. As for the weather, it was never trustworthy. Wind could pick up at any time. Blinding fog shrouded the ocean for days on end. It required some careful navigation just to find one's way home.

As a way of life it was certainly not for everybody. The Salmon Hunter, climbing aboard the *Marina* at 4 A.M. in the morning, reflected that there were certainly easier ways of earning a living. Although, on that morning in late June, summer had technically started, no one would have guessed it from the prevailing temperature. A clinging fog covered the harbor of Bodega Bay and moisture dripped from the eucalyptus trees. The air was cold and still. The sound of the whistle buoy came from the harbor mouth. Men tramped heavily on the decks of their boats. There was a smell of diesel oil, the sound of marine engines coughing into life.

The Salmon Hunter peered into the fog and wondered why anyone in his right senses would venture out onto the Pacific at four in the morning and spend all day hunting for fish which might not be present. Whether you caught fish or not, you had your expenses, the boat, the ice, the fuel and twenty dozen trays of herring for bait. It was perfectly possible that one would return empty-handed. Why did one do it?

He did not bother to answer his unspoken question. He knew perfectly well why he fished for salmon. He made fairly good money, but the money was not really important. Out there on the ocean, alone, he had a sense of absolute freedom. No one could tell him what to do or where to go. He was a player of a challenging and difficult game, the rules of which were imposed not by man but by the sea. He was playing against a clever, discriminating fish, nor could he ever tell, from one day to the next, how the game would go. There were endless surprises. The unexpected was always possible. And on good days, when the fish were biting, there was never a dull moment.

He started the engine, turned on his lights, backed cautiously into the channel. All around him boats were moving, churning the oily water, their lights haloed by the fog. He was glad about that fog. A foggy ocean was a calm ocean and he needed calm. That day he intended to run north all the way to Fish Rocks off Gualala, a seven-hour run. It would be a shame to run so far only to get blown off the ocean.

A procession of boats was moving out of the harbor and he joined that procession. There were nearly a hundred boats of various sizes heading for the fishing grounds. Outside the harbor he stopped the engine and spread his poles, thirty-six feet of eucalyptus with three lines on each. Then, setting a course for the northwest, he switched to Iron Mike (the auto pilot), sat down on the gaffing hatch, and made bait. Deftly he speared each herring through the tail with the bait holder, inserted a brass pin through the head, and wound on a rubber band. The device was essential to keep the herring on the hook. He loaded every hook in the tackle drawer, set the bait ready, checked his course, lay down at the bow and communed with a white-sided dolphin that had picked up the bow wave and was riding the crest. The two large-brained mammals, human and cetacean, wordlessly exchanged notes.

It was nearly noon by the time he arrived at Fish Rocks. The ocean was flat, there was no need to put out the flopper-stoppers. Putting the gurdy in gear he began to let out line, snapping five to seven leaders on each line as it went past. There were three lines on each pole, the bow, the main, and the tip, and they were weighted with ninety pounds of lead between them. The line was seven-strand stainless steel with a breaking point of six hundred pounds.

Moving forward he watched the fathometer. Flashes on the screen showed signs that bait fish were in the area, and where there were bait fish one could expect salmon. He lowered his lines to twenty-five fathoms and began trolling.

The boat passed over a bait ball, a swarm of bait fish surrounded by feeding salmon. As the baited lines passed through the crowded fish, action at once became apparent. The Salmon Hunter watched the springs at the poles. He could tell by the way they vibrated how many fish he had caught and their approximate size. The bow line had something big and active attached to it, either a single large fish or several smaller ones. He put the gurdy in gear, removed the first leader. On the second a big fish about twenty-five pounds was doing its best to shed the hook. The Salmon Hunter grabbed the eighteen-foot leader and cautiously hauled the fish to the side of the boat. It required delicate judgment. One could lose a fish either by bringing it in too fast or by letting it fight too long. Moreover, by the behavior of the line, it was clear that at least one more fish had been hooked.

The Salmon Hunter leaned over from the gaffing hatch, brought the fish to the boat side, grabbed the gaff, hoisted the fish aboard, and bashed its brains out with one well-aimed blow. With a single deft movement of the gaff he removed the hook. He meticulously avoided touching the fish. The fish slime was notorious for producing infected wounds and so slippery that it made handling the gaff almost impossible. Swiftly he straightened out the leader and unclipped it, brought in the second fish and repeated the sequence. The pace, as he passed through the school, became increasingly frantic. There was a fish on one of the other lines and the spring was dancing. He put on new baits, returned the first line to the water, hauled in the second, removed the fish, rebaited. He was dancing around doing several things at once. Once you were over a school, action could be so lively that a man lost all sense of time. The problem was to stay over it.

Action slackened. The Salmon Hunter made fresh baits, left the gaffing hatch, went forward to the cabin, took a Loran reading for position, checked his fathometer, turned the *Marina* through one hundred and eighty degrees to get back over the bait ball, made four more passes, then lost the fish. He hunted around in the fog trying to find them. Only as darkness approached did he realize that he was tired and hungry and the day was ending. He determined to anchor at Fish Rocks. It was an unfamiliar anchorage and he carefully followed the other boats as they made their way shoreward, set his anchor, lit his stove, and cooked himself a hamburger. Bone-weary, he fell into his bunk in the forecastle, but first of all rigged an alarm to awaken him in case his anchor came adrift. Dropping a weighted line over the side he tied the other end to his tea kettle and balanced it above his head. If the boat moved, the line would pull the tea kettle off its perch. It would fall and awaken him.

Next day he set out again at 4:30 A.M., nearly killing himself in his struggle to lift by hand his sixty-pound anchor. He had no winch on the *Marina*. Out beyond the steamer lanes he set his lines in ninety fathoms, fished all day, and spent the night on the ocean drifting in one hundred fathoms, his mast lights turned on. The wind rose in the night and the fog dispersed. At daybreak he found he had drifted fifteen miles to the south. He was too far from Fish Rocks to return, so headed for home. Off Salt Point he moved shoreward to check the coastline. It was a lovely day, sunny and clear with a northwesterly wind. The fishing had been good. He was satisfied. But no fisherman is ever really satisfied and nearly always dreams of just one more fish. So the Salmon Hunter, though ready to

head for home, nonetheless checked his fathometer. There, sure
enough, were signs of bait.

He lowered his lines. He was in an ideal situation, had a
school of salmon all to himself. There was not one other boat in
sight. For the next eight hours he worked frantically. It was
the best fishing he had ever experienced. In addition to salmon
he was catching rockfish in fantastic variety. On one haul he
found every one of his seven hooks occupied, one salmon and
six rockfish, every one of which was different in color from the
others. The line looked like a string of Christmas tree orna-
ments. This unexpected bonanza off Salt Point turned a good
trip into a great trip. He returned to Bodega Bay with eight
hundred pounds of salmon in the fish hold. It was not a bad re-
ward for three days of hard work.

# XII

## *Homo aquaticus*

From time to time, members of the Church of the Earth would consider scenarios with an aquacultural theme. There was, for example, the great Blasket scenario. The Blaskets are a group of islands off the west coast of Ireland and were for centuries inhabited by hardy fisherfolk who made a livelihood fishing from open boats in a frequently stormy and always treacherous ocean. For extra food these islanders trapped rabbits, grew modest crops of potatoes, and raised sheep. Their language was Irish. Their way of life had been described by two native writers and translated from Irish into English in the 1930s. There was *Islandman* by Tomas O Crohan and *Twenty Years A-Growing* by Maurice O'Sullivan.

What books! What true Whole-Earthers! A breed of peasants and poets. But the Shulamite and Britannicus who visited the islands in 1972 found them uninhabited. Unlike the Aran Islands, they had not been able to hold their population against the manifold attractions of the mainland. Would it not be a worthy enterprise to recolonize the empty Blaskets with sturdy young Americans? It would certainly be a fine way of screening out dabblers and dilettantes and developing a population of true Whole-Earthers.

Then there was the Scottish sea loch scenario. The sea lochs of the west coast of Scotland are deep inlets having access to the sea. They would, the Gardener decided, be ideal places in which to raise the Atlantic salmon, a valuable species in danger of becoming exterminated. An aura of romance hung over the sea lochs. They were, in one case at least, ornamented by a castle of great antiquity and impressive strength, the Eilean Donan Castle of the MacRaes situated opposite the Isle of Skye. What a location for a salmon hatchery! Surrounded by shades of Prince Charlie, lairds, bards, crofters, fishermen, and poets, the true Whole-Earthers could blend science with the sea. Salmon in the loch, sheep on the hills, potatoes in the croft. There were abandoned crofts throughout the Highlands and the Islands. Indeed the whole area was in need of a boost, and a good salmon-raising project would be just what it required.

The sea loch scenario gathered just enough momentum to induce the Gardener to draft a letter to J. D. H. MacRae suggesting that the somber outlines of Eilean Donan Castle would be enormously improved by the addition of a salmon hatchery. But the dream went no further. The Gardener was prone to rheumatism. In sunny California the affliction remained more or less dormant, flaring up only during periods of fog and damp. There were many such periods on Sonoma Mountain, times when the ocean fog blew in and lingered, but such fog spells rarely lasted long, were followed by clear skies and hot sun. But how would one fare in Scotland, where fog and damp cold were perpetual? At the thought of it, the Gardener's joints ached and the sea loch scenario lost its romantic aura.

Then, of course, there was the South Sea Island scenario.

> Breathes there a man with soul so dead
> That never to himself has said:
> "I will now abandon my dull life and go to the South Seas and
> live among brown-skinned girls, corals and coconuts"?

The Gardener, an imaginative soul, had cherished the dream ever since he had seen *Tabu* back in London in 1933. He knew the names of all the islands from the Marquesas to Rarotonga, had a set of books on island adventures and a large map of the

Pacific. But somehow, since coming to California, he had lost interest in the Paradises of the Pacific. They were paradises no longer, overrun by American tourists, exploited, polluted, vulgarized. The blight that had stricken Hawaii had spread to the other islands. The French authorities, who had fought the tourists for so long, had finally capitulated. There was an airstrip and a luxury hotel on Bora Bora. As for Tahiti, the less said the better.

There remained the Sea of Cortez and Baja California. The Baja scenario had one great advantage over all the others. One could at least visit the scene without spending a fortune on travel. From Santa Rosa to Calexico was about six hundred miles, from Calexico to San Felipe another hundred. It was within reach.

The Sea of Cortez scenario began to bloom. Its blossoming was hastened by a gift to the Gardener of Ray Cannon's *The Sea of Cortez*, a book that scintillates with pictures of sapphire blue waters and enormous fish. The Gardener began to visualize himself as one of *los vagabundos del mar*, the sea gypsies who roam the Sea of Cortez alone in a weatherbeaten dugout canoe with a tattered sail. Of them Ray Cannon had written that, apart from the canoe, "their only other earthly possessions are confined to heavy hand lines and hooks for fishing, an arpon for spearing sharks, turtles, and fish, a bucket, a couple of pots for cooking, a machete, wine bottles for water, a blanket and a coil of rope . . ." All major foodstuffs come from the sea and the shoreside hills. Every few months, when additional supplies are needed, they take live turtles or salted shark meat to the nearest town for trading. Even in this contact they feel beholden only to the freely giving sea. Their only conflicts are with the sea's storms. And when they feel ready to stop their roaming and die, they so do, and are buried on the southernmost tip of the Isla Cerralvo.

A tribe of true Whole-Earthers! There were people one could respect.

It seemed, however, too soon to become a vagabond of the sea. Instead a more ambitious project began to bubble in the Gardener's mind. The fantasy centered around *Homo aquaticus*, the water-man. Concerning this water-man the Gardener had written as follows:

> *In a study remarkable for its foresight [The Maracot Deep] Arthur Conan Doyle portrays an underwater human community that has not only learned to live in an aquatic environment but also developed psychologically far beyond the level attained by land-bound man. Today we have very good reason to believe that land-bound man is headed either for extinction or for a very severe reduction in numbers. If he becomes extinct he will be succeeded, as the most intelligent being on earth, by one of the aquatic mammals (whales or porpoises whose brain to body ratio is as high as his own). If he does not become extinct he may return to the aquatic environment from which life came in the first place, evolving into a new species,* Homo aquaticus, *as at home in the water as a sea lion or a seal.*
>
> *It is not necessary for man to wait for several millions of years to develop by the gradual process of evolution the adaptations necessary for existence in a new medium. Man can become* Homo aquaticus *very rapidly by using the artificial devices available to him that will enable him to exist in or under water longer than many aquatic mammals. Studies already begun by some members of the Church of the Earth have shown that the aquatic environment is not only extraordinarily interesting in its own right but also very therapeutic. The absolute quiet of "the Silent World," the weightlessness of the body in water, the complete relaxation that can be obtained in this medium, the mastery of breathing, the freedom of movement all combine to induce a state of awareness totally different from that experi-*

*enced in ordinary life on terra firma. Warm ocean water is the most health-giving medium there is. Its therapeutic effects in cases of muscular spasm, spinal adhesions, rheumatoid arthritis are attested to by many skin divers who took up this sport primarily on medical advice. But the psychological effects of steady quiet exercise in a warm ocean environment are even more remarkable. To say that such exercises are an adjunct to yoga is an understatement. They can be used as a form of yoga in their own right and form the basis of a new way of life, lived largely in or under the water, sustained by the products of the sea.*

*To further the exploration of this mode of existence the Church of the Earth proposes to create a sea-based commune. Its members will*

*(1) study the therapeutic effects of a variety of underwater exercises involving both free diving and scuba techniques;*

*(2) study the effect of raising children to be more aquatic than terrestrial;*

*(3) study various aspects of underwater farming with a view to feeding an aquatic community largely on the products of the sea;*

*(4) investigate various devices making possible prolonged existence on or under water.*

The sea-based commune had so far remained a dream. It was, however, a dream that could be turned into a reality by any group willing to exert itself. That man would outgrow the land and be forced to colonize the ocean had been predicted by more than one farsighted observer. Paoli Soleri had drawn the details for Novanoah I, a floating city for forty thousand. Kiyononi Kikutake had proposed, in his book *Marine City*, that man should model his floating city on the *velella*, a floating jellyfish that maintains stability by means of concentric circles of hanging tentacles.

Obviously it was high time for man to return to the sea. Seventy percent of the planet's surface was ocean. The needed technology was already available. Indeed a model of the floating city had already been prepared by students of the University of Hawaii. Certainly, if any state needed to expand into the ocean it was Hawaii. Overcrowded to bursting point, its rich agricultural land being guzzled by the developers at a rate which would cover the islands solidly with houses if allowed to continue, it had no alternative but to push its surplus population onto the ocean.

The Sea of Cortez, however, was nearer than Hawaii, and a trip would make a nice change during a damp March. So the decision was made. The Gardener and the Professor would travel in the Saab with two fiberglass kayaks on the roof. The Shulamite and Britannicus and the Patron would travel in a camper, the Patron's fiberglass kayak on the roof and the folding, two-place Klepper in the interior. The plan was to drive to Puertecitos, then go by kayak to Las Islas Encantadas, a group of islands about thirty miles to the south. They were called the Enchanted Isles because of the mirages that made them appear to be floating above the water, because the ocean currents ran in opposite directions on either side of the isles, and because the rocks broken from their edges floated on the water (they were formed of pumice, a spongy volcanic glass). There were six of the islands, San Luis, Cantada, El Cholludo, Coloradito, El Muerto, and Huerfanito. The Gardener was especially attracted to El Muerto, the Island of Death. It was infested with a particularly dangerous form of rattlesnake. He thought it would be a fine place to practice *chöd* (see Chapter 28).

So on March 19, at five in the morning, the Saab drove down the mountain and turned south. San Francisco in the early dawn was a ghastly mixture of electric light and gray twilight, a hungover city with the highest percentage of alcoholics in the United States. The A.A.A. had warned the travelers to avoid Los Angeles. An earthquake had shattered its celebrated freeways, leaving overpasses tangled like so much spaghetti. They avoided it, heading east through Bakersfield. Over the high desert the wind blew cold and gritty. A few dry bushes quivered as if in pain. The landscape was about as attractive as the backside of the moon and not a house was in sight. And yet it was neatly staked out, and here and there signs proclaimed "Lots for Sale." The Gardener, who had long cherished the theory that the Southern Californians were becoming collectively insane, took these signs as further confirmation of the correctness of his view.

"Who on earth," he muttered, "would choose to live in such a place?"

The Professor, concentrating on the road, for the Saab's speedometer was registering a steady eighty, muttered something to the effect that water was to be brought into the high desert, water which no doubt would be stolen from Northern California, to which the Gardener replied it was high time Southern California seceded from the Union, sank into the Pacific, or suffered the fate of Sodom and Gomorrah.

Silence returned. The Saab descended into San Bernadino, gulped a bellyful of gas, set off along a multi-laned highway among shiny, pompous, preposterous, streamlined air-polluters, all moving at eighty and going where? Palm Springs presumably. There seemed no other explanation for the roaring exodus. Past Palm Springs the pace became less hectic and the affluence of the Affluent Society slightly less offensively evident. Instead, as they approached Indio, there were dates, dates, and more dates, gloomy groves, often interplanted with orange trees. Indio, date capital of the world, offered its products to the traveler, date milkshakes, date cocktails, date ice cream, date cookies, dateburgers. The Professor stopped and bought a plastic bagful of the famous dates. They were small and dry and rather tasteless, a low-grade product kept specially for sale to the tourist.

Beyond Indio endless vistas of irrigated flat lands spread to the horizon, alfalfa, sugar beet, corn, tomatoes, cotton, row upon row, perfectly spaced, cultivated by machines, harvested by machines, fertilized by thousands of tons of chemicals, kept disease-free by clouds of insecticides and fungicides sprayed from the air. One could feel the pollution pouring into the biosphere from these endless acres of agri-business. They were not farms at all. There was not a trace of soil love, no farm sense, no manual labor, only science, machinery, pollution, and irrigation. There were not even any farm workers. What place had a man with a hoe among all those machines?

By the Salton Sea once again the theme song of Southern California became strident. Lots for sale, lots for sale, lots for sale. Low down payments. Own your own speedboat. Boating–fishing–swimming. The Salton Seaway a dying remnant of the ocean that the movement of the earth had dropped below sea level. The Southern Californians were hastening its demise.

Brawley, El Centro, Calexico . . . the end of California. From five in the morning to five thirty in the evening they had been rushing through space. Now the Professor, who liked the comforts of civilization, made the most of those that remained, before facing the deserts of Mexico. In the heated pool of a luxurious motel he swam gravely to and fro like a porpoise. The rest of the party arrived, having collected a ticket for speeding somewhere in the desert. Next day they crossed the border into Mexicali, hung around for a while waiting for officials to validate their tourist cards, then set off for San Felipe.

A cloud of dust mingled with smoke of burning garbage hung over Mexicali. The road had been torn up, but no one seemed interested in restoring the ravaged surface. A totally different culture enveloped the travelers. It even smelled different. Mangy dogs of various sizes lay in the dust of the road. The town's main industry, apart from the manufacture of a fairly palatable beer, seemed to be the production of painted tombstones. Examples of this art, in varying degrees of hideousness, were displayed along the road to San Felipe.

Then the tombstones faded out, the dust and garbage smoke vanished, the last halfhearted attempts at irrigated agriculture ceased, and they were in the desert, under a limpid sky looking at distant mountains or red-flowered cactus or salt flats shimmering in the heat, a deserted land. Across it the blacktop road, the only respectable stretch of highway on the Peninsula, ran straight and hot, a black line on a blue desert. Near San Felipe the first human habitations appeared, a few stakes of crooked cactus walled in with bits of cardboard around which strayed ragged children, scrawny hens, mangy dogs. Under the blazing sun the little groups seemed threatened with immediate extinction, as if they had chosen the wrong ecological niche and fully deserved to be wiped out for their temerity.

Beyond San Felipe began the road for which Baja California is famous. The Saab charged a sand drift. Both kayaks came adrift from their moorings and hurtled over the end of the car. The expedition ground to a halt after only a half mile of Baja road and there were fifty-two more to come. They rearranged the cargo and proceeded. The road grew steadily worse. It changed from a sandy track into a boulder-strewn obstacle course on which even a speed of five miles an hour was hazardous.

"I think," said the Gardener, "that I will do the rest of the trip by sea."

Protests were voiced. The Shulamite's rich buddies, who lived in San Diego, had flown over the area in their own plane and declared that there were no safe havens between San Felipe and Puertecitos. Ray Cannon had said the same. The Sea of Cortez was famous for horrendous currents, enormous tides, sudden winds, and a variety of sea monsters, not to mention rattlesnakes on the beaches. To these croakings the Gardener turned a deaf ear. He gave not a hoot for the warnings of the

Shulamite's rich buddies. As for Ray Cannon, his advice was directed to powerboat operators not kayakers. And in any case, said the Gardener, he very much doubted if the waters of the Sea of Cortez could be one half as dangerous as those boiling breakers on the California coast, tides and currents notwithstanding.

As the Gardener had clearly made up his mind, the expedition detoured briefly to the seacoast, the Gardener unshipped his kayak, fishing rod, and a few supplies, and launched on the sea after dragging his boat across an acre of clinging mud flat exposed by the recession of that fabulous tide. The Patron, who had announced that "someone should keep an eye on the old boy," after endless delays also managed to get afloat. By that time it was four in the afternoon. They were thirty miles from Puertecitos. The Saab and the camper proceeded by road, the Gardener and the Patron by sea.

"What a joke!" said the Gardener.

He was referring to the croaks of the various birds of ill omen. Nothing could have been more placid than the Sea of Cortez. Under that limpid desert sky it was smooth as a dance floor. To the west the mountains glittered in the sun. The air was crystalline, one could see forever. And as for there being no place to land, why the whole shore was one long sandy beach on which anyone could land a kayak with the greatest of ease. The Gardener blithely decided that they would paddle ten miles that afternoon and the remaining twenty next day.

The Sea of Cortez, however, had some tricks up its sleeve. As the sun dropped toward the horizon the Gardener began uneasily to realize that he was paddling on an enchanted ocean. The strange properties of the desert air caused islands to rise and float mysteriously above the sea. They also fantastically distorted distances. The sandy beach on which he had decided to land failed, after an hour of paddling, to come any nearer. He changed course, headed for a second nearer beach. Still he made no progress. Finally, as the sun was getting uncomforta- bly near the mountains, he turned directly toward the shore. Five minutes hard paddling, he estimated, would see the kayak safely ashore.

There was not a breath of wind. The sea was like glass. Five minutes, ten minutes, fifteen minutes. Still the shore seemed as far off as ever. The Gardener had an uneasy im- pression that he was in the grip of some sort of spell. He was, after all, an experienced ocean kayaker, had fought his way home through whitecaps and a head wind on more than one occasion in the old homewaters around Fort Ross. And here he was on an oily, waveless sea, held seemingly motionless as if in a bath of glue. Was it the tide or the currents that were against him? But the tide had been low when they set out and should be incoming now. And the kayak seemed to glide over the water with as much speed as one would expect. Why then did the sandy beach fail to come nearer?

The Gardener put forth more effort. Against enchantments, he recalled, nothing is as effective as one-pointedness. This was the secret of yoga, the key to liberation from the bonds of *maya*. And the effort was effective. Suddenly, as if released from some underwater chain, the kayak moved forward. Its bow hit the soft sand. The Gardener leaped out and dragged his boat up the beach.

But the enchanted sea still had some tricks to play. Scarcely had the Gardener finished stretching his aching muscles be- fore he realized that the Patron had totally vanished. In his one-pointed effort to break out of the sea's enchantment he had forgotten about the Patron. Now, in the fading twilight, he got back in his kayak and searched the sea, which was perfectly calm, utterly silent. Not a trace. Not a sound of the paddles. Like a conjurer with a rabbit, the Sea of Cortez had "vanished" the Patron.

The Gardener cursed. He was tired. The light was fading.

And really, taking care of the Patron was none of his business. The Patron had come along to "take care of the old man." Which was a joke, as the Patron had only been out in a kayak once. Some sort of search seemed in order, however. A murmur of Spanish came across the water, and the Gardener realized that some Mexican fishermen were nearby. They were lowering gill nets into the water from an ancient motorboat. He paddled out to them, striving to compose some phrase in Spanish. *Ha perdido mi amigo. Dónde está mi* fishing buddy? The inquiry came out in a mixture of English and Spanish. One of the fishermen pointed to the beach and lo and behold, there was the Patron in the act of landing. The other fishermen roared with laughter and started the outboard motor.

"How many horsepower has your boat?" he yelled in excellent English.

"One hundred," said the Gardener, paddling shoreward much relieved, though much bewildered. How on earth had that fantastic ocean contrived to hide the Patron? It was by that time practically dark. They ate raisins for supper and crawled into their sleeping bags. It had been quite a day.

Next morning the Gardener woke in the early light. He had acquired a healthy respect for the Sea of Cortez, a place full of tricks and enchantments and hidden dangers. He could well understand why an area near the island of Tiburón was called *Sal si Puede* (get out if you can). The Sea of Cortez was not brutal like the old home ocean. It did not hit you with its big breakers as with a fly swatter. It was tricky, like a magician. Now you see it, now you don't.

It was also, as the sunrise approached, exceedingly beautiful. The blending of reds, oranges, blues, and greens promised a day of stillness and great heat. Mindful of the tricks of the sea, the two kayakers kept within easy reach of the shore. They rounded point after point, always expecting to find Puertecitos. But Puertecitos eluded them. At intervals they stopped to fish.

The Gardener, who had a picture in his mind of Ray Cannon hauling in a baya grouper which must have weighed two hundred pounds, lowered his hook with some trepidation. He anticipated a frantic tug, line screaming from the reel, a sweating, straining, rod-bending, adrenaline-releasing fight. Realities were very different. A series of dainty little twitches and nothing on the hook suggested to the Gardener that he was dealing with minnows rather than monsters. He changed to a smaller hook, brought in three spotted cabrilla, about half a pound each.

Well, cabrilla were better than nothing and at least they were plentiful. The kayakers paddled on, the sun grew fiercer, the glare off the sea was ferocious. They deluged themselves in suntan lotion, drank copiously, paddled, fished, fished, paddled. Where was Puertecitos? Once again the sun was descending, and no sandy beach was offering them welcome. Instead they landed at low tide on a rock-covered expanse and sloshed and slipped over an obstacle course of boulders, struggling to carry the kayaks above tide level.

They camped in the desert. At least there was some dry cactus, enough to light a good fire. On the glowing coals the cabrilla were duly barbecued. They were really delicious little fish and made an adequate supper. The desert was still enchanted. Strange shapes stirred across the fire as the darkness descended. Spirits? Allies? Guardians? The Gardener recalled Castaneda's encounters with the latter and wondered if, after all that paddling, they were going to be disturbed by ghostly visitors. He was too tired to care and crawled into his sleeping bag muttering a fragment from the Tibetan *Book of the Dead*:

> O nobly born do not be distracted.
> The things you see are nothing but illusions.
> Out of the mind they arise, into the mind they return.
> All that you see is mind created.

That should take care of the Allies.

Actually the trouble in the night came from quite a different quarter. It must have been close to two in the morning when the Gardener awoke. The stars were brilliant overhead. Far out at sea the lights of shrimp boats were visible and the sound of their engines could be heard through the still air. But from closer at hand came an ominous clunking which caused the Gardener to scramble from his sleeping bag and go slipping and staggering to the shore. The great tides of the Sea of Cortez were playing their tricks. The kayaks they had lugged so laboriously over the rocks were now afloat and banging about in the waves. The Gardener dragged his boat shoreward and awakened the Patron who merely groaned. As far as he was concerned, his kayak could sink and he'd walk the rest of the way to Puertecitos.

The sun, that inexorable taskmaster, returned to drive them, and Puertecitos continued to elude. The Gardener began to wonder whether this was yet another trick of the enchanted sea. Was there really a Puertecitos? It was reputed to be owned by an elderly Mexican and inhabited exclusively by affluent Americans.

Signs of the latter now began to appear, accompanied by the noise and gasoline-stink that is the hallmark of the Affluent Society. Along a stretch of sand roared a couple of dune buggies shattering the stillness of the desert into quivering fragments. A small plane buzzed the kayakers. A big speedboat roared out of the little bay, an almost naked girl on the prow, poised, as if in an ad, a can of beer in one hand. Totally inconsiderate, the noisy monster zoomed past the Gardener's kayak, almost swamping it in its wake.

The Gardener, steadying his rocking kayak, cursed the speedboat, its makers, owners, operators, and the whole culture that had spawned them. The Affluent American at home was bad enough, but God deliver us from the Affluent American abroad! In Mexico especially. Strutting, noisy, untidy, in-

considerate show-offs! Here they were in the desert, tearing up
the sand with raucous dune buggies, driving their ostentatious
campers along the atrocious roads with a "look-at-us-aren't-we-
heroic" expression on their faces. In the little bay of Puertecitos
two young men and a girl on water skis shattered the peace
with a gas-guzzling powerboat, totally indifferent to the safety
of all other occupants of the bay.

The Gardener thought of the dirt-poor Mexican fishermen
in their cardboard-covered shacks. What did they think of these
noisy, rich invaders from the north? When would they reach
for their knives and cut the throats of every *gringo* within
reach? Alas, it was far more likely that the *gringos* would invade
the whole peninsula, desecrate the desert, dispossess the fishermen, smother the place in hot-dog stands and marinas. Only
the appalling roads had protected Baja California from the
Affluent Americans. As soon as a good road was built, that
would spell the end of peace. The monied dregs of Los Angeles and San Diego would drain into the long peninsula and
proliferate there like pus in an infected appendix. And the
theme song of Southern California would be repeated in the
Baja. "Lots for sale. Lots for sale. Lots for sale."

So strong were these misanthropic sentiments that the Gardener was tempted to bypass Puertecitos and continue paddling
in the hope of finding a stretch of desert beach unpolluted by
the *gringos*. But he was dirty, tired, unshaven, thirsty, and had
forgotten, in his haste, to pack his toothbrush in the kayak. It
was still in the Saab. What he wanted, more than anything,
was to clean his teeth. So he landed reluctantly on the Puertecitos beach to be greeted by a fat effusive woman with a Middle
West accent and a voice like a buzz saw.

"We watched you coming round the point. The Mexican
Eskimos, we called you. That thing is a kayak, isn't it? That's
what Tom said. Never seen one before. Hey, Tom, you were
right. It is a kayak."

Mom to all the world! Where do they breed these types? Des Moines, Iowa? Kalamazoo, Mich.? The Gardener staggered into the bar where he found the Professor deep in a glass of Mexicali beer. The Professor had had experiences too. He was pissed off at the Shulamite and Britannicus who had assembled their Klepper boat and shown off most disgustingly, running rings around his lumbering kayak and taunting him with his slowness. He called them the Beautiful People with an edge of contempt in his voice that classed them among the speedboaters and small plane operators, blatant show-offs and polluters of the environment.

"And they nearly got swept out to sea," said the Professor with satisfaction, relating how the Beautiful People had spread out their sleeping bag too far down the beach. He, the Professor, cautious soul, had camped higher up. He had awakened to the sound of lapping water. The enormous tide had totally filled the little bay which had been bare sand when they had gone to bed. The Shulamite and Britannicus were afloat on their air mattress, sound asleep in each other's arms.

"I was tempted to let them drift," said the Professor. "I was really tempted."

The Gardener rummaged in his baggage in the Saab, extricated his toothbrush, and began cleaning his teeth. It had never occurred to him that that homely chore could attain the status of a sensual orgy. These are the things one learns by a trip into the desert. And a glass of ice-cold beer in the bar of Puertecitos was certainly another sensual indulgence, but one he felt he deserved after thirty miles of paddling. However, it was urgently necessary to extricate the Professor from the bar before he became demoralized by its luxuries like Hannibal's troops in the suburbs of Rome.

They set off south toward the Enchanted Isles.

That night, however, the Sea of Cortez showed another of its tricks. A violent wind descended on the camp. Sand flew, covering the sleeping bags, making sleep almost impossible. In the dawn the Enchanted Isles seemed very remote and the formerly placid Sea of Cortez was covered with whitecaps. The Professor had become dubious. His musculature, stiff and creaking, generated power with difficulty at the best of times. And suppose, on the way to the Enchanted Isles, that violent wind sprang up again? The Professor could clearly manage very well without a trip to the Isles of Enchantment.

So the trip ended. The Enchanted Isles had eluded them. The Beautiful People and the Patron remained on the peninsula for three more days. They did not voyage to the Enchanted Isles but spent an instructive night on a Mexican shrimp boat. The Gardener and the Professor returned along the rocky road to San Felipe, thence to Mexicali, thence to Calexico, where the marijuana-obsessed watchdogs that guard the Land of the Free delayed the tired travelers while they endlessly searched their baggage for the wicked weed.

Next day they returned to the north. The weather grew steadily colder, the skies grayer, and in Modesto it was raining. Ah, the rain! Never had it sounded more lovely. The Gardener reveled in it. He had had enough and more than enough of the deserts. Despite their blue skies, clear air, and endless distances they were, on the whole, dreary places, monotonous and impoverished. The Gardener went to bed listening to the rain and dreamed of rich harvests. The desert was not for him.

And the *Homo aquaticus* scenario? Somehow it had become mislaid. It was not until some days later, when the others returned from Mexico, that the Gardener remembered the original purpose of the trip. But his limpid image of the Sea of Cortez had been tarnished by the squalors of Puertecitos and its noisy *gringos*. What good would it do to create a sea-borne commune in those tropical waters? The taint of the Affluent Society would quickly infest it with beer cans, powerboats, small planes, dune buggies. It would turn into another Puertecitos or a squalid replica of Miami Beach. The tropical sun seemed to bring out the worst and weakest in Western man. A cold, harsh climate was what he needed to keep him healthy.

Perhaps, after all, the sea lochs of Scotland . . .

# PART FOUR

## The Garden

# XIII

## Gathering Grapes

Clear sky and dancing heat. A vague sense of menace.

Always toward the end of September or in early October California took on this hostile, sinister aspect. Not a drop of rain had fallen since March. The country was dusty and tinder dry, the grass on the hills brittle and dessicated, bleached to the color of flax by endless hours of sun. Even the redwoods, normally dark and cool, were wilting in the heat and seemed dusty and flammable. Black scars on their massive trunks bore witness to old holocausts, but it took a lot to kill the coastal redwoods. *Sequoia sempervirens*, the ever-living Sequoias.

Huge fires had already started in the south. The curse of the southland, the Santa Ana winds, had gusted in from the desert like blasts from an oven. Hundred-thousand-dollar homes in Malibu and Topanga Canyon were going up in smoke. Whole mountains were exploding into flame. Half a million acres were ablaze, energies were being released equivalent to 12,000 atomic bombs (Hiroshima vintage). You could always trust Southern California to go to extremes.

The smoke blew north over five hundred miles and reached Sonoma County. The Gardener, stretching a sprinkler-hose on the roof by way of a precaution, observed the brown smudge that dirtied the horizon. He turned on the sprinkler, listening to the rainlike drip of falling water, strange in the ninety-degree heat. Vividly he recalled the great fire of 1964 when the mountain was ringed by flames and Sonoma County was declared a disaster area. It happened at just the same time, during the grape picking. But the flames never spread to Sonoma Mountain. There were those who maintained that the mountain was under divine protection mediated by the Reverend Swallow who lived on top of it and had a direct line to God.

It was a consoling thought, but still wise to wet down the roof, if only to cool the house.

Meanwhile the grapes had to be gathered. The road down to the vineyard was ankle-deep in hot white dust. From it, one could look across the Valley of the Moon to the dry hills of Napa County, dancing in the fierce heat. A small fire had started in the valley. The borate bombers were swooping and turning, white clouds of fire retardant spreading like tails behind them. Fortunately the air was completely still and the fire just beginning. The big burn of '64 had taught the fire fighters a lesson which they had not yet forgotten.

*Get in there fast while it's small.*

It was about a mile from the ranch house to the vineyard. One walked past the garden, the orchard, the upper pond, specially stocked with Sacramento perch, swarming with bullfrog tadpoles, visited from time to time by kingfishers and blue herons.

Below the top pond was the Tulgey Wood which contained a Jabberwocky and some other mythical beasts. It had the air of a place about to spring a surprise on people. In the middle of the wood was Kublai's ravine. Its sides were practically vertical, carved by a creek which was a piddling trickle in September but swelled to a raging torrent during the rains. The mountain, in spots, was mushy beyond belief, like a partly rotten apple. Pockets of volcanic ash were scattered among the rocky areas, white leprous patches that eroded with extraordinary speed. The creek had cut into those soft patches to form a miniature Grand Canyon, undercutting the redwoods which had fallen down the steep slope and lay in a tangled mass at the bottom.

Indeed the whole mountain was slippery and unstable, and seemed at times on the verge of sliding down on top of itself. Such massive slides had occurred from time to time, and well-drillers told of coming upon perfectly perserved redwoods buried three hundred feet under the surface. The place quivered with a restless instability and, during the earthquake that had recently shaken Santa Rosa, seemed to be dancing on its toes. A very lively mountain, full of strange spirits.

Below the Tulgey Wood was the lower pond, a misplaced excavation, bulldozed out of white volcanic tuff, easily eroded and porous as a sponge. The owner, an enthusiastic conservationist, had stocked the pond with pup fish from the Salton Sea, another species menaced by man's misuse of the environment. But the lower pond had dried, not a drop of water left in it. The pup fish had fried in the cracked mud. Even the cattails were dying.

By the time he reached the vineyard the Gardener's shoes were white with hot dust and his feet were burning. The vines, however, seemed cool in the hottest weather. They were huge, powerful, sprawling plants, by some called Palomino, by others Golden Chasselas. Their luscious clusters, golden or pale green, were so big that one could fill a grape box in a few minutes. They flourished in the cooler climate of the hills, producing a phenomenal ten tons to the acre (as against one to three tons for such shy bearers as Pinot Noir or Cabernet Sauvignon). They were really a sherry grape, originally from Spain, but they flourished in these Californian coastal ranges like weeds. They were without distinction, producing, for those who wished to try the experiment, a dull, sour wine almost totally lacking in aroma. Quantity but not quality.

So aggressive and big were the vines that the grape pickers seemed lost in the foliage. The long trailing growths enveloped

them like tentacles of sea beasts, the big palmate leaves, re-
dolent of sulfur, closed over their heads as they knelt to gather
the lower bunches. Halfway down the slope the blond head of
Primal Scream emerged from the greenery. She had been picking grapes under the blazing sun for the past two weeks, dis-
daining a hat, flaxen hair bleached, skin fried to a rich golden
brown. She picked fast, with a kind of furious energy, as if
angry with the vines, her body exuding a rich odor of girl-
sweat. The Gardener, looking into her eyes, found her far away,
dreaming.

Where was Primal Scream? Such a promising kid. So full
of energy.

But Primal Scream was not ready for the rather tame existence prevailing in the Church of the Earth. Her need was
for suffering and plenty of it. She only felt really alive when
living in the midst of some horrendous emotional crisis. Though

not yet twenty-one, she had experienced enough *Stürm und Drang* to last most people a lifetime. She had lived in communes, blacks and whites mixed, done the whole trip, drugs, gonorrhea, abortions, suicide tries, and endless, endless encounter groups. She was well on the way to becoming a guru herself. In her head, if one listened carefully, one could hear the slosh of the great Theosophical mishmash—a jumble of astrology and magic, of tantras, yantras, mantras, auras, root races, Mahatma letters, and akashic records. The Gardener had foretold a colorful future for Primal Scream, if she managed to avoid dying young.

"You will be a second Blavatsky, a second Blavatsky! You will develop a bosom like this and your eyes will pop and you will lean on your hand and gaze hypnotically."

At this he would illustrate that look, recalling as he did so the photographs of the old lady hanging in the headquarters of the Theosophical Society in London. Good Lord, how long ago? 1935! The year before he met Ouspensky. He had been just twenty-two, seeking in Theosophy a key to the locked rooms of the psyche. But the Theosophists did not have any keys to anything. Only fairy tales. Tales of Lemuria and lost Atlantis, tales of akashic records and Mahatma letters that fell through the ceiling. Something had gone wrong with Theosophy somewhere. It was too bad, because the starting idea was a good one.

Primal Scream in her sixties, heavy of bosom with hypnotic eyes. Blavatsky II. How the archetypes recur!

But that was far off. Primal Scream at twenty had small, neat breasts, almost virginal. She fucked freely, without fuss. Down below she was clear and her energies were free-flowing. The blocks were higher up—in the heart or in the head? Perhaps she would emerge from the occult jungle and find the way. One remembered how Krishnamurti had risen out of the Theosophical fog, to become a burning and a shining light.

*Be lights to yourselves. Find the master in yourselves.*

The boxes of grapes, stewing in the Californian sun, attracted swarms of bees and yellowjackets. They hummed like hives. The Coal Man, stripped to the waist, dust-grimed and sweaty, made swooshing motions with both hands to fend off the hordes of insects. He grabbed the grape boxes and hefted them onto the truck where his helper dumped them into the hinged gondola. Time was, only four years before, when the grape boxes themselves had been stacked on the truck, and were driven, bumping and sloshing, to the winery, leaving behind a trail of grape juice. A wasteful method. The gondola was an improvement. It held three tons, juice and all, was emptied at the winery by a large crane that grabbed one edge of the container and tilted its contents into a bin. The Coal Man took one load a day to the Cooperative Winery in Windsor. One hundred and fifty dollars a ton. The mountain growers were benefiting from a late frost that hit the vines in the valley, leaving them leafless in May. A real devastation. Even the pear orchards had been damaged.

But the frost spared the mountain vineyards. The cold air drained down into the valley floor. There were advantages to growing grapes on slopes.

The Gardener picked grapes, slipping the curve of the grape knife around the stems, letting heavy bunches fill the bucket, then packing them in grape boxes. Only nine years previously, when he first came to California, he received a puny twenty-five cents per box. Now the pay was better. Forty-five cents if one agreed to stay through the harvest. It was still quite inadequate. In the general scream for more money, which rang through the country like the squeal of a million hogs, the farm workers had been forgotten. They gathered the nation's food, wandering like nomads from south to north following the harvests. When attempts were made to improve

their lot, the growers responded as did everyone else. Get rid of the workers. Use a machine.

So they had machines to pick lettuces, machines to pick tomatoes, machines to pick grapes.

At least, the Gardener reflected, no one would be able to get picking machines into that vineyard. The vines, planted for horse cultivation, were too close together, the slope was too steep. And vines, to be picked by machines, had to be trained neatly on trellises, every grape bunch at the same level. The machines were not very smart. They were quite incapable of ferreting out the bunches in the tangle of heavy foliage produced by the Palominos.

The Gardener returned to the ranch house to find that the Winemaker had arrived with a raucous collection of his buddies in varicolored jalopies and battered trucks. The Wine-

maker had bought two tons of Pinot Noir (five hundred dollars a ton) plus a second-hand press, and four new barrels of French oak, beautiful cooperage from the forests of Ardennes. The Winemaker sparkled and bubbled, a gangling blond with the eyes of a riverboat gambler, a passion for cock fighting, and a colorful reputation with the local cops. He was alleged to have planted a whole hillside with marijuana, but the charge was never proved. Later he cut his hair and swore off drugs. Not worth it, said he. The local narks were proud of him.

Now he had put his precious Pinot Noir through the crusher and had left the grapes in large open barrels to ferment for a day on the skins. The brew was quietly bubbling, the skins floating like a raft. The next step was to put the whole crushing through the press, squeeze out the blood of the grapes, reject the pips and skins. But before work started, there was always a tasting ritual, just to see how earlier batches were coming along. The Gardener, arriving from the vineyard, was swept into the small dark wooden building that was all the Winemaker had by way of a winery. Bungs were removed from barrels. The long glass wine stealer was poked into the contents. The Winemaker sparkled with enthusiasm. He was in raptures. Wine was in his very blood. He fired off short sentences like sky rockets in praise of his product.

"This Cabernet—two years old—nearly ruined it by blending —nearly made the worst mistake of my life—what color—note the aroma—a little harsh—needs two more years in the wood.

"And now—look at this . . ."

The glasses were rinsed, dried, polished. The wine stealer plunged into another barrel. The Winemaker was bent on proving, in response to skeptical comments from the Gardener, that one can make a drinkable wine from Golden Chasselas. And certainly the product he now fished out of the barrel was pleasant enough and had a beautiful amber glow, like evening sun on the vineyards.

"But now, try this—try this . . ."

Really, considering the generosity with which the Winemaker sampled from his barrels, it was a miracle he ever had anything left for the bottling. But he always had spare wine somewhere, stored in five-gallon Alhambra water bottles, ready to repair the depredations of the wine stealer. The ceremony was turning into a Bacchanal. In the dark little winery the light glinted on the hand-blown bottles which the Winemaker treasured and on the skull he had dug up from somewhere and placed on a shelf from which it watched the proceedings with its vacant orbits.

*Alas, poor Yorick! To this same likeness shall we all come in the end.*

Soon the whole company was as jolly as a herd of hogs and almost as noisy. The thick raft of skins was broken on the barrel of bubbling Pinot Noir and plastic buckets were plunged

deep into the brew. Purple juice slopped and splashed as the frothing bucketfuls were poured into the slatted wine press. Grape blood gushed. More buckets. A vinous flood. The Wine-maker developed as many arms as Shiva, grabbing buckets, pouring juice through a makeshift funnel into the white oak barrels, dashing here, there, everywhere, intent on not wast-ing a drop of the precious stuff. To help the free flow, the Winemaker's daughter, six years old, redhead, feet carefully hosed down, was hoisted into the press, jumped around like a Bacchante, splashed to the crotch of her panties in grape blood. The Winemaker's son, aged three, put his hands in the purple gush. With his round cherubic face he looked like a miniature Winston Churchill.

All the crush was now in the barrel and all the free flow had flowed. It was time to remove the Winemaker's daughter and apply more forcible pressure on the pips and skins. The

Winemaker's buddies hurled themselves on the press as if they intended to strangle it. The Winemaker played life fast and furiously, *presto agitato*, declaring that none of the males in his family lived much past thirty, and seeming determined to maintain the tradition. His buddies were like him. Several were members of the Hells Angels.

So they hurled themselves on the press and started twisting its neck, exerting huge pressures on the pips and skins, gaining leverage by the use of the Gardener's crowbar, which he had been rash enough to leave in the line of sight. Before long they had not only bent the crowbar but also broken the casting on top of the Winemaker's press. At this point the Gardener retreated from the scene of battle, taking the crowbar with him. The Winemaker was an enthusiast, almost a fanatic, but there was one thing he could not seem to realize. Men and machines both had their breaking points, and nothing could be gained by going beyond them.

# XIV

## *Seedtime and Harvests*

"Shall we leave out the wheat?"

The question hung in the air, mingling with the rustle of dry bean pods. The Whole-Earthers were sitting in a circle shelling beans from the previous harvest, red kidney beans, white navy beans, brown Italian beans. They popped open the dry pods and dropped the beans into bowls. The husks were composted, the beans eaten—reluctantly, for few of the Whole-Earthers were willing to give the bean its due as a good source of protein of vegetable origin. They complained that beans tasted dull and induced flatulence.

Meanwhile the problem of the wheat hung in the air. The Gardener had raised the question, prefacing it with a reference to Tolstoy and the peasants.

"This wheat-growing scene isn't practical but it is satisfying. It gives us a chance to make like genuine peasants, to swing a scythe or sickle and bind the sheaves by hand. This lets you know firsthand where your bread comes from. I admit it is cheaper and easier to buy the stuff. God knows how many man-hours we put in to raise a few hundred pounds by our primitive methods. But at least we've mixed our sweat with our bread and can eat it knowing where it came from. And it hasn't been sprayed with some foul insecticide, herbicide, fungicide, or pesticide. So I say, keep the wheat."

They kept it. A modest plot 100 by 100 feet. The position of next year's wheat was marked on the crop map and the Whole-

Earthers passed on to consider other needs. There were peas, beans (limas, white, Italian, kidney, and green and yellow beans eaten in the pods), potatoes (red and yellow), field corn, Indian corn, sweet corn, squash (summer and winter), cabbages and other brassicas (including cauliflower, broccoli and kohlrabi). These were the major crops, the chief food-makers. Then there were tomatoes, peppers, eggplant, ground cherry, celery, dill, cucumbers, onions, carrots, beets, chard, turnips, melons. As they all had to be watered and the sprinkler hoses were fifty feet long, each row had to be fifty or one hundred feet.

There were other considerations. Some crops like recent and heavy dressings of manure. Others did not. Put tomatoes on freshly manured ground and you will harvest a tangle of magnificent leafy plants without a single tomato. But the potatoes needed almost unlimited manure. The heavy clay soil on Sonoma Mountain was unsuited to this crop. The manure opened up the soil and let the tubers expand.

Eleven one-hundred-foot rows two feet apart would give half a ton of potatoes. Sixteen one-hundred-foot rows of green peas (Little Marvel) would give nine hundred and forty pounds of peas in the pod to be harvested in late May. There would be seven successive sowings of sweet corn (April 15, May 1, May 15, June 1, June 15, July 1, July 15), the biggest sowing (ten fifty-foot rows) on May first. The Indian corn (ten rows), the field corn (ten rows), would also be sown on May first. Despite the mildness of the Californian winter it was not until May that the soil warmed sufficiently to receive warm weather seed (corn, beans, squash, melons). The tomatoes and peppers would be started in the greenhouse in March. The green peas, which hate heat, would be sown in February, as soon as the ground was workable.

These sowing dates reflected the laws of the biosphere, the vast machinery of which operated in strict accordance with cosmic cycles. Among all primitives (and the Whole-Earthers liked to consider themselves primitives despite the fact that they owned cars and a washing machine), an acute awareness of the cosmic cycle was part of their being. A Navaho sand painting, the Four Houses of the Sun, expressed this awareness. More correctly the sand painting could be called the Four Houses of the Year, separated by the solstices and the equinoxes. In the House of Rest (winter solstice to spring equinox) there was a pause in the activity of the biosphere. In the House of Renewal (spring equinox to summer solstice) the great machine of the biosphere began to move and moved more rapidly with each lengthening day, like a giant flywheel gathering momentum. In the House of Fruition (summer solstice to autumn equinox) the biosphere generated its highest energy substances, the concentrated foodstuffs in seeds and fruits, gathered in by men, mice and squirrels, and stored against the coming cold. Then, in the House of Decline (autumn equinox to winter stolstice) the great flywheel on the biosphere lost its momentum as days shortened, temperatures dropped, and leaves fell from trees.

Corresponding to the Four Houses of the Year and measuring time with bloom was the Procession of the Flowers. In harsher climates it started with the earliest snowdrop boldly forcing its way through the February snow, passing on into the full panoply of spring through daffodils to cherry blossoms, on into the blooms of high summer with petunias and zinnias, hollyhocks and begonias, on into the fall-blooming dahlias and the last late chrysanthemum boldly opening its petals to the first snowflakes.

But in sunny, sea-warmed California the Procession of the Flowers never ceased. The jonquils bloomed in December, there were roses open on Christmas Day, and the fragile flowers of the almond opened in February. So the desperate springtime rush that follows the thaw in harsher climates turned into a more leisurely operation. But though there was no frost there was much rain and it was rarely possible to start spring plowing before March.

One could, however, almost always dig, except immediately after the heavy storms. There had been, in San Francisco during the Flower Children epoch, an outfit that called itself the Diggers whose members, apparently, did almost anything except dig. The Whole-Earthers could have called themselves Diggers with justification, for they one and all knew how to dig and were more or less adept at this ancient art. Single trenching, double trenching, spading, forking, they had moved dirt by the ton and enjoyed it. Is not digging one of the ancient, primordial rhythms? Is any sensation more satisfying than that of sinking a fork to the hilt into the rich fat earth, watching the worms, burying the weeds, leaving a clean level bed ready for seeding?

Certainly there was no better way to prepare soil for a crop, but the diggers found themselves confronted with the inescapable laws imposed by the limitations of man's musculature. Though he dig from dawn to dusk, a man cannot prepare enough ground for the crops he will need. A practical realization of this fact forces the digger to turn to the plow and to impose his will on a horse or use a tractor. High-minded Utopians, of whom Bronson Alcott was surely the archetype, may refuse, on moral grounds, to compel a horse to work for them. So what was the result? Picture Bronson Alcott at Fruitlands solemnly refusing to extort labor from a horse. He is going to sow ten acres with barley (it is already June). How will he prepare the ground? He will dig it.

Dig! Dig ten acres!

If a man works from dawn to dusk he will be doing well if he digs 30 by 30 feet. No wonder Fruitlands was a failure and the Alcott family nearly starved that winter. This lack of practicality was the curse of the New England Transcendentalists.

The more practical builders of Creative Communities, the Mennonites, the Amish, the Hutterites, the Shakers, knew more about the laws of the biosphere and the limitations these laws impose. If you try to break these laws, you perish. It's as simple as that.

The Whole-Earthers had some understanding of those laws. Their garden measured 400 by 100 feet, divided into eight fifty-foot plots. There was the Kennedy plot at one end and the Burke plot at the other, named for former occupants of the ranch. The rest were named after women, for the earth that receives the seed is surely female. There was Alice, Betty, Charlotte, Diana, Eloise, Flora, each 50 by 100 feet with a six-foot divider between them. Two would be occupied by wheat, one left fallow. The corn and vegetables from the rest would suffice for most of the group's needs.

As for seed, they saved their own wherever possible. Seed of onions, peas, chard, beans, even such brassicas as cabbage and broccoli could be saved easily. The hybrid corn seed (golden cross bantam) they preferred to purchase.

The plots were plowed as soon as the first rains came in October or November. As soon as the weed seeds germinated, the ground was worked over with a rototiller and the wheat was sown broadcast in November. This sowing was biblical—"a sower went forth, and, as he sowed, some seed fell by the wayside." An ancient and satisfying rhythm, the arm swinging in a smooth circle, the seed spraying out in an even arc and falling, just overlapping the previous seed. It was an art, a dance, the feet pacing evenly, the whole body taking part in the rhythm. Later the seed was buried by the harrows and then, after further rain, the shoots would appear.

> *One for the pigeon,*
> *One for the crow,*
> *One to wither*
> *And one to grow.*

So went the old rhyme apropos of broadcasting seed. Which would suggest that one should sow four seeds for every one that survived.

And it did indeed seem, when the shoots showed through the soil, as if the seed had been applied too thinly, and the birds certainly took their toll, swooping down from the fence to eat the shoots nearest to hand, the quail and mourning doves being the worst offenders. Nevertheless, by late April, when the plants really began to enlarge, the ground was well covered, and later, as the ears shot up in May, the crop seemed, if anything, too dense.

The peas were sown early in February during a dry spell which made it possible to open the furrows. Seed was poured in thickly, one and a half pounds of seed per hundred-foot row, protected from birds by screens of wire netting. They sprouted green and thick in a warm spell in March. The sweet corn and carrots had also to be protected from the birds. Their seedlings were attacked by quail and blue jays and red-eyed vireos and mourning doves and sparrows. Meanwhile gophers assaulted the crops from underground, digging holes that neatly followed the row and left gaping gaps. And the deer broke through the fence and ate the young beans. And they likewise broke into the vineyard and devoured great quantities of young vine shoots.

The harmony of nature? No. There was no harmony. The place was overrun with quail and deer whose natural enemies had been destroyed by man and who were not even shot any-more during the hunting season. There was war, unending struggle. But at least, under the clear Californian sky, the fungal and insect pests were minimal and could be controlled with sulfur or pyrethrum. After April, rain was a rarity and the dark adobe soil grew drier and drier, cracking and wrinkling like the skin of an old man. Then there would be days of bril-liant sun interspersed with foggy mornings when the breath of the ocean swept over the coastal ranges and the redwoods dripped moisture.

All in all, the crops were remarkably healthy as long as they were protected from the birds, the gophers, and the deer. By May the wheat was green and tall, by June it was golden. That year two varieties of wheat had been sown, a soft wheat, early maturing, suitable for pancakes, and a hard red wheat high in gluten, suitable for bread. The soft wheat had grown too luxuriously. In a heavily manured section near the road the tall stems proved too weak for the heavy heads. A late rainstorm accompanied by wind caused it to "lodge," which meant it lay flat on the ground and was difficult to cut. The hard wheat proved unsuited to California. It matured too slowly and the drought caught up with it, forcing the grain to ripen before it was fully formed.

However, in that clear Californian July it was relatively easy to bring in the wheat harvest. There was no threat of rain or storm, no danger of wheat rotting in the damp. The heads of the wheat were crisp and dry in the sun, and the grains were hard and low in moisture. The Gardener, a lover of plants, would pluck the heavy heads, rub out the grain in his hands, reproach his fellow workers for their lack of enthusiasm about this marvelous grass by which whole civilizations had been nourished. And as for the city-born man-swarms, what did they know about the source of their bread? Had they ever opened the flowers of this life-giving grass, parted the awned glumes to see how the heads were constructed? Had they ever sweated in the sun with a sickle or watched the yellow straw bow before the blade in that rhythmic dance which went back to the Neolithic? Their wheat was harvested by huge machines. Their bread, untouched by human hands, was over-refined into a soft white pap, precut and wrapped in plastic, an emasculated product not fit for a hog.

By their bread shall ye know them, for the bread is the

life of man. And the soft white pap produces a soft pale people, a degenerate race.

The Gardener, his scythe over his shoulder, looked across the plot of wheat, hot and crisp in the sun. His scythe, twenty-five years old, had an English blade (Americans, who can land men on the moon, cannot make a good scythe blade), and his whetstone, of Oxford limestone, came from England also. Above the blade he had attached a wooden cradle, a device that gathered the stems of the wheat together and ensured that they fell in a neat pile. It required a special movement to hold the stems together and cause them to fall at the right angle.

Working along the eastern edge of the wheat, uphill toward the road, he found his body falling again into the old pattern, the strong circular swing, the rotation of the body, the hissing, satisfying bite of the scythe blade through the straw, the contented rustle of the stems as they fell in a heap. Every year the same rhythm, the same hot sky, the same bird songs, even the same mental images. Every year as he scythed the wheat he remembered that passage from *Anna Karenina*: Konstanin Levin mowing in the meadows among the peasants. Levin was surely Tolstoy himself, seeking refuge from an artificial society in the ancient rhythms of the land.

There's therapy for you. Fold up your phony encounter groups, you sorry head-shrinkers, and send your patients into the hot fields. Let them swing a scythe all day in the blaze of the sun. Then ask them how they feel. Tired, relaxed, free of their miserable egos—too tired to fuss any longer over their neuroses. Full of fresh air and ready to eat and sleep.

It worked for Tolstoy.

It would work for them.

Far better, in any case, than sitting up all night in a smoke-filled room chasing each other through the rat holes of the persona. Give them a scythe and send them into the wheat fields.

But of course they will not go into the wheat fields. Out there, under the hot sun, they would lose the thing they love best—their imaginary sufferings—their precious little egos—their endless dreams about themselves and their "personal problems." All these would dissolve in the acrid bath of their own sweat and they would be left—with what?

With the realization of their utter nothingness, a speck of life in the biosphere cast between earth and sun in a sea of wheat and a bath of sweat. The drama of seed time and harvest —death and rebirth. The taste of liberation—the ultimate mystery.

Anything but that . . .

In the upper part of the field where the wheat was flattened, the scythe was abandoned in favor of the sickle. The harvesters worked with sickles in one hand and small rakes in the other. Though the sickles were of steel, their form mirrored

that of the oldest of all farm instruments, the curved blades
made of baked clay or flint used by Neolithic farmers in the
fields of the Fertile Triangle where agriculture was born. It was
back-breaking work bending over the lodged wheat, severing
the stems at ground level, raking them together into bundles.
The wheat had lodged because it was given too much nitrogen,
which caused the stems to grow sappy and too tall.

Next year the Whole-Earthers planned to experiment with
short-strawed Gaines wheat, less apt to lodge. Meanwhile they
had to bend their backs, both to cut the wheat and to bind it
into sheaves. They used binder twine to bind the sheaves,
peeled from a large roll and precut to length.

There was no shortage of sweat in the wheat field. The
Shulamite, swarthy and tough, dripped sweat on the sheaves as
she bound them. She built them into shocks, like little tents,
scattered over the field. The Shulamite once worked on a *kib-*

*butz* in Israel. Dark and sunbrowned, with a sheaf under each arm, she looked like an Israeli poster extolling the joys of the simple life.

After the shocks had stood for a week in the sun the sheaves were carted to the barn and more sweat was shed. How does one separate the grain from the straw if one lacks a threshing machine? The classical instrument is the flail but no one in the group knew how to use one. So the Whole-Earthers resorted to the grain dance, a sort of one-legged shuffle, like a chicken scratching. They untied the bands of the sheaves, spread out the straw on the barn floor on a day of low humidity when the temperature was in the nineties. Then, holding the straw in place with one foot, they would roll the heads under the other foot, thus separating the grain from the straw, leaving it mixed with chaff, to be swept up and dumped in a bin. Even that was not the end of the process of separation and purification. How does one separate the wheat from the chaff? The New Testament, which is full of references to harvests, recommended a fan.

*Whose fan is in his hand, and he will thoroughly purge his floor, and will gather the wheat into his garner; but the chaff he will burn with fire unquenchable.*

The Whole-Earthers took a dim view of burning the chaff, *streng verboten* in fire-conscious California and contrary to the principles of conservation. They had no fans either but waited for a brisk wind, poured the grain-chaff mix back and forth between two buckets, put the grain in sacks, gave the chaff to the chickens to peck over. Duly impregnated with chicken shit, it was worked into compost heaps and returned to the soil. The straw was similarly operated upon by Jill and Cinderella, the two goats, and also found its way back to the soil. Only the wheat, eaten by humans, ended in an unproductive septic tank and failed to return whence it came. (The Whole-Earthers were not sufficiently fanatical to dispense with flush toilets. More rugged groups that had dared to use their own shit to manure their vegetables had been roughly treated by the local Department of Health whose bureaucrats were horrified by such practices.)

The five hundred pounds of wheat which resulted from all this was certainly expensive stuff, if one considered the man-hours involved in its production. Nor was the process completed after the winnowing wind had removed the chaff. The wheat had to be ground. No doubt, had the Whole-Earthers been purists, they would have ground it in a *petate* (more sweat) or built a windmill or a watermill. And they could have baked the bread in a brick oven fueled with wood. But they were not entirely consistent. They ground the whole wheat, a few pounds at a time, in a neat little electric mill. The resultant whole wheat flour, mixed with milk and duly leavened with yeast, was shaped into loaves and baked in an electric oven. Which placed the Whole-Earthers, like almost everyone in California, in a condition of dependence on the gigantic P.G.&E., whose power lines spread through the state like a spider's web, whose plans for atomic generators were regarded with disfavor by hosts of conservationists (who nonetheless continued to buy the company's product).

Often the wheat in the little mill was mixed with Indian corn of many colors, which the Whole-Earthers grew because it was nice to look at. The corn was a noble grass, a gift of the New World, cultivated for so long by man that its wild forms could not even be found. Its vigor was fantastic. Sown in May when the soil had warmed, it raced to maturity, its sword-shaped leaves feasting on the body of the sun. By August the corn plant generated its special sex organs, the corn-boy and corn-girl so revered by the Indians. The tassels expanded against the sky, gold-dusting the air with pollen, inviting swarms of bees that busily packed their pollen baskets with this abundance. The female organs, lustrous as silk, were pollen-covered and the whole obscure sexual drama took place within the ovary, nuclei fusing, endosperm and embryo beginning to grow. Sometimes pollen from the Indian corn blew onto the sweet corn and a dark mahogany kernel appeared in the rows of gold.

As the kernels fattened and filled, all the stored reserves of the plant were poured into the grain, converted into starch or protein that the embryo, on reawakening, might have food to grow on. By October that process was completed. All life had been drained from the corn plants, gaunt skeletons remained, the pale dessicated leaves rustling in the wind. The heavy ears, encased in dry husks as if wrapped in parchment, hung down to shed the rain. On warm October days the Whole-Earthers gathered them, throwing them into piles. Sitting in the sun they would strip off the papery rusks, revealing

the rich variegation of the Indian corn, multicolored grains, white, yellow, blue, mauve almost black. Later, sitting in a circle in one of the houses, they would separate the grain from the cobs, pressing off the kernels with their thumbs, gathering the grain into a sack, dumping the cobs on the compost heap. Stalks, husks, cobs were food for the earth—grain was food for man.

This process of separation was a part of every harvest. The first harvest of the year was the green peas that offered their fine substance packaged in boat-shaped pods that had to be popped open between finger and thumb. The pods were composted, the peas were eaten. Then came successive batches of sweet corn, carefully gathered while the kernels were sugary, stripped of their husks, plunged into boiling water, the kernels sliced from the cobs with a sharp knife. Between the successive waves of corn came the potato harvest, each plant carefully

dug by hand, the tubers picked up, sorted, and put into bags. Later in the year the pumpkins and squash were harvested, massive globules of food, silver Hubbards, acorn squash, butternuts. Stored in straw in the barn, they would keep till spring. The onions were gathered also as their tops died down and were carefully plaited and hung up in strings in the barn, purple Bermudas, brown Spanish the color of old varnish. The dry beans were gathered also, their pods removed from the plants and stuffed into sacks, to be opened later and the seeds extracted.

On each plant a different part yielded the life-giving food. In peas, beans, corn, wheat, the food was in the seed. In squash and pumpkins, in the fleshy walls of the ovary. In cabbages, it was in the leaf, in broccoli and cauliflower, the flower. Carrots and beets had their food stored in the roots, celery in the leaf stalks, potatoes and Jerusalem artichokes in the tubers.

But in every instance the collection of the food involved both gathering and separating. This was the basis of all harvesting processes. *Carefully separate the fine from the coarse with wisdom and foresight.*

# XV

## *The Soul of the Harvest*

Fellow Whole-Earthers!

Our wheat crop has now been gathered.

Those who ride by in their shiny cars and observe our labors from the road probably consider us insane. Why should we go to all this trouble to gather wheat, using virtually Neolithic methods, when red Montana wheat can be bought for eight or nine cents a pound, all clean and ready? Why bother to grow wheat at all?

The superficial answer is because the wheat is our bread and bread is our life and we prefer to gather our bread with our own hands, in the sweat of our brow, than receive it at second hand from some monstrous machine, polluted with a variety of chemical additives. The deeper answer is because the wheat tells a story and this story is very old and very sacred and it is worth a little sweat and hard work in order to hear it.

What is the story it tells? Consider this version.

> In the meanwhile his disciples prayed him, saying, Master, eat.
>
> But he said unto them. I have meat to eat that ye know not of.
>
> Therefore said the disciples one to another, hath any man brought him aught to eat?
>
> Jesus saith unto them. My meat is to do the will of him that sent me, and to finish his work.

*Say not ye, there are yet four months and then cometh harvest?*

*Behold, I say unto you, Lift up your eyes and look on the fields; for they are white already to harvest.*

*And he that reapeth receiveth wages, and gathereth fruit unto life eternal: that both he that soweth and he that reapeth may rejoice together.*

*And herein is that saying true, one soweth and another reapeth.*

*I sent you to reap that whereon you bestowed no labor: other men labored and ye are entered into their labors.*

In this story is expressed one aspect of the Work. The wheat is the food of man, the bread on which his life depends. Only a small part of the wheat plant becomes grain. The rest is straw and chaff. Only the grain can be transmuted into bread, and the bread transmuted into life. So, in the mystery teachings, all mankind was regarded as a harvest field but only a small proportion became grain.

The gathering in, or concentrating, of this grain was the work of the inner circle of humanity. This work was handed on from teacher to disciple, and continues to this day. The chain has never been broken. It is proper that those who labor be aware of this fact and sense the work of the past stretching back to Eleusis, to Egypt, to Babylon, to the very dawn of history. *Other men labored and ye are entered into their labors.*

From this standpoint mankind can justify its existence. It provides food for beings of a higher order. Only a small fraction of the human bio-mass is thus transmuted, just as only a small proportion of the wheat plant is transformed into grain. Fully developed man is thus regarded as food for something higher, in the sense that he blends with and becomes part of a higher order of being. He dies on one level and is reborn on another. This is referred to in one teaching as "becoming food for archangels."

This is one part of the story of wheat. The other relates to the harvesting process itself. As you sweat in the harvest field one fact must be clear to you. The wheat won't harvest itself. Much work is involved. The stalks must be cut, the grain beaten out of the heads, the grain separated from the chaff.

Again we see an analogy with the inner work. Man can transform himself into food for higher beings but the transformation won't happen by itself. Nature has made no provision to guarantee that man will develop all his latent powers. Quite the reverse. Owing to an error in his evolution man must confront and overcome inner obstacles which prevent his development. These obstacles are so formidable and so deeply embedded in his psyche that only exceptionally honest and determined people can overcome them. The obstacles are referred to in one teaching as *the consequences of the properties of the maleficent organ Kundabuffer*. They take the form of suggestibility and credulity. They make it difficult for man to break out of that state of hypnotized sleep that he calls his "normal state of consciousness." They prevent him from realizing the Terror of the Situation and thus awakening.

You must realize that these elements in the human psyche are very powerful. They constantly operate at every level to bring the harvest to a halt. Even people who sincerely wish to transform themselves and to assist in the transforming of others can lose their way because of credulity, because they would rather believe blindly than test things for themselves. All attempts, therefore, on the part of those who have attained inner freedom, to liberate men from their bondage, tend to become frustrated by the credulity of man, coupled with his laziness and reluctance to think for himself.

So, no matter how powerful the teacher, his followers can always be trusted to make a mishmash of his teachings and bring his work to a halt. This they generally do by creating a cult of personality around the teacher himself, and fossilizing everything in exactly the form in which it was given. Using this fossilized teaching they engage in mechanical repetitions of certain patterns of behavior assuring themselves and each other that they will attain liberation and higher consciousness as long as they never, never make the slightest change in anything the master taught.

But life is change, and what is appropriate for one period is not necessarily valid for another. So all this effort to hold on to certain forms only results in the arrest of development. So another teacher has to appear, smash the fossil, start all over again. This, of course, causes shrieks of indignation among the True Believers, whose sleep is thus disturbed and whose comfortable habits are disarranged.

Now you must decide whether you wish to be True Believers or liberated beings. I assure you they are not at all the same thing. The inner circle of humanity is made up of liberated being, not True Believers, and the characteristic of members of the inner circle is that *they cannot misunderstand each other and cannot work against each other.* They have attained objectivity and can *see* in the fullest sense of this word. From such a one it is worthwhile to seek guidance if you have courage enough to go with him. But he will not let you worship him or become dependent on him. He is one with the poet Rumi when he says: *Don't look at me. Take what is in my hand.* He can indicate the way but you are the one who must tread it, and the sooner you can find your way independently of him the better pleased he will be.

# XVI

## *The Practical Gardener*

Fellow Whole-Earthers!

I must ask you to be reasonable and stop behaving like religious fanatics. You talk of things you don't understand as if you understood them and voice opinions as if opinion were the same as knowledge. What says our favorite poet on the subject? Refer to Rumi.

> *Knowledge has two wings, opinion only one.*
> *Opinion is defective, curtailed in flight.*
> *One who has been delivered of Opinion to him knowledge*
>     *shows its face.*
> *The one-winged bird becomes two-winged and spreads his*
>     *wings.*
> *He flies aloft with two wings like Gabriel,*
> *Without opinion, without peradventure, without disputes.*
> *Though the whole world say, "You are in the Way of God,"*
> *He will not become more fervent in his faith,*
> *Or if they all should say to him "You are astray"*
> *He will not fall into doubt because of their taunts.*

All mankind goes astray because of this craving for opinions, because of beliefs which men prefer to facts. Even in an age of science where facts are available, men prefer opinions. "This I have heard, that I read in the newspaper and I am firmly convinced that it is so." Why is he so convinced? Is it because he has sifted all the evidence? Because he has performed some exclusive experiment which proves the truth of that which he chooses to believe? Not in the least. He happens to like that particular set of opinions. They tickle his fancy. They may be utter nonsense from start to finish but he believes them and will hotly defend them against attack.

Credulity and suggestibility once again. The hypnotized sheep, bleating of its dreams and delusions.

> *The worst infirmity of the human mind is to believe that a thing is so because one wishes it to be so.*
>
> BOSSUET

I wish to relate this to the belief some of you have in what is loosely referred to as Organic Gardening. I hope to prove to you that Organic Gardening is a mixture of misunderstood plant nutrition and a quite laudable desire to protect the environment. What was originally quite a sound idea has been turned into a sort of religion by starry-eyed "health food" fans, most of whom would not dream of soiling their hands at the shit heap. As practicality and discrimination are necessary, let us apply them to this cult (Organic Gardening) to see what in it is of value and what is superstition.

Let us look back for a moment.

As recently as 1800, people had only the foggiest idea what plants ate. Some people thought they ate humus, some that they lived on air, or on water or on phlogiston. It was the careful experiments of Lavoisier, Liebig, Lawes and Gilbert, and de Saussure that finally solved the riddle, What do plants eat? The fact, as every even half-educated educated person should know, is that they eat air, the salts of the earth, and the light of the sun. From the air they take the gas, carbon dioxide, which is present only in very small amounts (0.035 percent in normal air). From the soil they take water and various mineral salts. From the sun they take photons, tiny packets of energy of certain wavelengths. This is all they need. These are the raw materials of life on earth.

No mention of organic matter. It is quite unnecessary for the nutrition of the plant. You don't need to take my word for it. Just try an experiment. You can grow plants perfectly well on sterile washed sea sand containing not a trace of organic matter. All you need to do is supply them with the major and minor chemical nutrients dissolved in suitable concentrations in pure distilled water. You can even dispense with the sand and grow them in the solution (hydroponics), but the sand is better because it provides aeration for the roots. As long as light of the right wavelength and air with the usual percentage of carbon dioxide are provided, the plants will grow perfectly well on this solution of salts. There is not a shred of evidence to suggest that they will be defective in vitamins, nutritionally inadequate, in any way different from plants which have been "organically grown," whatever this means. This is fact. It has been proved again and again by meticulously conducted experiments. Of course if you prefer to reject the facts in favor of opinion, this is your decision. But as the poet says, "Opinion is a bird with one wing."

You may well protest at this point. You may ask me why we spend time building compost heaps, why we haul great quantities of cow shit from the few dairy farmers who have not been driven out of business by the developers. Why do we pour organic matter into the soil if it is not a plant food? I will try to answer these objections.

First consider the soil. Soil is not a simple material. It is a very complex mixture of the dead and the living. It teems with life, bacteria, protozoa, fungi, insects, worms, even mammals (the mole and the gopher). This marvelously intricate substance has a life of its own, and this life makes the difference between a rich soil and a poor soil. A rich soil is dark and smells good. It has spongy texture, holds moisture, is well aerated. It is neither soggy with clay nor thin with sand but has both ingredients in balance. It has plenty of humus (the black organic material that gives to soil its characteristic aroma) but not so much as to render the soil too acid (as happens in peat bogs where the soil is almost entirely organic).

Now focus on this humus, the organic portion of the soil. It is concerning the role of humus that the so-called Organic Gardeners have become confused. *Humus is not a plant food.* No green plant can absorb it. But humus is vitally important to the fertility of the soil. It is important because it improves the consistency of the soil, makes it lighter, more spongy, better able to hold water and plant nutrients which must always be in solution. Our own garden tells us directly the importance of humus. This heavy clay would be practically unworkable if we did not pour in organic matter. What a difference is produced by a layer of well-rotted manure! Without the manure the ground puddles when wet and sets like concrete when dry. With the manure it stays open and workable. The soil has *good tilth,* it is *in good heart.* These expressive phrases from an older and sounder agriculture really have meaning, and any good peasant would understand that meaning.

Your Organic Gardener of the sensible variety will be making good sense as long as he talks about tilth. He will be making sense also when he declares that heavy dressings of artificial fertilizers plus intensive irrigation damage soil structure besides over-fertilizing lakes and streams. But the Organic Gardener of the religious fanatic variety goes far beyond this. He boldly states that all chemical fertilizers are bad, completely forgetting that the word chemicals includes every form of matter and that a load of manure contains the same chemicals as are obtained in a bag of 10–10–10, namely the vital plant nutrients NPK in that order, N being the symbol of nitrogen, P of phosphorus, K (kalium) of potassium.

I laugh when I hear that some so-called health food store refuses to buy our surplus vegetables because, now and then, we use 10–10–10. It makes not the slightest difference to the wholesomeness of the product whether the nitrogen, phosphorus, and potash needed by the plant come out of a bag labeled 10–10–10 or 5–10–5 or out of a load of cow shit imported from one of the surviving dairy farms. We use cow shit too, and plenty of it. And if we can get enough of it, we will dispense with 10–10–10. But the notion that NPK somehow becomes poisonous when put in a bag called 10–10–10 but is wholesome and "organic" when applied in the form of cow shit is an example of credulity and suggestibility. It is a reversion to the age of superstition, the era of witchcraft and belief in the evil eye. It totally ignores more than a century of painstaking research and puts us back to the days of Jethro Tull who believed that plants ate humus and had "lacteal sucking mouths" in their roots. His book *Horsehoeing Husbandry* was all the rage in England in the reign of George III. Like the contemporary concept of Organic Gardening, it combined several good ideas with some nonsensical theories.

You will avoid all this nonsense if you remember the following facts. 1. Plants cannot use the nitrogen of the air, but members of the legume family (peas and beans) can "fix" nitrogen with the help of bacteria that grow in their roots. So a legume crop will enrich the soil with nitrogen, but if you don't grow legumes you must add nitrogen either as nitrate, ammonia, or urea. Or you can add it as manure, provided all the nitrate has not been washed out of the manure by rain.

2. Potash and phosphorus can be obtained by plants only from the soil. The plants can no more make these elements from organic matter than they can make gold. If your soil is short of potash or phosphorus you must add them. Phosphorus is available as bone meal, but this form is expensive and not very soluble. Super phosphate, invented by John Bennett Lawes, is prepared from rock phosphate by treating the mineral with sulfuric acid. It has the advantage of being soluble in water and readily available to the plant. Potash is mined in various parts

of the world in the form of potassium salts. Of course both potash and phosphorus are present in well-made (nonleached) manure, derived from the urine and feces of the animals. Potash is also present in wood ash (whence the name), so all wood ashes should be returned to the garden.

Nitrogen, potash, and phosphorus are the only elements that need to be added to most soils. There are soils in some parts of the world deficient in trace elements like boron, cobalt, manganese, or molybdenum. There are also soils that are deficient in iodine, but iodine is not an essential element for plants, though it is for some animals, including man. So the intelligent gardener, at least in these parts, will improve the tilth of his soil with well-made compost but will not disdain the various mixes of NPK if he can show by experiment that they improve his crops.

A lot of the passion of the Organic Gardening cult is due to its distrust of various dusts and sprays. The distrust is well justified of course, but here again discrimination is necessary. We in California are blessedly free from many pests. Even so we must take steps to protect certain crops and use chemicals to do so. I refuse, for instance, to let my peach trees be totally defoliated by peach leaf curl when I can control it with a spray of relatively harmless Bordeaux mixture. I do not hesitate to use lime-sulfur against aphids on the apples, sulfur against mildew on the grapes, pyrethrum against flea beetles on the eggplant or the cabbages. The corn earworm I accept, as well as coddling moth in the apples. I will not use chlorinated hydrocarbons of the DDT type, and compounds containing mercury are utterly taboo. One has to spray and dust or lose certain crops. But one also has to use discretion or just plain common sense. Fanaticism, whether applied to gardens or religions, is always disastrous because it substitutes opinion for knowledge and passion for discrimination.

# XVII

## *Arts and Crafts*

Rain!

It fell relentlessly, drumming on the roof, a subdued but unvarying roar supplemented by the voices of rain-swollen creeks filled to the brim or overflowing. Inches and inches of rain. The storm clouds rolled in from the south, gray curtains over the hills. They engulfed the slopes completely from time to time, swirling mist-shapes like white dragons that curled and hovered over the sodden trees. The saturated soil quivered on the hillsides, held back only by the tree roots from plunging down into the valley. Millions of gallons of muddy runoff poured into the Russian River which was now coffee-colored and rising by the minute. On the front page of the Santa Rosa *Press Democrat* were pictures of people in boats floating among partly submerged buildings.

It happened yearly.

Fires in summer, floods in winter, with an earthquake or two thrown in for good measure.

Californian delight!

The Whole-Earthers had retreated indoors. They had secured their precious topsoil against the raging rain under a cover crop of oats and winter wheat. Moreover they had terraced the slope and built up a row of rocks to hold back the soil. Nothing more could be done. The elemental force of the rain was gouging great canyons in the softer parts of the mountain, cutting into it like a drill into a rotten tooth, carving the edge of the continent, sculpting and smoothing the curves of the coastal ranges. There were landslides on Route 1. A large chunk of the Redwood Highway had fallen into the Russian River.

Members of the Church of the Earth were engaged in arts and crafts.

It was an article of faith among the members that somehow or other, sooner or later, they would find an art or a craft that would enable them both to enjoy themselves and make money, thereby fulfilling the command, "Strive to combine the profitable with the pleasurable." So far this endeavor had not been very successful. A man-mass, trained to prefer the synthetic to the real, bought mass-produced objects turned out by the million in molds—from some plastic designed to look like something else.

So the Whole-Earthers were turning to art for art's sake, echoing, as far as the market was concerned, Beethoven's scornful comment to a roomful of talkative listeners: "I refuse to play for such hogs."

Foremost among the practitioners of art for art's sake was Sailor's Yarn who had labored for months with two knives on a piece of seasoned beechwood. The result was a series of designs of extraordinary intricacy constituting what was known in Holland as a mangel board. No one had any idea what such boards were used for. The prevailing theory suggested that Dutch housewives ironed their husband's shirts on such a board, imparting the design to the fabric in bas relief.

Sailor's Yarn did not know what the mangel board would be used for and did not care. Bending over his work with a sort of fierce concentration, he resembled a reformed pirate, home from the Spanish Main and settled down. He was full of tales, like a character in Conrad. He talked of ships and seas and storms and brothels and fourteen-year-old Korean girls who can rejuvenate a man by walking along his spine, relaxing the strain in each vertebra with their subtle toes.

The Designer, who had a PhD in psychology, was at work on a beechwood panel of rare distinction, based on the cover design from the copy of the Koran in the British Museum. Designs of all kinds fascinated the Designer; Islamic, Celtic, Polynesian, Egyptian, Greek. If you studied designs long enough, you discovered archetypal forms, primordial rhythms corresponding to certain basic hungers of the human soul, like the so-called mandalas drawn by Jung's patients, which were not really mandalas at all, but symptoms of a hunger for harmony.

Recently the Designer had discovered the Pictish knots. They really turned him on. He glowed with enthusiasm over their balanced intricacies, demonstrating examples from the

Book of Armagh in which the work attained a fineness of one hundred and fifty-eight interlacements in a quarter of an inch. The Celtic artists did their work for the eye of God and would be satisfied with nothing less than perfection. Without optical aids they could draw designs so intricate that the unaided eye could scarcely resolve them. By the pious these designs were thought to be the work of angels.

But what about the Tibetans? The Gardener had a hanging scroll (*thanka*) in his possession on which, in the heart of a lotus in an area less than that of a dime, were portrayed the Buddha and all the Bodisattvas in red, black, and gold, complete with facial expressions practically invisible without the aid of a lens!

And then there were Japanese artists who write poems on grains of rice. . . .

All of which, of course, was far exceeded by the intracacies of microcircuits printed on chips of silica by photographic techniques. Micro-bodisattvas to microcircuits, *thankas* to transistors. Progress?

The Gardener was copying a design from an Isfahan carpet. The intricate medallion, after weeks of study, had finally yielded its secret. Hidden in the pattern were the rotated squares, a favorite symbol of the Naqshbandi. The cupola in the Hall of the Abencerrajes in the Alhambra, at Granada, demonstrated what could be done with rotated squares. What a harmonious blending of triads, tetrads, octagons—an entire cosmology in stone, a marvel of craftsmanship! The Designer had brought picture postcards from Spain, along with a collection of travelers' tales, mostly about Naqshbandi, a mysterious order, still active throughout the East. Were they the designers of the Dome of the Rock at Jerusalem that stands in the place of the Temple destroyed by the Romans? Did they build the Taj Mahal? Were they the originators of the enneagram, the diagram of the nine? Are they associated with the Sarmouni, the

Brotherhood of the Bees, whose two communities in Afghanistan have so rarely been visited by Westerners?

But the quest for mysterious Oriental Brotherhoods was one of the fool traps spread in the way of the unwary. One could spend a lifetime wandering and searching, and many did, and never found what they sought. They were imbued with the same starry-eyed romanticism that compelled the Theosophists to fabricate mysterious mahatmas. It never occurred to such seekers that what they wanted might be right next door, perhaps in some Western city, London, New York, San Francisco. They had to have mysterious Orientals. They demanded Tibetan lamas with skull drums and thigh-bone flutes, with inscrutable faces and a capacity to fly through the air. The dull, ordinary, down-to-earth reality was not for them. So they never found what they sought. Because ultimately, however ornate the trimmings, the same dull, ordinary, down-to-earth reality was there in the background.

Down-to-earth reality which also contained all that man needed . . .

> How marvelously supernatural and how miraculous this—
> I draw water and I carry wood.

Both the Professor and the Shulamite were working on prayer rugs. There was much to the making of a prayer rug. Enjoined though they were to remain "within the tradition," the Whole-Earthers had sufficient freedom of choice in color and design to enable them to show themselves in the rugs they created. The stable rectangular *mihrab* appealed to the Professor who was, despite sallies of wit and a sense of humor ranging on the macabre, an orthodox soul, almost a square. The Shulamite was much more skittish, had unearthed from somewhere a curvaceous central design, suggestive of gourds or amphoras. Where the Professor wove cautiously with browns, blacks, and old golds, the Shulamite splashed among Turkey

reds and rich blues. There were delicate balances involved. Mute the colors too much and the prayer rug became merely dull, overdo the bright hues and it became distracting, garish, and distasteful.

Darling Lou had had dreams of her own private industry, coloring gourds and filling them with herbs, "organically" grown for the health food nuts. She had sowed and reaped a gourd crop of astonishing variety from plants that grew with unbelievable vigor, threatening to engulf the whole plot on which they had been let loose. There were calabashes of all shapes and sizes, drupes, pear-drops, boules, figures of eight. From the larger ones, so went the dream, pitchers for wine or water would be made, inscribed, in Persian perhaps, with a text from Rumi: *Love the water not the jug.*

The smaller gourds were to receive those "organically" grown herbs, with their aromatic essences, to be used for fragrant teas or to flavor food. There would be borage and chamomile, rue, mint, thyme, balsam, savory, tarragon, rosemary, catnip. There would be the pungent umbellates, dill, parsley, fennel, cardamom. There would be reeking members of the onion family, chives and garlic. There would be mace, nutmeg, and cinnamon imported from distant spice islands, and the exotic *kava kava*, base of the sacred drink of the Polynesians.

But the project remained at the dream stage. She had painted one gourd. The rest hung in the barn. They would probably end on the compost heap.

A similar dream was harbored by the Duchess who had visions of herself as a weaver and shepherdess. There was nothing impossible about the dream. To raise on the hilly pastures a small herd of Corriedales, to shear them, spin the wool, dye it, and weave fabric was well within the power of any woman with a certain amount of common sense and some spare time. And the Duchess had indeed gone so far as to buy, at an outrageous price, a small bag of raw wool from a local hobby shop which she spun on a simple spindle into thread. And she wove small designs on a hand loom. But somehow the larger plan seemed unlikely to materialize. The creative force was lacking.

This certainly could not be said of the Reverend Mother. Her project was jewelry, made from gold wire. She had really mastered the art and received quite large orders. She sat now before rows of crosses, dextrously curling the wire into rosettes, four of which would enclose a pearl or garnet at the center of the cross. The cross, that symbol of the Judeo-Christian guilt cult, had become very popular along with Jesus Christ, Superstar. There was a good market for crosses and the Reverend Mother made the best of it. She made the chains also, twisting the wire in figures of eight, nimbly connecting the links and bending in the ends. It took forty-five minutes to make a twenty-two-inch chain. The chain sold for seven dollars, the gold cost one dollar.

Then there was basket weaving. From time to time one or other of the Whole-Earthers practiced the art. Primal Scream, before leaving the group, had made a half bushel basket of coils. It was not a distinguished product but served its purpose, holding, when full, just thirty pounds of wheat. Others produced platters and bread baskets, always by the coil method, which was certainly not the fastest form of basket making, though also not the slowest. The Pomo Indians, who had roamed those hills before the white man came, had been the true masters of the art, weaving baskets so tightly that they actually held water. There were still, in Sonoma County, Indian women who taught this art, but none of the Whole-Earthers had taken the trouble to learn it. Such basket making took a prodigious amount of time and the result was hardly worth the effort.

Batik, tie dyeing, pottery, at one time or another they had tried them all. Was there not some small ecological niche they could occupy, some place inviolable by the great machines, some product they could make with their hands and sell, and thereby pay the electricity bills, the gas bills, the doctor, the dentist? Even if you did grow all your own food you still needed money. And it seemed natural to make that money doing something enjoyable, making something others needed. But what did people need? One could never compete with the machine product. Clothes? The machines had the edge. Jewelry? The Reverend Mother had found it possible to make money this way, but the going was tough. Pottery? You could never compete with the Mexicans. Silverware likewise.

Perhaps arts and crafts were not the solution. Perhaps one should experiment in a different area. But what? What could one sell to the Great Society? How could one serve it without becoming its eight-to-five wage slave? The Whole-Earthers had, on the whole, failed to solve this problem.

# XVIII

## *Thanksgiving*

Fellow Whole-Earthers!

Open your eyes and look about you. Throw away your books and learn directly from the biosphere. It teaches man all that he needs to know.

What does it teach?

First of all, interdependence. The biosphere is an exquisitely balanced system for converting solar energy. It converts this energy into transient, ever-changing entities that move and breed and feel and think. Finally it converts that energy into a being capable of mirroring in his consciousness the universal cosmic process itself.

In man, evolution becomes conscious of itself. In man evolution becomes potentially self-directing. So man is the crown of the biosphere. But man is also the bane of the biosphere, the poisoner able to destroy in a few decades forms that have taken millions of years to evolve. A sword has been put into the hands of this naked ape. He can use it either to free himself or to cut his own throat.

*Let us see if he turns out a warrior or a robber.*

Study the biosphere. Look at the plants and animals. Look at the ocean and under the ocean. Learn to see with your eyes and to hear with your ears.

The biosphere tells us that everything lives in accordance with certain laws. For some creatures these laws are very restrictive, for others they are quite flexible. Consider the kangaroo rat. It is perfectly adapted to life in the desert. It can do without liquid water. It has marvelously efficient kidneys. But the very specialization that enables it to survive in the desert boxes it into that special environment, makes it impossible for it to live elsewhere.

Consider the Weddel seal. What a marvel of adaptation! It lives in Antarctica for the most part under the ice in water so cold that unprotected man would perish in a few minutes. The pups are born on the ice in the total darkness of the Antarctic winter. What an uncomfortable ecological niche! And yet the Weddel seal flourishes. But the very adaptations that enable it to live in the Antarctic prevent it from establishing itself in other environments. Both the seal and the kangaroo rat live under restrictive laws.

Now consider man. For him the laws are very flexible. Look in the coldest climates, in the Arctic, in Siberia, there you find man. Look in tropical jungles, there he is. Look in the deserts, there he is. The Australian aborigine can survive in a climate as dry as that inhabited by the kangaroo rat. Man can invade even more hostile environments. He can penetrate the depths of the sea, climb the highest mountains, gather rocks on the moon. Of all the creatures in the biosphere man lives under the most flexible laws.

Does this mean that he is free of the laws? Certainly not. He *acts* as if he were free, violating, squandering, polluting, destroying. But in this he merely shows himself to be a bandit and, above all, a fool. A drunkard may smash all the furniture in the house and set fire to the house itself because he imagines himself to be all-powerful and above the law. This does not alter the fact that he will find himself without a house. The fact that you are intoxicated, whether with alcohol or a sense of your own power, does not free you from the laws. The sober man must pay for all that the drunkard has smashed—if he can pay for it. Some kinds of damages are irreparable.

Look about you. See how the laws are broken. What has happened in these United States? A nation of fat cats, 6 percent of the world's population guzzling and squandering 35 percent of the world's resources, strewing the land with junk, scattering empty beer cans, beer cans that symbolize all that is lowest in the American way of life, glittering, vacant, smelling faintly of intoxicants.

Look at our own Santa Rosa. The town grows like a cancer, as if eager to become a second Los Angeles. Orchards and vineyards are bulldozed out of the way. Groves of walnut trees are desecrated. Dairymen go bankrupt because they can't pay the taxes. Developers won't be satisfied with the thin land up in the hills that is relatively worthless for agriculture. If they built on the hills they would have to spend money to make level sites. So they use up the good flat valley lands, burying the rich earth in concrete and forming a huddle of houses, squashed together like cells in a honeycomb, burying the rest in gigantic parking lots. By the year 2000, if this keeps up, 50 percent of California's farming land will be buried under concrete.

And don't think this is confined to California. It is taking place all over the country. It is regarded as some sort of progress. And what happens when the urban sprawl takes up all the good land? That is in the future. Let our grandchildren worry about it.

By the way things are going, those grandchildren will have plenty to worry about.

Look about you. Open your eyes. The laws are firm, harsh, utterly inescapable. Each link in the chain is connected to the one above and the one below. Break one link and you break the chain. But although payment has to be made, it is not always made immediately. Sometimes payment is delayed. And those who make the mistakes are not the ones who must pay.

What else do we learn from the biosphere? We learn that

there is a certain kind of order regulating the relationships between living things. A given square mile of earth or ocean contains just so much life, and each organism has its place. On the ocean rocks there are just so many starfish, so many mussels, sea anemones, seaweeds. They fit in their place like parts of a jigsaw juzzle. On land there are just so many plants, so many mice, so many skunks, hawks, predators in general.

What applies to the biosphere applies to man both collectively and individually. There are patterns within human communities. The mosaic of occupations has an ecological basis. Farmers and fishermen are the first links in the food chain. Without them the entire social process would grind to a halt. For there's no other wealth in the world than what is grown on the soil, dug from the earth, or fished out of the sea. So the farmers and fishermen bear the whole social structure on their shoulders, and mighty little thanks they get for bearing it.

Time was when these farmers and fishermen were quite independent. They drew their food directly from soil or sea. In good years they ate well, in poor years they went hungry. But they were sturdy and self-reliant. They dealt with nature directly.

Those days are over. In most cases the farmer is independent no longer but merely a cog in a vast industrial complex. In order to survive he is forced to farm more and more land. To farm this huge acreage he must buy more and more machinery. To buy the machines he must borrow more and more money. He is bound hand and foot by his dependence on banks for credit, on oil companies for fuel, on heavy industry for his machines, on a host of mechanics who must service these machines. So vast and complex has the whole process grown that the individual farmer has become a thing of the past. His farm is being replaced by huge impersonal agricultural empires that employ managers and pay them salaries. Such a manager has none of the old-time farmer's personal link with nature. He poisons the soil with huge dressings of chemicals and with spray residues, influenced only by a need for higher yields, which will please the men who pay his salary and probably result in a raise. He has no love for the good earth. For all the feeling he has about the soil he might as well be working for General Motors.

The fisherman is going the same way; bigger and bigger boats, more and more expensive machinery, sonar, radar, depth-finders, even small planes to spot the schools of fish. The latest thing in tuna boats, the super-seiner *Apollo*, cost $3 million and has enough capacity to carry two thousand tons of tuna. With a fleet of such monsters guzzling the world's tuna crop, how long will it be before the tuna go the way of the great whales, hunted to extinction by huge factory ships manned chiefly by Russians and Japanese? Meanwhile the small fisherman in his modest boat can barely make a living. Costs go up, fishing gets worse and worse. The Japanese and Russian factory ships scoop up everything from sardines to salmon, regardless of size. So the independent fisherman follows the independent farmer into extinction, and in his place is the paid manager of the factory ship, sea-borne equivalent of the paid manager of the factory farm, and an even worse desecrator of the environment.

So what can we do? Go to Washington and demand that the government protect the fisherman by imposing a two-hun-dred-mile limit? The government is totally indifferent. Who cares about the fisherman? There aren't enough of them to affect the elections. So the foreign factory ships scoop up huge loads of fish under our very noses.

We can do nothing through governments. All we can do is work on ourselves. We can fish. We can farm. We can offer an example. We fish from about the smallest boat you can safely take on the open ocean (a fifteen-foot kayak) and we take only enough for our needs. We farm with due regard for the soil and the other creatures that share the planet with us.

We grow what we need. We replenish the earth and treat it with respect. We try to train others to do likewise. For what the earth gives us we try to be thankful.

Thanksgiving. It is a truly American festival and has honorable origins. But what can these city-bred man-swarms of today know about the meaning of Thanksgiving? What is this feast but an excuse for burdening their already overloaded systems with huge gobs of cholesterol, thereby increasing their chance of developing atherosclerosis? What did they have to do with producing the goodies they guzzle, the store-bought turkey raised in a turkey factory, fed, killed, plucked by machinery, the canned cranberry sauce, the mass-produced vegetables grown on factory farms? They do not know where the food came from. They had nothing to do with its production. They are not even aware of the forces that generated their food, the sacred triad, soil–sun–biosphere.

Thanksgiving! And only once a year at that! The feast has become a farce.

Let us try to do things differently. Let us base our behavior not on that of the overstuffed white men who have raped the continent but rather on that of the Indians whom our fellow whites have herded into reservations and who now live on the edge of starvation on the poorest lands in the States. These men lived in harmony with Nature. Morning and evening they gave thanks to the sky for giving them shelter, to the earth for giving them food, to the sun for giving them light. Such men truly understand the meaning of Thanksgiving.

# PART FIVE

# The Universal University

# XIX

## The Star of the Show

Fellow Whole-Earthers!

What do you see in the morning when you climb the hill among the apple trees, turn to the east and await the appearing of the star of our show, the all life-giving Sol, the blessed sun? Let me remind you that different people experience Sol differently according to whether they look or they *see* (I use this term as don Juan would use it).

Said Blake, who was a mystic and poet, to Crabb Robinson, who was a lawyer and collector of painters and poets:

> *I assert for myself that I do not behold the outward creation, and that to me it is hindrance and not action; it is as the dirt upon my feet, no part of me. "What," it will be questioned, "when the sun rises do you not see a round disc of fire, something like a guinea?" Oh no, no, I see an innumerable company of the heavenly host crying: "Holy, holy, holy is the Lord God Almighty."*

This is called seeing with the third eye, which is the eye of wisdom. But even if you only see a "round disc of fire something like a guinea," at least you are aware of the sun, the giver of life. For it is characteristic of the sleeping mass in our great man-swarms that they are totally unaware of the star of the show on which their lives depend. They neither greet his appearance at dawn nor bid him farewell in the evening. If they ever see him at all it is probably on television.

How very different is the attitude of peoples we call primitive. Consider this description by Jung of the Pueblo Indians:

> As I sat with Ochwiay Biano on the roof, the blazing sun rising higher and higher, he said, pointing to the sun, "Is not he who moves there our father? How can anyone say differently? How can there be another god? Nothing can be without the sun." His excitement, which was already perceptible, mounted still higher; he struggled for words and exclaimed at last, "What would a man do alone in the mountains? He cannot even build his fire without him."

Of course it would be a mistake to give Sol all the credit. He is indeed the giver of force, but it is the biosphere that captures the force and gives it form. So the joyful sun-worshippers of northern India saw Surya, the sun god, as the embodiment of *purusha* (the male force) and earth as the embodiment of *prakrti* (the female force) that receives unto itself the seed of the male and gives it form. Hence the riot of copulating figures that swarm over the sun temples such as the one at Konarak. Hence the devadasi, temple girls, servants of the god, who gave to the sexual act the quality of a mystical and cosmic experience.

But we, who are children of a different age, are bound to view the sun against a wider background. He is indeed the giver of life and the source of all our energy. But he is one among billions. We cannot blind ourselves to the realities revealed by astronomy.

So what are the realities?

A modern cosmology, taking all that is known into account, can be constructed within the cosmic egg which we call the Absolute. The Absolute is Alpha and Omega, the beginning and the end. Outside of it nothing can exist. It is inconceivable to our minds except as a philosophical concept.

The laws of symmetry suggest that two universes exist in

the Absolute. Universe I is composed of matter in time, universe II is composed of antimatter in antitime. If the two mixed, there would be an explosion and matter would be annihilated, transformed into radiation. Somehow the two are kept apart, like a man and his mirror image.

Universe I, "our" universe, began, it appears, with an explosion which, for reasons hard to explain, occurred 12 to 13 billion years ago. This was the big bang that started the show. The radiation of the big bang is still around us and can be detected by suitable instruments. The big bang theory of the cosmos leads us to suppose that this explosion is the essence of the cosmic drama. Universe I explodes, differentiates, and evolves worlds within worlds. Universe II contracts, falls in, dedifferentiates. As one unfolds, the other folds up. Or perhaps there is only one universe that alternately unfolds and folds up, corresponding to the days and nights of Brahm (a cycle that some cosmologists think may have a rhythm of 15 billion years).

This drama is on a scale inconceivable to our minds. Inconceivable also is the second order world, the super-galaxy. It is a galaxy of galaxies so huge that even our greatest telescopes cannot tell us of its structure because, as they look out into space, they also look back into time. So the remotest galaxies (about 2 billion light-years away) are seen not as they are now but as they were two billion years ago.

The next level of cosmic differentiation, worlds of the third order, are visible to us. These are the galaxies, cosmic concentrations built up of huge aggregates of stars, perhaps a hundred billion stars per galaxy.

Let this figure sink into your minds. One hundred billion, 100,000,000,000! And the super-galaxy may contain one hundred billion galaxies. This is the background of the cosmic drama, this gigantic quantity of worlds within worlds. With so many actors in the drama you might speculate that everything that conceivably can happen will happen. If an event is not forbidden by some physical law, it is sure to occur somewhere. Even events which seem so unlikely as to be virtually impossible will happen sometime because the scale of the drama in space-time is so enormous.

Eighty percent of the galaxies take the form of flattened discs with spiral arms. Our own galaxy has this form, so has the nearby (it is about a million light-years away) nebula in Andromeda. Galaxies of this kind commonly measure 100,000 light-years across. They contain two populations of stars, old stars in population II, young stars in population I. The young stars are born in the spiral arms of the galaxy from interstellar gas, chiefly hydrogen.

This brings us to the fourth order worlds, the suns or solar systems, for along with the sun we must include its satellites. Our sun with its planets is a relatively young system. It arose along with a group of other stars about 5 billion years ago when a mysterious shock wave triggered movements in the interstellar gas of one of the arms of the galaxy. The gas condensed into aggregates. These aggregates contracted under the influence of gravitation until, at a certain density, the enormous pressure caused the hydrogen in the aggregate to start to "burn." This burning was not of the sort that takes place when hydrogen burns in oxygen to form water. This burning involves fusion of the protons in the nucleus of the hydrogen atom, which gives an atom of deuterium (heavy hydrogen) a positron and a neutrino. The energy evolved in the process heated the aggregate to incandescence. So the sun was born.

Having been born, will the sun go on shining forever? Certainly not. All that is born must die and this includes the stars and even the galaxy. The life of a star such as the sun has six stages. (1) It contracts for about 140 million years. (2) It burns hydrogen quietly for about 10 billion years. (3) It flares up into a red giant, then contracts again for 500 million years. (4)

Having exhausted its hydrogen, it starts burning helium and carbon for 500 million years. (5) It contracts again for 13 million years. (6) It shrinks to an incredible density, becoming a white dwarf which radiates the energy left in its mass while gradually fading into a cold corpse of a star. Or it may become a "black hole," contracting to such a density that its gravitational field prevents any radiation from escaping.

The star called Sol has by now lived through half of stage two. It will continue to radiate heat at a steady rate for another 5 billion years. At the moment Sol has a diameter 109 times that of the earth, its mass is 331,950 times that of earth, its surface is 6,000°K. (compared with an electric arc, 4,000°K.), it transforms its matter into radiation at a rate of 4 million tons per second. It is located far from the center of the galaxy (about 26,000 light-years), and it takes 200 million years to rotate about that center at a speed of 600,000 miles per hour.

Within solar systems, planetary systems or worlds of the fifth order may arise. We have no reason to think that the development of planets around a star is a rare event. It may be quite common. Even if only one in a hundred stars develops planets there will be a billion planetary systems in our galaxy alone, many of which may have developed biospheres. Our home planet, Earth, is the third planet from the sun and differs from the others in having a biosphere, a thin film of living matter that intercepts and transforms a small fraction of the solar energy that reaches it.

This, then, is the framework within which we exist, the cosmic background of our small drama. We find ourselves reduced to total insignificance. Our individuality, our whole species, our planet, solar system, even our galaxy becomes unimportant. The universe seems extravagantly, almost preposterously, big, and its limits, if it has limits, are forever beyond our reach. We shall never be able to escape from our own solar system. We are tied down in space and in time, and all the fantasies of our science-fiction writers will not alter this fact. If there are other intelligent beings in the universe (and it would surely be presumptuous to assume there are not), then they exist so far from us that meaningful communication is almost impossible. Every reliable form of communication now known is dependent on electromagnetic radiation. And all electromagnetic radiation travels at the same rate (186,000 miles/sec). If our near star neighbor (Alpha Centauri) has a planetary system and one of the planets has evolved an intelligent race of beings capable of sending signals into space, then each message will take 4.4 years to reach us. At this rate, merely to decipher their code would take us centuries.

There are, however, no signs of meaningful signals coming from interstellar space. The radio astronomers seek in vain. For a time the curiously rhythmic emissions of quasars seemed like signals, but the theory that they were sent out by "little green men" was not offered seriously and quickly abandoned.

There are consolations, however. The immensity of interstellar space precludes any cosmic catastrophes from affecting more than a small part of the universe. And such catastrophes occur. Stars explode. Horrendous quantities of energy are suddenly liberated, as happened in 1054 A.D. when a super nova, the remains of which are known as the Crab nebula, blazed in the sky so powerfully as to be visible even in daylight. Even whole galaxies can explode. On a smaller scale, intelligent beings whose evolution has taken a wrong turn (this might include *Homo sapiens*) could, by their meddling, touch off explosions that might disrupt planets and even solar systems. Again the immensity of interstellar space limits the mischief such beings might do.

But there is another reason why we can be thankful for the immensity of the universe. Our very existence depends on this immensity. A perceptive cosmologist has observed that we exist by grace of a series of hang-ups. The first of these hang-ups is the fantastic distance between galaxy and galaxy, star and star, star and planet. Gravitation, the universal attractive force, would pull the whole universe back into the primordial atom were its density much greater than one atom per cubic meter. At this density the "free-fall time" is about 100 billion years. If Universe I is about 12 billion years old this gives us another 90 billion years.

Within the galaxy, matter is about a million times as dense as it is in the universe, but the galaxy is saved from collapse by the spin hang-up. Anyone who has swung a ball on the end of a string knows that the ball will not fall as long as it swings at a certain speed. So it is spin that prevents the collapse of the galaxy, spin that prevents the earth plunging into the sun and the moon from falling into the earth (though the comets, by the irregularity of their orbits, represent a permanent threat of cosmic collisions).

Then there is the hydrogen hang-up. Stars like our sun burn in a reasonably placid, steady fashion instead of exploding like thermonuclear bombs because they are made up preponderantly of ordinary hydrogen. If they contained substantial amounts of heavy hydrogen (deuterium), they would burn by the "strong nuclear reaction" and our show would have ended in a violent explosion long before life could have evolved on the planet Earth. It is the heavy isotopes of hydrogen (deuterium and tritium) that operate in man's thermonuclear bombs, giving him power to wipe himself off the earth. The sun burns by a process so much slower (proton to proton fusion) that to heat a cup of coffee by the sun process would take years. The sun's high temperature is due to its huge size that prevents the heat from escaping readily.

So the size hang-up, the spin hang-up, and the hydrogen hang-up plus a number of other hang-ups not mentioned here have made possible our existence in this relatively quiet corner of the universe. There are other corners of the universe that are by no means placid, and violence on a fantastic scale is common. These observations have led a perceptive cosmologist to conclusions more genial than those entertained by the *avant garde* intellectuals of the garbage can school whose sickly dreams have poisoned our spiritual lives.

> *If sheer distance had not effectively isolated the quiet regions of the universe from the noisy ones, no type of biological evolution would have been possible.*
>
> *I believe the universe is friendly. I see no reason to suppose that the cosmic accidents that provided so abundantly for our welfare here on earth will not do the same for us wherever else in the universe we choose to go. . . .*
>
> *Nature has been kinder to us than we had any right to expect. As we look out into the universe and identify the many accidents of physics and astronomy that have worked together for our benefit, it almost seems as if the universe must in some sense have known that we were coming.*
>
> F. J. DYSON, "Energy in the Universe," *Scientific American*, September 1971, p. 51.

# XX

## When the Walls Come Tumbling Down

Fellow Whole-Earthers!

The Decline and Fall of Industrial Man is a popular topic among purveyors of gloom and doom. I talk about it merely to awaken thought, not to make you worry. The subject is somewhat speculative at best. We are aware that all is not well. The Tower of Babel gets higher and higher but also appears to be less and less stable. We live in the shadow of the tower and are apt to be damaged if it falls. We need to estimate just how unstable it is, when it is likely to collapse, whether it will fall all at once or bit by bit, and where we can go to get out of the way. It's a matter of self-preservation.

Let us try to analyze the forces at work. Let us look at some possibilities.

Will the tower crash because the sources of industrial energy become exhausted?

This seems bound to happen sooner or later. An industrial society like ours uses and squanders energy like a drunken millionaire. Like most drunken millionaires it suffers from the illusion that its wealth is inexhaustible. But it isn't. I can give you some figures to prove it. Let me quote from a recent paper:

> Last year the U.S. achieved a gross national product of just over $1,000 billion with the help of $69 \times 10^{15}$ British thermal units of energy, of which 95.9 percent was provided by fossil fuels, 3.8 percent by falling water and .3 percent by fission of uranium. CLAUDE M. SUMMERS, "The Conversion of Energy," *Scientific American*, September 1971, p. 149.

189

This is the fact. It shows us that great Babylon guzzles oil and coal at a rate corresponding to the use by every one of its people of 2,700 gallons of gasoline or 13 tons of coal per year. And if the past is anything to go by, this rate of consumption will double every ten years!

At this rate, how long will the coal last and how long the oil? Let me quote an authority.

> The earth's supply of minable coal is estimated at 7.6 trillion metric tons. Of this we can forecast that all but 10 percent will be used between the year 2000 and 2300. Oil supplies are estimated 2,100 billion barrels (but may be as low as 1,350 billion). All but the last 10 percent of this will be used in 58 to 64 years, peak production being the year 2000.
> M. KING HUBBERT, "The Energy Resources of the Earth," *Scientific American*, September 1971, p. 61.

So much for the fossil fuels. They were accumulated over millions of years. They will be all exhausted by industrialized man in, at the most, a few centuries.

So what happens then? *Homo mechanicus neobarbartus* (the mechanized barbarian) switches to uranium and nuclear fission for his energy needs. How much uranium is available? If one takes into account the low-grade uranium ores such as the Chattanooga black shales, we are led to the conclusion that "the energy potentially available from the fissioning of uranium and thorium is at least a few orders of magnitude greater than that from all the fossil fuels combined."

Then there is nuclear fusion. It is, let us remember, the reaction from which the sun draws its heat, and from which, as children of the sun, all living things draw their life energy. *If the technologists can ever control this process (which all concede is a stupendously difficult task), then 1 percent of the amount of deuterium in earth's ocean would suffice to supply

500,000 times the energy of the world's initial supply of fossil fuels.

Saved? Will Great Babylon live on indefinitely, its city lights fed by an inexhaustible flood of deuterium?

Hardly. For the prospect of unlimited power drawn from the ocean brings with it a second prospect that is much less jolly. Which is that all energy ends in the form of waste heat. And this heat has to go somewhere. If you pour it into the air it will overheat the air. If you pour it into the streams it will overheat the water. Great Babylon will cook in its own waste energy. The whole biosphere will cook. For waste heat ultimately is as much a pollutant as are the toxic gases that pour from the nation's 100 million motor vehicles. Even now the waste heat from the 1,550 billion kilowatt hours of electricity used by the U.S. in 1970 is enough to affect the temperature of the environment. Ninety-nine years from now, at the present rate of increase, this heat will cook us all.

Out of the frying pan into the fire.

But the controlled fusion reaction, using deuterium, is very difficult to maintain. Perhaps it is even impossible. So what will the Great Society do for energy when it has guzzled all its own oil, coal, natural gas, and uranium? Its own and that of others?

Well, it could use sunlight, which is free and strikes the earth anyway. If one covered a tenth of the area of Arizona with heat traps one might convert enough solar energy to electrical energy to supply the whole country. Which looks like a solution because it is technically feasible, does not pollute either with heat or waste products, and draws energy from a fire likely to go on burning steadily for the next 5 billion years. And by using sunlight to power a photolytic reaction one could derive hydrogen from water, of which, on the planet Earth, there is an abundant supply. No one can deny that hydrogen is the perfect fuel. You can run a fuel cell on hydrogen and get electricity with an efficiency that far surpasses that of any other method of generating this commodity. And hydrogen does not pollute. Burned with oxygen it goes back to the state from which it came, namely water. So hydrogen is the perfect fuel, and if sunlight can be used to generate hydrogen, then a long-term, nonpolluting, energy-generating system will be available.

Reprieve? Perhaps. But only if we succeed in limiting growth. The water–sunlight–hydrogen–water cycle could fuel a *stable* economy indefinitely. But it can fuel it only if the economy stops growing. No energy-generating system can provide fuel for an economy that doubles its energy requirements every ten years. This kind of growth will end by exhausting any energy system.

Obviously this growth cannot continue. Obviously stopping this growth, which has long ago ceased to be healthy and has now attained the status of a cancer, is the most urgent task faced by the industrialized nations of today. Obviously no one is in a position to stop this growth because this would mean changing the habits of living and thinking of huge masses of people. Equally obviously, if this growth continues, the technological Tower of Babel must crash as soon as the demand for energy becomes impossible to satisfy.

As with fuel so with food, which is nothing more than the fuel of the human machine. Enough food for a *stable* human population could be generated by the biosphere for millennia to come. But no food-generating system can provide enough fuel for a human bio-mass that keeps getting bigger and bigger and bigger. Food is generated in the biosphere by the transmutation of sunlight. This transmutation is wasteful in the extreme. Let us look at some figures.

The beef-guzzling American, a carnivore without a carnivore's excuse, consumes on the average 183 pounds of meat per person per year (compared to eighteen pounds a year eaten by the average Japanese). To get his 183 pounds of flesh this carnivore devours the equivalent of 1,830 pounds of corn, which corn was generated by the use of only about 1 percent of the solar energy that fell on the cornfield. If this were a typical diet of the whole human race, then nothing could save us from starvation within the next year.

Fortunately this meat-eating is restricted. The human biomass lives mainly on grain. Even so, there are only on the surface of this planet 3.5 billion acres under cultivation, which gives one acre of cultivated land for each one of the 3.5 billion people now living. Perhaps a total of 8 billion acres of arable land might be found and the earth could support 8 billion people. Ten to 12 billion probably represents the limit. This would give a very crowded planet.

We must try to be rational. We must consider objectively the fate of *Homo sapiens*. Here is a picture that might perhaps be accurate.

The fall of the technological Tower of Babel is not inevitable. Large natural energy sources are available that do not pollute and are virtually inexhaustible. Food enough for a population of 8 billion could be produced from the arable land and could be further supplemented by an intelligent program of aquaculture (farming the sea). Before the 8 billion population figure is reached, ways may well be discovered of controlling man's tendency to multiply. Such mechanisms exist in nature and man may be no exception.

We *could* see *Homo sapiens* last a long time.

Or again—we could see him destroy himself in a sort of frenzy, driven mad by overcrowding and, ultimately, by sheer boredom. Or he might start fighting over the diminishing stores of earth's goodies, destroying what remains of the goodies in the process.

We of the Church of the Earth are bound to rely as little as possible on the products of the Industrial Society. But we still do rely on them to some extent. We *could* do without our deep freeze, our refrigerator, our tractor, and our various cars.

We *could* make candles for light or go to bed when it gets dark. We *could* (but this would be far more difficult) irrigate the garden by carrying all the water instead of letting an electric pump do the work for us. But I maintain it would be stupid to go to such extremes. We have to live on the best terms we can with the Industrial Society, accept the benefits (and it confers many) while, at the same time, avoiding the temptations it offers to turn oneself into a human punch card.

Total retreat into the woods after the manner of Thoreau is not called for at the moment.

We have to realize, however, that the Tower of Babel is a very shaky structure. All that is needed to make it crash is another outburst of mass insanity such as occurred in 1914 and again in 1939. Such outbursts occur for reasons that are not at all clear, but the symptoms of the coming storm can always be detected. These take the form of lies and violence. Whenever the level of general untruthfulness and the level of violence reach a certain point, then the society in which this occurs is headed for disaster. Lies and violence, not lack of energy sources or lack of food, are the forces that will bring down the Tower of Babel. It was the confusion of tongues, the inability of men to understand each other, that caused the downfall of the original tower.

Two other factors will contribute to the fall of the Tower, boredom and self-alienation. Boredom is inevitable. An increasingly efficient technology steadily replaces men with machines. All the simpler jobs are taken over by the machines. For millions this means that there is literally nothing for them to do. They are technologically unemployed, forced to live on relief, degraded to the level of beggars in a society more interested in accumulating wealth than developing its members.

So what will happen to all these bored beggars who have nothing to do? Their boredom is potentially dangerous. Their anger is also potentially dangerous. They may start blowing up the machines that have made them redundant.

Alienation from the self is even more dangerous. An aimless man-swarm, its inner life nonexistent, constantly dependent on external stimulation, a mere appendage of a television or radio, may suddenly realize that it has been duped, that its life is aimless and idiotic; that the technological Juggernaut is rolling nowhere, an insane machine journeying from the empty to the void, crushing beneath it as it goes those who supposedly benefit from its progress.

If such an awakening occurs, will they not blow the Juggernaut sky-high, even though they themselves will be buried in its ruins? For the roots of the destruction of our new Tower of Babel lie deeply embedded in the soul of man. If you make him too idle, too comfortable, something in him revolts. He suddenly demands challenge, hardship, suffering, may blow up all the comfort-giving gadgets, turn his back on the easy life and start again at the Stone Age.

# XXI

## *The Balanced Life*

Fellow Whole-Earthers!

What is the balanced life?

The balanced life is like the balanced diet. It supplies all the components necessary for man's completion.

Man is an incomplete being. Nature ensures his growth as far as puberty, then leaves him to his own devices. He develops further only if he chooses to develop. To do this he must select the right environment, the right impressions, the proper balance of activities. In short the balanced life.

To understand what are the right conditions for development it is useful to consider what are the wrong conditions. Consider the slave of the assembly line. All day he works in the din of a factory. Around him are bricks, concrete, noise, distractions. And what does he do? Here's an article in *Time* entitled "The Blue Collar Worker's Lowdown Blues." A striker outside General Motors' assembly line is talking in Tarrytown, N.Y.: "Do you know what I do? I fix seven bolts. Seven bolts! Day in and day out, the same seven bolts. What do I think about? Raquel Welch."

I ask you, how can a man attain his full development on a diet of seven bolts and a dream of Raquel Welch? You might as well expect a child to grow by feeding it on paper pulp. This is the perfect example of the unbalanced life. It doesn't matter how much you pay this poor fellow. He's living in an impoverished environment and all the dollars on earth won't change this fact. He isn't getting the proper quality of impressions. How can he take any pride or pleasure in his work when that work has been so fragmented by "efficiency experts" that he's hardly aware of what he is producing? Efficiency experts! Let them try for themselves the effect of living on an exclusive diet of fixing seven bolts. Maybe they'd learn a thing or two about real efficiency, which is to say the human use of human beings.

Turn now to the balanced life. What are its features?

First, variety. If man is to develop fully and harmoniously he needs to be fed through all his functions. Thinking, feeling, moving, emotion, sex—all these are areas in which growth can occur. Through these channels he receives the impressions that nourish his being.

Impressions are food. Man can no more live without impressions than he can live without food. But just as food can vary in quality so can impressions. They can be rich, nourishing, beneficial, or poor and inadequate or downright poisonous. A man's level of being is shown by the kind of impressions he seeks and absorbs. The muddled members of a degenerate man-swarm love poisonous impressions and swallow them in great gulps. Crime, violence, scandal, gossip, degraded sexuality, all these they feed on. If they can't get them firsthand they get them in packaged form via newspapers or television.

This craving for poisonous impressions has always been characteristic of the man-swarm. Think of the Romans gloating over the butchery in the arena or our pious ancestors enjoying public hangings or witch burnings. This inborn appetite is part of the chain we carry about our necks as a result of an error in our evolution.

He who lives the balanced life has no need for these poisons. He arranges his affairs in such a way that all the channels of awareness are used in a creative manner. This balanced use of the functions is only possible for one who has freed himself to some extent from the law called "eight-to-five." This law, which binds a man to certain limiting forms of repetitive activity (like tightening seven bolts), is so much a part of our social structure that we regard it as almost inescapable.

"He works from eight to five, a forty-hour week."

For millions, this is the accepted structure on which daily life is built.

We aim to change this structure, and we can do so. The key to the change is the balanced work program based on the principle that man must grow through the harmonious exercise of all his functions. This involves structuring one's daily life around a much more varied program of activity than is made possible by the eight-to-five law. It involves working with far greater intensity on a much greater variety of projects than does the slave of "eight-to-five." It is this demand for skilled work of many kinds performed at a high level of intensity that gives to life its richness and variety. Activity of this kind is governed by two principles.

1. *Work at the highest possible level of intensity.*

2. *Do it right.*

In short, this is no place for idlers, dreamers, muddlers, or starry-eyed devotees seeking mystic experiences.

Work is holy, but only if you do it with intensity, know why you're doing it, and understand the significance of the work.

What is our work at the Church of the Earth? How is the program designed?

The day starts with exercises. Why? Because the body must be awakened, charged, warmed up, vitalized. You drag it out of bed half dead, still lost in dreams. So you wake it up. Shake the bottle. Inverted jogging we call it. Stand it on its head and do a hundred and forty-four kicks to a breathing rhythm determined by your capacity. Follow this with *nauli* and *aswini mudra*. These force air into the system, stir up the guts, activate the adrenals, bathe the brain with blood, and generally activate the biochemical machinery.

Fuel the machine. Cleanse the machine. Empty out waste. Use *basti* (the yogic method of cleansing by drawing water into the rectum and expelling it). Think of what forests would be spared if everyone used *basti* to cleanse after defecation. Think of the myriad trees sacrificed merely to provide a pampered man-swarm with tissues on which to wipe its collective anus! The practice is not only wasteful, it isn't even sanitary. It merely smears the perineum with fecal matter, whereas *basti* cleanses both outer surface and inner. You rinse out your mouth, so why not the other end of the tube?

What about fuel? You are probably aware that a large part of the world's population suffers from malnutrition. You are probably not aware that *mal*nutrition (which means bad or wrong nutrition) applies to those who overeat as well as those who undereat and to those who use the wrong kind of food. Millions of Americans suffer from this second type of malnutrition. Americans are becoming a nation of sitters. Machines do the work, humans sit. And as they sit they degenerate, just as the fat, pampered Romans degenerated when all their needs were tended to by slaves. Americans have machines in the place of slaves. The machines do practically everything, so all the Americans have left to do is sit around and watch the machines and fix them when they go wrong.

What a life!

Obviously these sitting Americans will rot. They violate the laws of their own organism, for the body of man is a vehicle built to travel on rough roads. To stay fit it needs shocks, strains, challenge, exercise, and a rather sparse diet. With a sparse diet and plenty of exercise a human vehicle can remain in good shape for eighty to one hundred years.

Look at that fine old physician, Paul Dudley White, chasing after the electrocardiogram of a whale at the age of eighty. That

is a man who knows how to treat his vehicle. He knows, and
has said it again and again, that overeating plus underexercis-
ing is as sure to result in premature death as any of the pesti-
lences that decimated our ancestors. And why? Because it
wrecks the arterial system. Man's body is totally dependent on
these arterial tubes. They not only carry his oxygen but also the
food and fuel for every cell in the body. So what happens when
you live the unbalanced life, stuffing yourself with rich food
and taking no exercise? The great gobs of unused fatty material
circulating in the blood (particularly cholesterol) start gum-
ming up the arteries. The result is atherosclerosis, a disease
which has reached epidemic proportions in America. It kills
more people than does cancer, but, unlike cancer, is largely self-
inflicted. It is the price the American fat cat has to pay for being lazy, greedy, self-indulgent, and stupid.

Yes, stupid. Because there is absolutely no excuse nowadays
for anyone to be ignorant about the laws of sound nutrition.
The body requires four kinds of materials: fuel, building
blocks, vitamins, and minerals. You can get fuel from sugars,
starches, or fats. You get your building blocks (amino acids)
from protein. You get your vitamins and minerals from various
sources. The building blocks can be broken down and used as
fuel, but the fuels (sugars, etc.) cannot be used as building
blocks. You *must* eat a certain amount of protein. You don't
have to eat sugars, starches, or fats. But protein is rather an
expensive form of fuel and eliminating its waste products puts
some strain on the kidneys. So a balanced diet gives the body
sugar and starch to burn and enough protein to rebuild worn-
out tissue. Growing children and pregnant women need extra
protein.

Meat, eggs, milk are all sources of protein, but they carry
with them much fat or cholesterol. Fish of the non-fatty varieties is probably the best source of protein. Soybeans are good

but rather low in tryptophan. One can run the vehicle safely on a simple diet of fish, beans, potatoes, and green vegetables.

And plenty of exercise.

If you're fool enough to get stuck with a job which keeps you immobile in an office chair all day, then at least stand on your head at intervals to drain the the blood out of your legs and do a hundred and forty-four kicks as briskly as possible. If our large corporations who value their top executives would train the latter in this simple technique they would not have them dropping dead like flies from coronary thrombosis.

But of course no true Whole-Earther would ever let himself be tricked by fate into sitting all day in an office. The true Whole-Earther shapes his life to suit himself to assure his proper development and growth of being. Those splendid Whole-Earthers, Scott and Helen Nearing, long ago defined the goal in *Living the Good Life*. When they fled from New York City to a Vermont farm back in the thirties they plainly stated that work falls into two parts. First there is bread labor. If you grow your own food, as they did and we do, this should not take more than five hours a day. The bread labor should not be allowed to take all of a man's life. Man must have bread but he cannot live the balanced life if he spends his whole time getting it. He must have time for other activities. And he must try to keep those activities in balance.

The morning hours—for some these are the hours of maximum energy, the best time for creative activity, the best time for thinking. For others they are the best hours for hard physical work. What do we at the Church of the Earth do with them? The rule here is flexibility and variety. Whenever possible, divide activities so that more than one function is exercised. Suppose we have to dig a ditch for a water pipe, hard, heavy work swinging pick and shovel. Very well—work in the ditch—give all you have to the ditch—do as much as you can. But you don't have to bury yourself alive in the ditch. Give it two hours hard labor, then change over to another activity. Maybe art work. Maybe a seminar. Whatever has been planned.

But suppose the job is urgent—has to be finished?

Very well. Then it has to be finished. There are laws escapable and there are laws inescapable. We have to cooperate with the biosphere if we want it to feed us. This means that certain jobs must be finished by certain times. Ground must be prepared, crops must be sown, water must be supplied, and all by a certain date. In this area we have no choice. We are not free agents.

So it goes.

If the roof leaks, you fix it. You don't give a seminar on the theory of roofing. If a pipe bursts, you turn off the water and repair it. You don't offer a lecture on plumbing.

Prolonged toil of the back-breaking variety is rarely called for. It is not necessary, pleasurable, or profitable to overwork the musculature. A switch to an entirely different form of activity gives the muscles a rest and exercises the mind instead. In this lies the secret of the balanced life. The well-rounded student never gets stuck in a rut. He may dig a ditch from 8 A.M. to 10 A.M. and attend a seminar from 10:15 to 11:30. Balance is everything.

Activities fall into six categories.

First, those requiring hard muscular work but not much skill: ditch-digging, wood-chopping, land-clearing, and so on. Second, those requiring both physical strength and skill: various forms of building, repair of heavy equipment, etc. Third, those requiring manual dexterity but little strength: various forms of crafts, cooking. Fourth, those requiring artistic skill: the designing of pictures, jewelry, etc. Fifth, those involving inventive capacity: designing special apparatus, planning scientific experiments. Sixth, those involving various kinds of purely intellectual effort: solving mathematical problems, learning a new language, etc.

These categories of activities employ different centers and different energies. They involve different triads of activity. This applies especially to the third force of the triad, the directing or balancing force, seen mainly as point of application or "skillful means." Notice that the activities become increasingly difficult as the third element becomes predominant. Anyone in reasonable health can dig a ditch, chop firewood, or mow the lawn. But not everyone can build a house, repair an engine, design and make a fine jewel or a musical instrument, plan and carry out a meaningful experiment, or solve a problem in mathematics.

What we try to do here is to strike a balance between all these activities and to give everyone a taste of all of them. So the day includes many activities, so much ditch-digging, or its equivalent, so much art, craft, intellectual effort, music, dance, interpersonal interactions. This rich and varied diet applies to the children as much as to the adults. The children have their own small gardens, can undertake projects, attend seminars just like the adults, and, where possible, along with the adults. For there is no definite point where childhood ends and adulthood begins. We are all learners, and he who ceases to learn ceases to grow.

# XXII

## Man and Woman

Fellow Whole-Earthers!

As we drift further and further from our biological moorings, the man-woman relationship becomes increasingly unstable. A primitive people rooted in tradition has no problems in this area. Consider the Elgonyis, whose mode of living (then still unwrecked by the whites) was so sympathetically described by C. G. Jung. During his travels in Africa he was introduced to the second wife of the chief, a placid, dignified woman of about thirty with four children. From what did the dignity flow? From a secure and tradition-hallowed place in the scheme of things. Each of the chief's two wives had her own *shamba*, a garden in which she grew bananas, sweet potatoes, and maize. Each had her own *boma*, a hut in which she and her children lived. The husband's hut stood midway between those of his wives.

Jung had no doubt that this was a biologically sound arrangement. There were none of the stifling intimacies that make married life such a drag, with male and female crowded together, tripping over each other and the children. The husband's whereabouts was of no great importance to either of his wives. He was sometimes home, sometimes not. That he would move around was taken for granted, but when he came home he was welcomed. What really mattered was the wife's stability, with her children, her garden, her chickens, and her goats. She provided the geomagnetic center for the husband who wandered

over the land with his herds; a real earth-mother with no need
for Women's Lib.

The Elgonyi living arrangements are based on the premise,
as old as the Paleolithic culture, that the man wanders, the
woman stays in the cave (or whatever form the home shelter
happens to take). They are also based on the premise that too
much intimacy between male and female is damaging to both.
Among the Elgonyi, men speak to men, women to women.
Anything else signifies lovemaking. The elaborate games of one-
upmanship, the endless bickerings, the stifling intimacies are all
eliminated. The man has his hut, the woman hers. There is
no danger of their seeing too much of each other.

Are our sexual relations wrecked by too much togetherness?
What can we learn about this from our fellow inhabitants of
the biosphere? Consider the mammals. They vary in their appetites for sexual togetherness. Among the shrews, the shortest-
lived and worst-tempered of the mammals, mutual avoidance is
the rule. They meet only to mate, then separate immediately.
Stoats, weasels, minks in general avoid each other. Mating,
when it takes place, looks more like fighting than fucking. The
male springs on the female, as if he intended to devour her. His
long sharp teeth pass completely through the skin of her neck.
For a time the animals engage in what seems to be a violent
battle. Union, when it finally occurs, may be maintained for
several hours, then the couple separates and the two have no
more to do with each other. The same pattern is seen among
bears. No family life there, Goldilocks notwithstanding. Bears
copulate rarely, separate completely. If Poppa bear so much as
goes near the cub he is chased off by the female.

We look in vain among the mammals for evidence of what
might be called married love. Among the great apes harems
dominated by one old male are the rule, and stable pairs seem
unknown. It is the birds rather than the mammals that have
evolved stable pairings. The jackdaws, Konrad Lorenz assures

us, mate for life and bring to their relationship a tenderness
rarely found among contemporary humans. Their affection in-
creases with the years instead of diminishing. They are long-
lived birds and become nearly as old as human beings. They
become betrothed in their first year, marry in their second.
Their union may last even longer than that of humans. But
still the male feeds his wife with solicitous care and "finds for
her the same low tones of love as he whispered in his first
spring of betrothal." There are no dirty games of one-upman-
ship, no violent arguments about children, politics, mothers-in-
law, no trips to the lawyer or expensive divorces. Happy jackdaws!

Have these birds discovered the key to marital harmony
that man seeks in vain?

Or is the jackdaw pattern of monogamous devotion hope-
lessly unsuited to man? Does man's nature partake more of the
bear than the bird—of a bear, however, with a persistent and
insatiable sex urge, which forces him to mate almost incessantly
instead of rarely and in a definite season, as a well-regulated
mammal should?

If we wish to have a stable creative community then surely
we must discover what pattern of sexual behavior is normal for
man and shape our lives accordingly. But where shall we find
this normal pattern? I have read more than my fair share of the
deluge of sex books currently flooding the market. I have even
contributed to that flood a book of my own (*Sex Energy*). I have
delved into the findings of anthropologists, read Frank and
Beach, Malinowski, Margaret Mead, Kinsey, Masters and John-
son, etc., studied the sexual patterns of so-called savages and
primitives. Never does a single pattern emerge. Polynesians
fuck freely whenever they meet, provided they are not related.
Papuans are as sour about sex as the Puritans. Ancient Greeks
put their wives in the gynaeceum and got their fun from
*hetaerae* (male chauvinist pigs?). The legendary Amazons

killed the males after mating and had a totally female society (female chauvinist sows?). And so on and so forth. The variations on the theme seem endless.

So where do we stand? Anthropology offers no guidance. Religion speaks with too many conflicting voices. Tradition carries no weight in a society that has come adrift, and even our instincts have become confused. There are, however, certain results of our experiment which suggest that a natural pattern may be found and that members of a commune in this day and age will more or less inevitably fall into this pattern, because, if they don't, the commune will disintegrate.

What is the pattern? It appears that, in a group of men and women, couples naturally form on the basis of affinities. So you get a collection of more or less stable pairs. From time to time the glue that holds a pair together loses its adhesive power. Don't ask me why. There are dozens of reasons. So the couple fall apart. We've seen it happen, also seen two couples split at the same time and each unite with the former partner of the other. So AB, CD becomes AC, BD. We have no rule of sexual "morality," don't even recognize the word as meaningful. Anyone can fuck anyone. The fact is they don't. Attempts to celebrate a group sexual orgy have always resulted in halfhearted affairs which gave pleasure to no one. Ventures into the realm of sexual yoga have not been popular.

So we have ended with a group of couples, some married, some not, which, though not as devoted as Konrad Lorenz's jackdaws, nonetheless stay together. There is very little switching of partners and no urge toward group marriage. The couples seem on the whole to want separate housing. Each wants its own lair or cave. And from time to time members of the pair start irritating each other and want to separate for a while. They become more bear than jackdaw. The spirit of man is a jungle, as Rumi says.

Does this mean that we of the Church of the Earth are just

a bunch of squares? Quite probably it does. We have tried to partake in the great Sexual Revolution, and not found it worthwhile. The stable pair relationship has developed naturally among us. It seems to be the normal pattern of sexual behavior, at least for the present.

Of course there are other communes that have adopted more adventurous patterns. We can all think of examples. Total sexual promiscuity goes with the "all is permitted" style of life that some imagine to be daring and therefore good. But is it? If the biosphere teaches us anything it is precisely the opposite. All is *not* permitted. There are natural laws everywhere, laws governing what plants will grow where and how many animals the plants will support. On a given piece of land there can be just so many plants, worms, insects, deer, mice, hawks, vultures, and men. Every food chain has just so many links, and every link is only a certain size. The whole idea of "all is permitted" is ecologically unsound.

So when it comes to sexual behavior I have to conclude that stable pair relationships are more in accord with the laws of the biosphere. Stable pairs and no more than two children per couple. Total sexual promiscuity is part of a sloppy life-style that may appear bold and romantic but is actually dangerous, disorganized, destructive. Followers of this life-style, if young and beautiful, may be admired as were the Flower Children of the Haight-Ashbury. But the Flower Children faded swiftly, blighted by a mixture of poor food, drugs, violence, hepatitis, and venereal disease. Their communes, when they migrated from city to country, were fertile breeding grounds for the clap and not much else. They degenerated into mere scavengers, living off the garbage of the Great Society, parasites who took without giving, neither food-growers nor food-gatherers but mere scroungers, living on welfare.

And what of the babies that result from these casual couplings? We have heard from our friends at Morning Star of the pleasures of turning childbirth into a sort of celebration. No doctors and nurses, no smelly anesthetics, a real party, and everyone participates by eating part of the afterbirth. Romantic? If you wish. Or is it merely idiotic? Let me quote a physician friend of mine, whose exasperation seems quite justified. "We've worked for years to make childbirth reasonably safe and these idiots go off and have their babies in the woods!"

Which does not mean that a woman should be scared half to death when confronted with the prospect of having a baby. Of course be relaxed about it. Of course exercise in advance. Of course avoid anesthetics if possible and regard the whole thing as a natural, exciting, enjoyable creative experience. And of course it would be much better if birth places could be separated entirely from hospitals so that the morbid atmosphere of death and disease could be excluded. But this isn't practical, and any normal woman should welcome the knowledge that, in case anything does go wrong, there is expert help at hand. Just how badly things can go wrong is made clear in a letter entitled "Scary Event Almost at Home" in the *Last Whole Earth Catalog* (p. 218).

> *One birth in ten shows complications. [writes this correspondent, after offering some hair-raising details of her own narrow escape from death in childbirth.] One baby IN FOUR shows a birth defect—which can be aggravated if birth is hard or prolonged. Unattended births show the most serious oxygen starvation/anoxia-brain-injury which leads to mental retardation. And three births in a hundred are so complicated that without EXPERT medical help you may have a death on your hands, without warning. Don't say "It can't happen to you." I said it couldn't happen to me— but if I'd stuck to it and fled to the hills to escape that dehumanizing hospital I'd be dead or at best seriously damaged with a dead child, or brain-injured baby to raise.*

So let those back-to-nature enthusiasts who contemplate giving birth in the woods, in a tipi, or on the living room floor
think twice about it.

Finally what about sex energy and the inner work? Can
man develop his full potential and still have a satisfying sex
life? Of course he can. I would even be inclined to put this
sentence in reverse and say: Man cannot develop his full potential unless he has a satisfying sex life. I am well aware of
the saying that there are those who have made themselves
eunuchs for the kingdom of heaven's sake. Jesus, however, did
not recommend this course of action. He simply stated it as a
fact. Nonetheless, the saying has been cherished by generations
of pallid monastics who could find no better use for their
penises than to piss out of them. What incalculable harm these
sex-shy priests have done! Not content with wrecking their
own sex lives they had to interfere with those of their followers
who were fools enough to let celibates rule their behavior. At
the height of its power the Church managed to induce such
anxiety about sex that it turned all Europe into a demon-
obsessed madhouse. It is a hopeful sign of returning sanity that
the servants of this guilt-obsessed cult are gradually revolting
against the practice of celibacy and insisting on living like normal human beings. Hopefully the day is approaching when this
whole celibacy nonsense will be a thing of the past, to be
looked back on with astonishment by a generation free of
sex-guilt.

# XXIII

## *City Interlude*

It was another world. The aged Chevy, which, despite its years, zoomed up the Waldo Grade as smoothly as any of the sleek moderns, nosed over the top, moved into the right lane, began the descent to the Golden Gate. The great bay glittered below. Looking across the water toward downtown San Francisco, the Gardener reflected how remorselessly space-greed was robbing the last of America's really distinctive cities of its distinction. With every year that passed, its skyline grew more like that of Manhattan, Chicago, Detroit, Dallas, Tulsa, an anonymous jumble of huge blocks of masonry reaching skyward under a veil of smog. On that particular day the cleansing wind from the ocean had failed to blow. After San Rafael the air had grown progressively more tainted. It hung over the city in a brown film of mingled soot and oxides of nitrogen, blanketing Berkeley and Oakland and extending south all the way down the peninsula.

The avalanche of cars poured into the tunnel, roared through it in a rising gradient of carbon monoxide, emerged on the other side to charge onto the sweeping span of the Golden Gate Bridge. The Gardener, who tried to keep his sense of wonder alive as an antidote to the aging process, did his best to feel impressed. The splendid sweep of the suspending cables, soaring verticals of the towers, the curve of the roadbed, all these were surely things of beauty in their way. They should have produced some sort of thrill, but they failed to do so. He had driven across the span too often, the traffic was too fast, everyone was rushing somewhere, quite unaware of the beauty of the great bridge. To the west the Farallons were blotted out in smog. The ocean was calm. It would have been a great day for fishing.

The Gardener sighed. The ocean always seemed perfect on the days when he had to visit the city. He surveyed the years, reflecting that it would make sense to retire at sixty, to give his attention to the Church of the Earth, expel the last of the city smog from his lungs, simply fish and grow vegetables, perhaps set up a small laboratory, nothing fancy, a lab concerned with plant tissue culture, the production of virus-free grape stock by meristem culture. He had been a student of plant tissue culture from its beginnings.

Now he was concerned with different problems. His original training as a botanist had led him to study the action of drugs of plant origin. It was an ancient archetypal interest, an aspect of his being that linked him to the world of the magician, the witch doctor, the sorcerer. Even as a child he had loved the dangerous plants, the poisoners. They exerted an intense, mysterious fascination. He learned about them early and admired them, the deadly nightshade, henbane, hellebore, aconite, the berries of yew, the scarlet fly agaric, the mottled hemlock. In a secret place in the woods he would prepare malodorous and often quite dangerous brews and murmur over them incantations, drawing from the thought of their deadliness a sense of power.

Later, as science replaced magic, the scientific study of poisons became a major preoccupation. He knew the formula and properties of every plant and animal poison and the latest synthetic triumphs of the organic chemists. But poisons, which merely brought the machinery of life to a halt, were of less interest than the power-substances that altered its working. And of all those power-substances the most mysterious were those that exerted their action on the mind.

He had experimented with most of the psychedelics, as they turned up in his laboratory and it seemed desirable to know their effects at first hand. None of them, with the exception of the hemp resin, gave any useful insights. *Peyote* made him sick, *ololiuqui* and *teonanacatle* even sicker. He could get no effects from *ayahuasco* or kava, he avoided the devil's weed as being too dangerous. LSD was interesting at first but its effects lasted far too long and became merely boring. But the hemp resin was benign and revealing if taken rarely and under exactly the right conditions. If anything deserved to be revered as a sacred substance it was that sticky resin. It had, however, one drawback. Even though taken rarely, reverently, and with proper consideration for the quality of surrounding impressions, it failed to continue to reveal secrets. The ally residing in the plant, a high priestess surely, My Lady of the Hemp, seemed to discourage indulgence and to withdraw further and further behind the veil when the devotee appealed to her too often. Her message was obvious. *I have shown you the hidden land; now find your way there on your own.*

Excellent advice. There were far better ways of exploring the secret places of man's inner world than eating hemp resin, or damaging one's lungs with its smoke. Benign though it was, it definitely weakened the will. And he who would penetrate the mysteries needs his will above all. Without it he is helpless, a mere leaf in the wind.

*Live like a warrior. A warrior cannot indulge.*

But though hemp resin did not offer a key to the mysteries or any shortcut to higher states of consciousness, it still remained a fascinating substance. Its effect on the mind, on the emotions, was so delicate, so unlike the violent effects of LSD or the other more toxic psychedelics, that it appeared to possess some quite unique mode of action. Chemically it was quite unlike the other mind drugs, most of which had vague affinities with serotonin or the adrenalines. The structure of its active component (tetrahydrocannabinol or THC) gave absolutely no clue as to how it exerted its effect. It was a mystery.

Which was why, on that smog-laden day, he was breathing the tainted city effluvia instead of the clean air of the mountain. The farmer-fisherman in his being despised the whole project as an example of senseless meddling, an insane misuse of time and energy. But as he entered the laboratory and donned his white lab coat he changed I's and the voice of the farmer-fisherman was muted. His greeting to his technician was standard. "What's new and exciting?" It summed up his attitude to research. In research there was always something new, something exciting. You asked a question of the experiment and, if you asked it properly, you got an answer. And the answer could be very, very different from what one expected. Which, basically, was what made the game worth playing.

The laboratory smelled of the smoke of marihuana. Though all the experiments were conducted in a fume hood, the odor escaped, permeating everything with the exotic aroma of hemp resin. On neat squares of waxed paper the little heaps of marihuana lay ready, each weighing a gram. It was high-class stuff, specially grown in Mexico for the National Institute of Mental Health. Its THC content was 1.5 percent. It was stored in a locked refrigerator in a locked laboratory in a vacuum dessicator under nitrogen. To get it, the Gardener had hacked his way through a veritable jungle of red tape. It had taken a year to get the starting material—all that trouble for an innocuous weed less toxic than tobacco. The great marihuana psychosis affected not the people who used it but those who feared it and made laws out of their fears. Far more lives had been damaged by the laws than by the marihuana.

Meanwhile the smoking-machine clanged and wheezed. It was programmed to force air mixed with smoke into a breathing chamber into which twenty mice, held in tubes, projected their noses. (It would never do to expose the whole mouse to the smoke. Who could tell what effects it might exert through the skin?) So the machine forced air through a gram of burning marihuana held in a glass pipe. The smoke was held in the breathing chamber for six seconds, then flushed out with fresh air, giving the mice a chance to breathe without being asphixiated. The mice which perished died of smoke, not the marihuana. It contained 6 percent of carbon monoxide and they died simply of carbon monoxide poisoning. The smoke of simple cigarette paper was just as toxic as that of the hemp resin.

The smoking cycle now being used kept deaths to a minimum, which was necessary as this was a chronic experiment designed to determine the long-term effects of the drug. The white mice emerged from the smoking chamber properly stoned. They staggered around, obviously slowed in their reactions, their whiskers brown with smoke like the tar-stained fingers of a heavy smoker. It was too early to say whether the treatment would shorten their lives, induce lung cancer or abnormalities in their offspring. It did interfere with their reproduction. The smoked mice produced half as many litters as the controls. A remedy for the population explosion?

The Gardener spent little time with the chronic experiment. It was a laboratory chore, necessary but dull. Of much more interest was the acute experiment designed to answer the question "How does it act?" In other words just where do the active principles of marihuana go in the body? Do they end up in the brain and if so, in what amount and in what form? The question was not too hard to answer when one injected mice with marihuana extract, but mice which had merely been exposed to the smoke held their secrets more tenaciously. The traces of the drug were hard to find even in the lungs. To obtain a detectable amount of the drug the marihuana had to be specially reinforced, its resin contents boosted and labeled with a special preparation of THC tagged in two places with a radioactive isotope of carbon ($C^{14}$). Even so, it was necessary to pool lungs, the livers, the brains of twenty mice at a time in order to discover traces of the drug.

The twenty mice, heavily stoned, so much so that they did not try to bite their executioners as did the more alert controls, were duly sacrificed. Which meant that their throats were cut with scissors, their blood collected in heparinized tubes, their bodies, held by the tail, dipped swiftly three times into a Dewar flask of liquid nitrogen. The liquid nitrogen boiled furiously around the warm bodies which were thereby rapidly chilled but not completely frozen. This inhibited enzyme action and prevented the further metabolism of the drug.

Twenty corpses stiff and stark, throats slit, tails frozen stiff, were laid out on a board ready for rapid dissection. Humanity, the Gardener reflected, would surely, if it had any gratitude, erect a monument somewhere to the laboratory mouse, sacrificed in millions in laboratories all over the world. But of course the stupid creatures (the humans that is) never even knew what they owed to the mouse, made monuments instead to militarists who organized the killing and maiming of their own species. Meanwhile the mice perished in their millions, injected with poisons, with carcinogens, with drugs of all kinds, grafted with tumors, exposed to smokes, gases, lethal radiations. And not only mice. Dogs, cats, goats, monkeys, even chimpanzees were involved in this orgy of slaughter in the name of science. Was it really justified? Was this arrogant naked ape, whose numbers were overrunning the planet like a cancer, of such importance that millions of other animals had to be butchered to keep him relatively healthy and prolong his life? Prolong his life for what?

*Are not five sparrows sold for two farthings, and not one of*

*them is forgotten before God? Ye are of more value than many
sparrows.*

But are we? And how many sparrows equal one man? And
how many white mice, dogs, cats, monkeys, chimpanzees? Who
will tell us the value of these lower animals we butcher so
blithely? Of course the Gardener, who had spent his whole professional life in laboratories of one sort or another and done his
share of butchering, knew the obvious answers when confronted
with indignant anti-experimentalists who objected to the use of
animals. Do you want your children to die of diphtheria,
whooping cough, typhoid fever, tuberculosis? How do you think
we made the vaccines that protect them? From animals—that's
how. And as for our mice, our Swiss White, highly inbred spe-
cials, why they would never even exist if we didn't raise them.
They are our creations. We can do with them as we wish.

Which did not entirely solve the problem. Nor was it easy
to escape from an unsettling suspicion lurking in the background. Was the whole of humanity, this strutting, arrogant,
planet-dominating *Homo sapiens*, itself the subject of a vast
experiment conducted by some force more ruthless and un-
sentimental than any human scientist?

All these thoughts lay in the background as he began,
swiftly and dexterously, to eviscerate the twenty cold little
corpses, peeling them like fruit, snipping the liver free from
its moorings and dropping it in a beaker, opening the chest
cavity, dissecting out the lungs into a second beaker, snipping
off the roof of the skull, peeling back the brain into a third
beaker, pouring liquid nitrogen, furiously bubbling, onto the
dissected organs to hold the enzymes at bay until extraction
could be started. Twenty mice. The remains of the mice were
gathered together in a plastic bag and dumped in the incinera-
tor. The organs were ground up, extracted with chloroform and
methanol. On its specially reinforced table, heavy with lead
shielding, the latest thing in scintillation counters ran up its

columns of luminous figures while the carbon isotope with its half-life of five thousand years decayed in its interior within vials of scintillant, its beta particles magically transformed to quanta of light and counted by a pair of photomulitplier tubes.

How quickly times changed! Only fifteen years before he had begun working with radioisotopes and used to count them a monstrous machine whose valves gave off so much heat that it had to be housed in an air-conditioned room. Now his machine was no bigger than a large suitcase, totally transistorized, and miniaturized. It was wholly automatic, changed its samples, counted them, printed the result silently, swiftly, and coolly. An amazing gadget.

What a slave one was to gadgets! One was helpless without them. He stood before the scintillation counter as if before an oracle. And the oracle spoke, printing out its message on a roll of paper. Yes, said the oracle, there was significant radioactivity in the lungs, rather less in the liver, a small amount in the brain. The scintillation counter had picked up the tiny traces of $C^{14}$, itself a man-made element, product of cyclotrons and atomic piles, creation of a new breed of alchemists who really knew how to transmute the elements.

All of which was interesting but vague. The drug was there, but in what form? To answer this question he turned to a different oracle, square sheets of plastic coated with silica gel, the thin-layer chromatograms developed in a mixture of hexane and ether on which, by a process of differential elution, the components of the tissue extracts were separated. Carefully dried and placed on sheets of X-ray film the chromatograms could make photographs of themselves by their own radioactivity. Or they could be sprayed with a special dye, revealing the components of marihuana as bands of color, blues and magentas.

There were many such bands. Clearly all sorts of things were happening to the drug in the lungs. Already, in the mind of the Gardener, a new research project was stirring, in the form of the inevitable grant application. Gone were the days when a scientist could simply do research of his own choosing. An army of bureaucrats and committees stood between him and the steadily decreasing flood of federal funds necessary to keep the laboratory in operation. Grantsmanship was an art in itself. Proposed research had to be practical, justifiable, feasible, and thought out to the last detail. It was a useful discipline.

So, even as he examined the chromatograms, the new plan unrolled. *Metabolic pathways of smoke from* Cannabis sativa. Too long? By bureaucratic edict one's title had to fit into fifty-three typewritten spaces. It would really be an elegant project and he would need the help of a good organic chemist. Tiny amounts of quite unstable compounds would have to be separated from the tissues of the lungs, the liver, and the brain. The brain especially. It was in the brain, presumably, that the hemp resins worked their peculiar magic. But extraction of the brain was especially difficult. And really what could one learn from the crude mash of brain tissue? That beautifully organized, unimaginably complex organ with its billions of nerve cells all interconnected was turned by the biochemist into a mere soup, ground up, extracted with solvents, its structure destroyed. And of course he would have to use mouse brains. You could hardly expect humans to donate their brains for such work. It would take years. It would involve endless trips to San Francisco, the dangers of the freeway, the obnoxious impressions of man-swarm, the tainted air.

Was it worth it?

The Gardener sighed. The components of his being squared off, confronting each other. The scientist, a tiresome meddler, wanted to chop up more mice, write more papers, penetrate more secrets. The farmer-fisherman wanted to grow vegetables and go fishing. The mystic wanted to explore the mysteries of locked rooms of the psyche and to penetrate to the crack between the worlds. The mystic mocked the scientist: What can you learn, you poor boob, by grinding up more brains and running chromatograms? That the drug occurs in the brain? That it takes such and such a form, that it is metabolized thusly? So what? Who cares? Can't you find anything better to do with your declining years than to chop the heads off mice and mash their brains? Leave them alone. Look into your own brain. It's right there in your skull and immediately accessible. What can you learn from this brain soup, this miserable mash? Better to practice *zazen* or *shikan taza* and try to see into your own nature. Time is running out.

Thus spake Zarathustra: *Man is a rope stretched between animal and Superman—a rope over an abyss. A dangerous crossing, a dangerous wayfaring, a dangerous looking back, a dangerous trembling and halting.* Can you afford to pause in this dangerous journey to mash the brains of these miserable mice?

The day was at an end. The Gardener removed his lab coat, climbed back into the old gray Chevy, sighing with relief at the prospect of leaving the city. From the Golden Gate Bridge he looked again at the ocean. Still very calm though the afternoon wind had set in. Tomorrow he would go fishing. Mice, scintillation counters, chromatograms receded into the background along with the plans for a new grant application. He would stick with the Church of the Earth, make that the main game of his later years. Vineyards, gardens, the ocean with its teeming life, not smelly laboratories reeking of marihuana, would provide his environment. And as for the scientist, he could potter around with plant tissue-cultures and work on propagating virus-free vine meristems.

So everyone in the inner household would be kept happy, which is, after all, the aim of the inner work.

# XXIV

## Three-Space and Four-Space

Fellow Whole-Earthers!

The Master Game is a game. How many have failed because they forgot this fact! They turn it into a terrible affair. They grit their teeth and roll their eyes and weep over their sins. It is the legacy of the Judeo-Christian Guilt Cult that keeps us uptight and sin-conscious. That image of a tortured man hanging from a cross haunts us in spite of our efforts to exorcise it. With such a symbol festering in our subconscious how can we enjoy the game? And if the game isn't enjoyable why should we play it.

Enjoy the game! Take as your symbol dancing Shiva, poised on one leg amid the circle of flames, serene, confident, his hands placed in the *mudra* that says, "Fear not, I am here." Or take the Juggler of the Tarot cards, playing with the sacred symbols, his head enhaloed with the sign of the Infinite.

Only by playing in this light spirit will you avoid becoming hooked on the Personal Salvation Syndrome, a formidable catch, one of the worst. Groaning over your sins, lamenting over your weaknesses, perpetually fussing over some vision of hell fire and damnation, how can you ever become liberated from the personal ego? This brand of religion makes men worse off then before. Better no religion at all then this sickly mishmash of guilt, fear, anxiety, and superstition.

Play the game lightly, because you enjoy it. Sure, it's a difficult game. So is chess. So is mountaineering. This doesn't stop people playing. They enjoy the difficulty. It's a challenge. Moreover, there are some aspects of the game that can never be understood unless you use the light touch. If you are stiff and rigid about it you merely end by tying yourself in knots.

Three rivers flow toward the ocean of self-transcendence, uniting to form one stream. For lack of better terminology we call the three rivers *hatha yoga, bhakti yoga,* and *jnana yoga.* They are concerned respectively with the physical body, the emotions, the mind. The great stream in which all three unite is called *raja yoga,* the king of the yogas, having to do with the control of the field of consciousness, the reblending of our separate consciousness with the whole.

You can start with any of the yogas, *hatha, jnana,* or *bhakti,* and, if you use them rightly, they will lead you to *raja yoga* in the end. If they do not, it means you have mistaken a mere side arm for the main stream and got yourself stuck in some muddy creek without an exit. So people who get stuck in *hatha yoga* turn it into mere gymnastics, and become totally identified with the mastery of physical tricks. Those who get stuck in *bhakti yoga* swallow religious dogmas and lose themselves in a fog of superstition and wishful thinking. Those who get stuck in *jnana yoga* wander in the deserts of scholasticism and waste their time on intellectual arguments and philosophical speculations. It is the role of the teacher to help his pupils to avoid getting stuck and to keep them always moving in the direction of the main stream.

Consider *jnana yoga. Jnana* can be translated as knowledge. The Greek word *gnosis* comes from the same root. But the knowledge referred to is not just knowledge of facts, the sort of facts that are stuffed into students' heads in our diploma mills. *Jnana yoga* is concerned with the mind itself, and the way in which the mind represents to us the world in which we live.

*All that we know is mind-created.* We carry a model of the

universe around in our heads. It is a mind-made model and usually a very defective one. *Jnana yoga* teaches the student to examine the mind which made the model and to challenge some of the basic assumptions with which the mind operates. The mind of man in the third state of consciousness has been compared to a system of darkened, misaligned lenses through which man perceives a world that has not much relation to reality. One who desires a more accurate picture of himself and the world in which he lives must first correct these errors.

Has the mind the power to correct its own defects? Yes, if it goes about it in the right way and is willing to recognize the defects in the first place. The mind of man is potentially a very fine instrument, but nature has mocked us by giving us the instrument without the instruction manual. So undeveloped man is like an ignorant savage who has been given a complex computer that he has no idea how to operate. Man has too much brain for his own good.

This does not alter the fact that the man-mind is potentially a magnificent instrument if the man possessing the mind can find the instruction manual and learn how to use it. The instruction manual can indeed be found, and it is the function of *jnana yoga* to lead man to it. In the process of finding it, man must master certain techniques. It is in connection with the mastering of these techniques that the light touch is required. You dance like Shiva among the riddles of space and time. You juggle with the elements from which your mind constructs its universe. You have to maintain the light touch or you will get giddy and drop everything. Even if you do drop everything it doesn't matter. You pick up the pieces and start again.

In forming its model of the universe our mind uses two qualities, both of them mind-created and having no objective reality. The first quality is three-dimensional space, the second is unidirectional time. A more sophisticated model combines these qualities into a single space-time continuum.

The fetters imposed on our thinking by the space-time concept can be considerably loosened by a series of specific exercises. These exercises are designed to loosen the mind and make it more flexible, just as certain exercises in *hatha yoga* are designed to loosen the body.

The first of these exercises is well known to certain *illuminati* in the West. It is called the genesis of the tesseract. Actually the tesseract itself is not important. The purpose of the exercise is to train the mind to understand the limitations imposed by the concept of three-spatial dimensions. Why three? Is reality really confined in a three-dimensional space mold or are three dimensions imposed by our minds, which, in this respect, can only count up to three?

To answer this question we will postulate that there exists a fourth dimension of which, because of the limitations of our mind, we are ordinarily quite unaware. Can we train ourselves to perceive this dimension?

The genesis of the tesseract enables us to make the attempt. Visualize a single point of light. Let the point move in a straight line for a unit distance, leaving behind it a trail of points. The result is a line of light. Our point has generated a figure in one-space.

Now let the whole line move a unit distance in a direction at right angles to the first, again leaving behind it a trail of lighted points. Our line has generated a figure in two-space, a symmetrical figure which we call a square.

Now let the whole square move a unit distance in a direction at right angles to that of its own generation. Our square has now generated a figure in three-space with a special symmetry which we call a cube. Our familiar geometry and mathematics are quite well able to define the cube. We can draw x,y,z, coordinates along the three edges that meet at a corner.

Using such coordinates we can label every point in the cube with an ordered triplet of numbers.

Let me now quote Martin Gardner: "Although our visual powers boggle at the next step, there is no logical reason why we cannot assume that the cube is shifted a unit distance in a direction perpendicular to all three of its axes. The space generated by such a shift is a four-space unit hypercube—a tesseract—with four mutually perpendicular edges meeting at every corner. By choosing a set of such edges as w,x,y,z axes, one might label every point in the hypercube with an ordered quadruplet of numbers."

Gardner points out that a cube, if cut along seven of its twelve edges and flattened out in two-space, forms a two-dimensional Latin cross, a popular floor plan for medieval churches. By analogy he suggests that if a tesseract could be similarly unfolded in three-space it would take the form of the three-dimensional Latin cross illustrated in Salvador Dali's *Corpus Hypercubus* and utilized by Martin Gardner himself in his story "An Adventure in Hyperspace at the Church of the Fourth Dimension" (*Scientific American*, January 1962, p. 136). You must realize, however, that the unfolded tesseract in three-space gives no conception of what the tesseract really looks like. To visualize what it looks like we must learn to "see" in four dimensions. *See* is in quotes because of course it is a purely mental form of seeing.

Actually, owing to the nature of the propagation of light, we do not even see in three dimensions. We only see in two. Our eyes receive the light that bounces off objects in our line of vision. Everything we see is flattened and represents only two dimensions of the actual object. This is why our ordinary field of vision can be completely represented on a flat surface, as in a photograph or a picture.

Learning to see in three dimensions rather than two is an exercise that is considerably easier than is the genesis of the tesseract. To learn this art we may employ Charles Hinton's cubes.

Visualize the cube with one corner directly facing you. You will at once realize a special spatial property of the cube, that you can see three, but not more than three of its faces at one time. Color the three faces with the primary colors, red, blue, yellow. Now move your mental point of view to the opposite corner of the cube and color the opposite three faces with the three secondary colors, green, orange, purple.

You now perform a trick which, in some respects, corresponds to moving into the fourth dimension. You relate to the six sides of the cube in such a way that they all become equally visible at once *without* flattening the cube and projecting it on two-space. This is only the first step in the move into a new dimension. It enables you to see past the front and back limitation, but it does not let you pass the inside–outside limitation. To do this, you must proceed to the next step of the exercise. This involves taking eight of the mental cubes colored as above and creating from them a cube of cubes. The outer surface of the large cube so formed will show a mozaic of colors, the complexity of which will depend on how you have arranged the cubes. But in addition to the outer surface composed of six groups of four squares your cube has an inner surface also composed of six groups of four squares. The pattern of these concealed squares will be dependent on the pattern of the exposed squares. By moving into four-space it becomes possible to visualize simultaneously all the twenty-four outer squares and all the twenty-four inner squares in their correct relationship. This is because the inhabitant of four-space can see inside three-space just as an inhabitant of three-space can see inside two-space.

It may help you to understand this concept if you use the analogy proposed by Charles Hinton. Imagine a world of two dimensions floating on the surface of a three-dimensional ocean.

All the beings in this two-dimensional world, which we will call Flatland, see only in one-space, just as we who live in a three-dimensional world see only in two-space. We can argue by analogy that the Flatlanders can form a concept of two-space just as we can form a concept of three-space though we see in two-space. What the Flatlanders cannot conceptualize is the ocean of three-space on which they float.

To the Flatlanders, we who live in three-space would seem to possess miraculous powers. We can see inside their houses and inside their bodies. We can cause them to disappear simply by lifting them out of two-space into three-space. To the Flatlanders we would appear to be gods.

Because of their confinement to two dimensions the Flatlanders would form a very odd picture of our forms. They would see only a line representing the point at which our bodies intersected their two-space. If we only had our legs in their two-space, they would see two lines. If we went on all fours and had arms and legs in two-space, they would see four lines. In fact our shape would be constantly changing in their space and we would appear to have the power of dividing like an amoeba. All of which would be very puzzling to the poor Flatlanders unless one of their number, by a truly prodigious feat of mental gymnastics, managed to conceive the idea of the existence of another dimension which would endow the beings existing in that space with powers that no Flatlander could possess.

It is easy enough to dismiss these exercises as mere mental tricks, an extension of geometry beyond the limits recognized by Euclid. Such a dismissal is not justified. The exercises take one way beyond geometry. They awaken, if used in the right way, certain quite extraordinary emotions and intuitions. They give to the investigator a taste of a world "wholly other" than that to which he is accustomed. And this "wholly other" world is not the special province of mathematicians. Far from it. The boldest voyagers into this world have been poets and mystics. The intellect alone may take the voyager a certain distance, but it will not by itself suffice to take him all the way. For the end of this journey is the experience of *total self-transcendence*, an experience which involves a special kind of emotion having to do with the expression of the will to self-transcendence.

This explains an extraordinary statement by Paul of Tarsus in the Epistle to the Ephesians: ". . . that ye, being rooted and grounded in love, may be able to comprehend with all saints what is the breadth, and length, and depth, and height . . ." A mathematician might argue that being "rooted and grounded in love" has nothing to do with mastering the concept of a fourth dimension. But a mystic or poet would certainly agree with St. Paul. A special emotional element has to be introduced if the jump is to be made. For the genesis of the tesseract or the juggling with Hinton's cubes is only a means to an end. This end Hinton himself described as the awakening of "higher consciousness," involving the "casting out of the self." By this means we can accustomize ourselves to know and conceive the world, not from a personal point of view but as the "thing in itself." And it is logical to start this training by beginning with simple geometrical shapes and learning to see them from all sides at once.

When we are able to do this, we can turn our expanded awareness on any subject we wish to study and begin to enjoy those insights into the nature of things that are the hallmark of the adept. In particular we can turn this awareness on our own physical organism and learn many of its secrets. The trick here is to move into four-space in relation to the physical body which enables us to contact all parts of ourselves with a probe of awareness that has little in common with our familiar mode of perceiving.

The procedure has much in common with what is called in some circles Astral Projection, though there is nothing particularly astral about it. It is based on the idea that the field of consciousness can be molded in three-space in such a way that it totally enfolds the physical body. In short, a man surrounds himself with his field of consciousness somewhat in the way in which a sarcophagus surrounds a corpse. In this state he is aware of his body from the outside. He feels himself to be out of the body, and can indeed recede from it, sensing not only the body but also its immediate surroundings. The experience induces a trancelike state in the body itself which, being drained of its field of consciousness, sinks into a condition that might almost be called suspended animation. Respiration becomes barely perceptible, the heart rate slows, all the muscles relax, and the mind becomes totally blank.

In this state the body floats in the midst of a three-space field of consciousness as a bar of iron might float in a powerful magnetic field. In this state of dissociation, the ordinary body-centered awareness vanishes. The knower, or observer, whatever this is, floats outside of its ordinary physical resting place. Sensations of this kind are often described by people who have taken LSD or hashish, but the drugs do not give man the power to dissociate at will or use the dissociated state to answer certain questions concerning space-time and the nature of the self. What is important about this condition is that it makes possible perceptions and insights that are ordinarily out of reach.

Skeptics may argue that this condition, in which the field of consciousness is experienced as being outside of and separated from the physical body, is simply a dream state, induced by certain special exercises. It is quite impossible to refute these criticisms. It is not even profitable to try. The point is that, starting with *jnana yoga*, we have entered the mainstream of *raja yoga* and are on our way to the great ocean. If critics insist that this great ocean has no objective existence, that we are merely traveling about in inner space and deluding ourselves into thinking that we are entering new dimensions, there is nothing we can reply. We have traveled far, we have seen strange lands, but if those that have never been away from home insist that we are liars, or that we dreamed the experiences, what can we say? We have no recourse but to keep silent.

As Chuang Tze puts it:

*You cannot speak of ice to a summer insect, the creature of a season.*
*You cannot speak of Tao to a pedant; his scope is too narrow.*

# XXV

## *All and Everything*

Fellow Whole-Earthers!

Consider the quest for the Universal Arcanum, the Diagram of All and Everything. On this quest men in the past have expended prodigious energies. It was assumed by those who had a taste for mystery that there existed some secret diagram that would answer all the riddles of the universe. Indian sages sought the secret in the *shri yantra*, tantric Buddhists in the *bhava chakra mandala* or the mandala of the great liberation. The Cabalists sought it in the *tetragrammaton*, the four Hebrew letters that make up the name of God. The Alchemists tried to find it in the names of the four elements of the ancient world, Earth, Water, Air, Fire, all of which are symbolic. Students of magic sought it in the names of the four spirits, gnomes, undines, sylphs, and salamanders. The Astrologers sought it in the order of the planets and symbols of the Zodiac.

There was, in addition to all this, a powerful instrument disguised in the form of a pack of playing cards, used by the Spanish gypsies for fortune-telling. This instrument was called the Grand Arcanum of the Tarot, a collection of twenty-two diagrams numbered and marked with Hebrew letters. Some of the cards referred to the microcosm (man) and some to macrocosm (the universe). This instrument Eliphas Levi described as the universal key of magical works by means of which he could "open the sepulchers of the ancient world, make the dead speak, understand the enigmas of every sphinx and penetrate all sanctuaries."

In a less bombastic vein, he declared, "The Tarot is a truly philosophical machine, which keeps the mind from wandering, while leaving it initiative and liberty . . . An imprisoned person, with no other book than the Tarot, if he knew how to use it, could in a few years acquire universal knowledge and would be able to speak on all subjects with unequalled learning and inexhaustible eloquence."

You may, if you like, dismiss Eliphas Levi as a grandiloquent fraud and his *Transcendental Magic* as a mishmash of absurdities. But what he said of the Tarot is true of the Universal Arcanum. It is a philosophical machine which keeps the mind from wandering while leaving it initiative and liberty. For this reason the elements of the Arcanum must always be symbols, and symbols having as wide a significance as possible. The aim of the Diagram of All and Everything is to enable the student to constate all the universal laws simultaneously. To do this, he must learn not to think discursively (proceed step by step from one concept to another) but simultaneously. This involves thinking on a different time-scale, or in a different dimension. The only way to do this is to think in terms of moving hieroglyphs. Such thinking is almost mathematical in that it uses symbols in the place of concrete images.

The search for the Universal Arcanum still continues, though it has almost been brought to a halt by the excessive specialization that is the curse of the contemporary scientist. In our age it must take a modern form. We would merely be fools or frauds to start trying to use the dusty symbols of alchemy or magic or the ludicrous misconceptions of astrology. These approaches have lost any meaning they once had and are of historical interest only. The Grand Arcanum of the Tarot is still usable by those who understand the underlying principle, but several cards are missing and some have been transmitted incorrectly. In any case the cards are only a part of the Universal Arcanum. They are not sufficient in themselves.

In attempting to construct a contemporary version of the Universal Arcanum, all the most recent developments in the realm of science must be taken into account. Nothing can be more ridiculous than the notion that certain ancient people had a mysterious *esoteric* knowledge far in advance of ours. The knowledge of the ancients was defective, fragmentary, and unbalanced. Their cosmology was ludicrous, their chemistry absurd, their medicine disastrous. It is not an expression of *hubris* but simply of fact to say that we are infinitely better informed than were the wisest of the ancient peoples. What we have failed to do is to bring all this information into focus and use it for our own development. As a result, the flood of facts tends to engulf us. We are drowning in the ocean of knowledge for lack of a unifying principle.

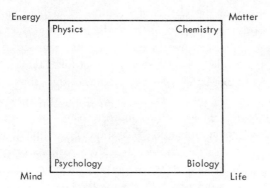

Figure 1.  The Universal Arcanum or
Diagram of All and Everything

The basis for a contemporary Universal Arcanum is a tetrad, as was that of the Cabalists and the Alchemists. The tetrad consists of the four basic manifestations of being—Energy, Matter, Life, Mind. Corresponding to these manifestations are the four basic subdivisions of contemporary knowledge—physics, chemistry, biology, psychology. Without going beyond these

categories you will be able to construct a complete model of
the universe, which is, of course, the Diagram of All and
Everything.

When you begin to think about the new tetrad (Energy,
Matter, Life, Mind), you see that all its elements are interdependent. They do not fall sharply into four divisions. They
overlap and blend. Energy and matter interact, and one is a
manifestation of the other. Life emerges from the interaction at
a point so vague that it cannot be defined. Mind emerges from
life also at a point that is indefinable. There is an uncertainty
principle involved. The edges of all the subdivisions are fuzzy.
It is a part of objective mentation to accept the fuzziness. Clear,
precise divisions are not part of the order of things.

Contemplation of the tetrad results in its subdividing. Indeed it has to subdivide in order to reveal its potential. But here
is the secret of the Universal Arcanum. You hold on to the
whole even while exploring the parts. So energy shows many
manifestations, heat, light, sound, electricity, magnetism, gravitation, the subtle "strong interaction" that holds the atomic nucleus together. Matter also subdivides, not only into chemical
elements but also into states (gaseous, liquid, solid) and degrees
of aggregation, molecules of different magnitudes. Life subdivides into plant and animal forms, into orders, phyla, genera,
species. Mind subdivides into a host of patterns of behavior
ranging from the simplest to the most complex.

But how, in practice, does one use the Universal Arcanum?
How does one avoid getting lost in mere speculation—the desert
of verbiage which is loosely called philosophy? Understand
clearly that the Universal Arcanum cannot be used as long as
you depend on words. Words are far too slow and too inaccu-
rate for any sort of objective mentation. How, then, does one
use the universal philsophical machine?

The starting point can be any real phenomenon. Suppose
we go for a walk in the garden. On our way we notice the sun-

flowers in all their glory, ten feet high, with discs two feet
across, golden against the blue California sky. Here is a universe, its links spreading in all directions. The great plant has
grown by trapping photons in its broad foliage, it has operated
on a level of molecules and atoms, capturing the very body of
the sun, locking the sun's substance into molecules of ever-
greater complexity. A whole series of worlds of differing orders
of magnitudes meet here and interact: subatomic, atomic, molec-
ular, planetary, stellar, even galactic for all we know. In the
sunflower the wave of life stands poised at its crest. The great
plant has grown from one seed, has accelerated, paused, slowed,
is pouring its life into its seed. The wave of its life rises and
falls in a single season. This is the law of its being. Soon it will
die, its life force locked and immobilized in thousands of seeds
which will either grow into fresh sunflowers or be devoured by
birds or beasts or men.

Finally one must take into account the mind of the observer.
The mind sees and shapes the sunflower. It makes a model of
the sunflower. Is it the real sunflower? Of course not. It is a
model constructed from streams of nervous impulses traveling
from the retina along the optic nerve, set in motion by those
omnipresent photons pouring out of the body of the sun. The
mind forms a model of the sunflower. An approximation. Part
of the model of the universe. All that we know is mind-created.
Reality lies beyond the reach of the mind. We live among ap-
proximations in a model of the real world, which is somewhere
out there, forever out of reach.

Start where you will. Go as far as you can. A stone, a tree,
a cloud, a pile of manure. Always you will come to a point
where a window opens on the inexpressible. And always written over the window is the same message. *All that we know is
mind-created.*

The diagram of the tetrad takes this into account. We have
energy–matter–life–mind arranged as a pyramid, with mind at

the top. Mind is the most recently developed of the four qualities, depends for its existence on special, highly organized kinds
of matter which, as far as we know, are generated only in living
beings. The cosmic process has a tendency to generate life
streams and these life streams have a tendency to develop
minds. In mind the cosmic process becomes conscious of itself.
We have no reason to think that man-mind is unique. As minds
go in the universe it is probably very defective. We can easily
follow the example of writers of science fiction and postulate
whole hosts of super-minds capable of communicating, forming
a collective entity, the mind of the galaxy. We can even hope
that man may become a member of the galactic club if he ever
manages to correct the obvious defects in his brain system. All
this, however, is speculation. All that we know for sure is that
the life stream, after about three billion years, has resulted in
the genesis of mind in one species and that this mind-genesis
has considerably altered the balance of life on the planet by giving its possessor an advantage over other forms of life.

The possession of mind by man puts him under a special
obligation. He must give account for his actions. He must try
to behave responsibly. At the same time, because his mind is so
obviously a defective instrument, he must try to correct its
defects. The defects could easily be fatal to him and other
forms of life on earth. The man-mind is a dangerous instrument.

So we come back to the starting point. Can the defects in
the man-mind be corrected, and if so, how? The answer is yes,
they can, but it takes a great deal of effort. The proper function
of the mind of man is the building of a model of the universe.
Through the building of such a model, man finds the key to the
fifth inner room, the state of cosmic consciousness. He becomes
at the same time an actor and a spectator in the cosmic play.
He understands his place in that play. He is a part of the drama
and yet outside of it. He is certainly very tiny, when compared

with stars and galaxies, but the importance of the role is not necessarily determined by the size of the player.

To awaken cosmic consciousness the mind must be stretched, exercised, trained to think in new categories. It is useless to sit around waiting for some Higher Mind to come suddenly into play. The way to Higher Mind is through ordinary mind. Make the most of what you've got and you will earn the right to use something better.

The arcana or sacred diagrams offer the student a means of stretching and exercising the mind. The diagram of the tetrad is only one of several. The diagram of cosmic concentrations that shows all entities from Absolute to Quantum is the Alpha and Omega of existing things in space. The *shri yantra* represents the cosmic process, the alternating phases of creation and de-creation, the days and nights of Brahma. These diagrams relate to the universe, and man's place within the universe.

The diagram called the Mandala of the Great Liberation (*maha nirvana mandala*) relates to the inner world of man. One who understands this diagram can learn from it the laws that govern his inner development. All the sacred mandalas, and there are several of them, contain one central idea. This is that man, as he is, is not completed. He is a king who has lost his kingdom. Like Nebuchadnezzar he eats grass with the beasts. The kingdom in the mandala takes the form of a palace having an outer and an inner court and a central "holy of holies." Each court is represented as a square and is entered by four gates. Each gate is guarded by a figure representing the guardian of the inner world. Man cannot enter that inner world unless he can pass the guardian.

The full complex symbolism of the mandala, combining as it does the monad, the dyad, the triad, and the tetrad, requires special explanation and will not be given here. Suffice it to say that man's level of being is measured by the place he occupies in relation to the mandala. Man in the third state of consciousness (waking sleep) does not even know that the mandala exists. He lives outside of the circle, lives and dies unaware of his own hidden powers. Man who has begun to awaken enters the first circle, which is called the circle of the eight places of pilgrimage. Here he can ask his way of the naked ascetic seated under the tree. The tree, the rock, the ascetic, the vulture devouring a corpse, the sun, moon, stars, planets, all represent entities of which he can ask questions. The stupa or Buddhist reliquary represents hidden power.

He who can ask the right questions can move on to the other circles, all of which symbolize the energies at man's disposal. The outer circle of flames represents the energy of transmutation which is derived mainly from sex energy. The circle of the bells and dorjes represents wisdom and will. Wisdom is useless without will. Will is disastrous without wisdom. The lotus petals of the inner circle represent objective love.

By drawing upon these energies man can enter the gate and confront the guardian. Man reaches this place only when he has attained a certain level of inner permanence. He must have permanent aim. He can no longer keep changing his direction. By virtue of his permanent aim he can confront and overcome the guardian, which represents all those forces in his psyche that together conspire to keep him in bondage. Once he has passed the guardian his whole life changes and he enters a new world, a new state of consciousness. This world has several levels, but it is impossible to describe them in words. To know them one must enter the inner courts of the mandala.

In addition to the Mandala of Liberation there is the Wheel of Existence, a Buddhist system of symbols that presents certain concepts not contained in the first mandala. On the outer rim of the wheel are the twelve interdependent causes of rebirth (the twelve *nadanas*). Within are the six *lokas* (states of being) symbolized by the worlds of the gods, *asuras* (warlike beings), *pretas* (hungry ghosts), the various hells, hot and cold,

the worlds of beasts and the worlds of men. Within this is the
path of ascent and the path of descent with the three poisons
at the center, greed, pride, and anger, symbolized by a pig, a
rooster, and a snake.

The wheel is commonly thought of as portraying the cycle
of rebirth, but this is a superficial interpretation and not good
Buddhism. According to the teaching of Sakyamuni there is no
ego. The separate self is an illusion. There is nothing to be reborn. A more sophisticated view of the wheel would represent
it as a picture of the jungle of man's psyche. It contains all the

six *lokas*, heavens, hells, hungry ghosts, beasts, humans, *asuras*. It contains both paths, the ascending and descending. It even contains the possibility of making friends with Yama, King of the Dead, who holds the whole contraption between his teeth and claws. The wheel is nothing more than a device to help those who wish to see to look into their own nature, a version of the Mirror of Karma which has the same function.

# XXVI

## The Book of Fate

Fellow Whole-Earthers!

Continuing our discourse on the Tarot cards we may say that the Tarot is a diagrammatic version of the Book of Fate. To read it properly we must know certain other diagrams.

First, consider the diagram of the four phases of life. It represents the wave of life as it rises and falls. Life-phase I lasts for about nine months from conception to birth, and is entirely devoted to the building of the physical vehicle. Life-phase II lasts from birth to the mid-teens, is devoted to the further growth of the physical vehicle and the development of the *persona* (and along with it, the false ego). Life-phase III lasts from the mid-teens to the early fifties. This is the householder phase occupied with mating, child-rearing, building a career. Life-phase IV lasts from the early fifties till death and should, in a spiritually healthy society, be devoted to the completion of the inner work. In our society it is wasted in more or less imbecile activities like playing golf.

Next consider the diagram of the four levels of being, represented in allegorical form as the Jungle, the Forest, and the Mountains. The Jungle is the lowest level, above this is the Forest, above this the Mount of Power, above this the Mount of Liberation. A map of these four is like a chart of the inner world of man. The place he occupies on this map shows a man's level of being.

The Jungle is represented by a circle and its Tarot symbol

is the Fool. The Fool does not know where he is going. He moves around in the same circle, lost in dreams. All those who live in the Jungle are prisoners of their dreams. Like convicts in an exercise yard they go round and round, never really getting anywhere. But they are worse off than convicts. At least a convict knows he is in prison and can make plans to escape. But the dwellers in the Jungle think they are free, so make no efforts to escape. They live under the law of dog-eat-dog. They fight incessantly for money, for fame, or simply to stay alive. They support a cosmic process which feeds on meaningless lives, but they do not realize that they feed this process. If they knew, they would strive to break out of the Jungle, would strive to awaken.

| Life Phase | Duration | Name | Purpose |
|---|---|---|---|
| I | Nine Months | Fetus | Development of Physical Body. |
| II | Birth to Puberty | Child | Completion of Physical Body. Growth of Persona. |
| III | Puberty to Year 50 | Householder | Raising of Children. Early Work on Second Body. |
| IV | Year 50 to Death | Sannyasin | Completion of Second Body. Liberation. |

Figure 2.   The Four Phases of Life

He who makes efforts to awaken passes out of the Jungle and enters the Forest. People in the Forest realize all is not well with them. They have not awakened but they are stirring in their sleep and cannot sleep comfortably. The chief characteristic of people in the Forest is that, from time to time, they catch a glimpse of the Mountains. They cannot see far because of the trees. The trees represent the many different I's in man, I's which do not know each other and are often in conflict. So those who have entered the Forest easily lose sight of the Mountain. Though they may have an inner aim, they tend to forget that aim. Sometimes they are worse off than they were before they left the Jungle. At least in the Jungle they knew nothing. Now they know a little and it spoils their sleep.

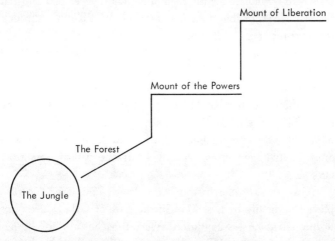

Figure 3.  The Four Levels of Being

This is particularly true of those who escape from the Jungle more or less accidentally as a result of taking psychedelic drugs. These drugs often give people a glimpse of the Mountain. It is a glimpse they did not earn and to which they had no right but, having had it, they can no longer sleep in peace. They do not know what to do, they wander lost in the Forest, hoping to get a second glimpse of the Mountain. To get it they try the drug again and again, but the drug won't work or only gives glimpses of the abyss. So the last state of such people may be worse than the first.

It is, however, quite possible to find guides in the Forest who know the trails and can help the seeker to find his way to the foot of the Mountain. It is quite possible also to find false guides. False guides are various practitioners of the world's oldest con game. They offer quick trips to higher states. They charge large fees. Three months' work, three thousand dollars, and there you are, on top of the world. There are lots of false guides in the forest. There are also a few true ones. The true ones take no money for their services. They never pretend that the way is easy or that there are any shortcuts. The trip through the Forest is always difficult.

What is this trip? It represents the first stage of the Way. On this part of his inner journey man learns certain truths about himself which the Fool in the Jungle does not know. He learns that he is not one but many, that his various conflicting selves have various conflicting aims, that he has no real permanent will and no permanent I, that he is at the mercy of all sorts of accidental happenings. Today he is one person, tomorrow another.

Next, this traveler in the Forest learns how large a part is played in his life by lies. Man in the state of waking sleep lies to himself about his condition. Every time he says "I," he lies because he has no I. When he says "I will," he lies. He has no will. The lies are quite unintentional. This is the whole trouble. If he lied intentionally at least he would know he was lying. But the lies of sleeping man are not even noticed as lies.

So man in the Forest still has the Fool in himself, but his position has improved in one respect. He now *sees* the Fool and can separate from the Fool. A new person is developing in him who is beginning to attain objective self-awareness. This new self is the Observer, who later, if development continues, becomes the Master.

At this point the traveler in the Forest is in a position to understand the diagram of the two circles of humanity. People in these two circles live under different laws, have different fates, and feed different cosmic processes. In the outer circle man lives under a triad symbolized by the Fool, the Devil, and

the Wheel of Fortune. The Fool represents man's habit of living in dreams, the Devil man's habit of unconscious lying, and
the Wheel of Fortune his servitude to accidental happenings
and lack of inner direction.

Man in the inner circle lives under a triad symbolized by
the Juggler, the Hierophant (or Priestess), and the Hanged
Man. The Juggler, also called the Magus or Sorcerer, represents *intentional doing* and is the sign of magic and power. The
Hierophant, or Priestess, is the sign of knowledge, and the
Hanged Man is the sign of self-sacrifice. This is the triad of
developed man, man who has attained a higher level of being.

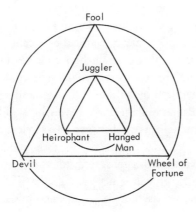

Figure 4.  The Two Circles of Humanity

The outer circle of humanity feeds the inner circle, but because of the laws that govern human evolution the number of
people in any generation that enter the inner circle is extremely
small.

Not everyone in the inner circle is at the same level of
development. One in whom the Magus predominates is primarily a man of power, a magician. One in whom the Hierophant
predominates is a man of knowledge. It is also possible for

certain people to break into the inner circle without the proper preparation. Such individuals may become black magicians or sorcerers. They have power but they use that power for the gratification of personal ends. They are ruthless, destructive, dangerous individuals. They live under a triad consisting of the Magus, the Chariot, and the Falling Tower. In such beings there is a struggle between the black and the white, symbolized by the two sphinxes of the Chariot. If black triumphs then the Falling Tower becomes the dominant symbol, for the black magician in the end is always destroyed by the powers he has evoked.

The traveler through the Forest becomes, as his insights deepen, an initiate of the first order and a candidate for higher initiation. His position may be clarified by means of the diagram of the mandala. In this diagram he stands in the entrance to the first of the inner courts. He is face to face with the guardian, symbolized by an armed figure standing in the gateway. In the diagram of the Four Levels he stands at the foot of the first mountain. He is between two circles, the inner and the outer.

It may take a man a long time to reach this stage of development. Inner growth is necessarily slow. The trip through the Forest is never easy but full of ups and downs and detours and stops and starts. It may easily take man the whole of life-phase III to reach the foot of the mountain even if he has the good luck to enter the Forest early in life and to encounter a reliable guide. The reason for this is obvious. First, man is a very complex machine and to understand this machine takes time. Second, our culture is opposed to inner growth, and conditions favorable to development are hard to find. Life-phase III is anyway a difficult phase, full of distraction and disturbance. Careers must be built, children engendered and raised. If he lives by the standards of the Affluent Society, man may have little energy left over for his inner work. Even if he lives in a creative community in which life flows at a more leisurely pace with plenty of opportunity for inner work, his progress will be slow. He will lose sight of his aim again and again, have to be reminded and redirected.

The fate of a man depends on the power of the various entities that operate within him. As soon as he leaves the Jungle and enters the Forest a struggle begins between the Fool and Devil on the one hand, the Magus and Hierophant on the other, the first two representing weakness and lies, the second strength and knowledge. This is the struggle between yes and no, between affirming and denying, between intentional doing and accidental happening. Here two processes meet and the balance between them determines the fate of man. The first process involves effort and exertion, a swimming against the stream; the second process involves easy drifting, downstream all the way. The first gives man strength, the second gives him weakness.

When he reaches the foot of the Mountain, he faces a decision. If he goes forward, he knows that he must ascend into regions that are full of danger and difficulty. Moreover he must ascend alone. The guide cannot help him much on the Mountain. A man does not have to go on. He can, if he wishes, sit down at the foot of the Mountain and look back over the Forest. He is, after all, a first-order initiate and already knows many things hidden from ordinary men. He has worked hard to attain this level. May he not rest?

He may, but, if he does, he runs the risk of entering a state called second sleep. Second sleep is worse than first sleep. A man in second sleep *dreams that he has awakened*. It is therefore almost impossible to emerge from second sleep. So, if this happens, man loses all that he has gained and his last state is worse than the first.

What happens if he goes on and climbs the first Mountain? This question cannot be answered in ordinary language.

A suggestion is given by the Diagram of the Four Points. In this diagram, the life of ordinary man is represented by a line connecting point 1 (thinking) with point 2 (sensing-feeling). The line which connects these points man calls his *understanding*. In the outer circle of humanity man spends his whole time moving back and forth between points 1 and 2. Points 3 and 4 play no part in his life. He does not even know that they exist. They are hidden from his awareness by a barrier in his own psyche, also called the guardian of the other world.

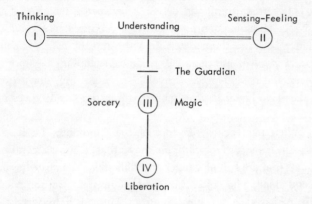

Figure 5. The Diagram of the Four Points

Points 3 and 4 lie outside space-time as we ordinarily experience it. One can say of point 3 that it represents magic or sorcery. He who attains point 3 has certain powers. In Sanskrit these powers are called *siddhi*, in Japanese they are called *joriki*. One who has these powers is a second-order initiate. He can do certain things and create certain phenomena not possible for ordinary man. He who has attained point 3 has access to the archives and can learn directly many secrets that are hidden from ordinary man. He cannot communicate these secrets to others even if he wishes to do so. They lie beyond the reach of man's ordinary understanding. Certain forms of sacred or *objective* art can transmit some information about point 3 but only to those already able to *see*.

Just as a man can stop at the foot of the Mountain, so he can stop when he has attained the top of Mount I. This is the Mountain of Attainment of the Powers, and the powers have an intoxicating quality. A man easily gives way to indulgence here and enjoys using the powers for good or for evil. He is a magician or a sorcerer. He can influence people and to some extent change their fate. His powers confront him with temptations that do not even touch an ordinary man. The Buddha never failed to warn his hearers of the danger involved in possession of the powers. They are doubly dangerous because they tempt their possessor with a vain "magical mastery of the world" and are likely to cause confusion in the minds of undeveloped people who are credulous, suggestible, and forever on the lookout for miracles.

To attain complete liberation a man must abandon the powers, continue his journey, ascend the Mountain of Liberation. One who ascends the second Mountain becomes a third-order initiate. Of him nothing more need or can be said. The Tarot symbol of this Mountain is the Hanged Man. He who fully realizes in himself this sacred symbol has gone to the end of the journey. Beyond this there is no way that can be seen or described.

# PART SIX

# The House of Death

# XXVII

## Death and Resurrection

Dawn, Easter Sunday, a moment of blending of traditions . . .
From the tradition called pagan came an echo of a sigh of relief.
The sun had returned. The pulse of life was growing stronger.
From the tradition called Christian came the story of death and
resurrection embodied in an ancient hymn.

> *Christ is risen from the dead.*
> *He has conquered death with death*
> *And given life to those that were in tombs.*

The members of the Church of the Earth, who had fasted
since the previous noon and spent the night in meditation,
stood on the leading edge of time, looking across the Valley of
the Moon to the wooded hills to the east. The air was still, ex-
pectant. Birds from various vantage points sang songs in praise
of the territorial imperative. The second-growth redwoods
brooded over the past when forest of enormous trees had covered the slopes, all long since cut down, victims to the white
man's greed. Over the State of California, on which the sun of
resurrection was about to rise, hung a tenuous film of pollutants.
Several million Easter bonnets waited for women, still asleep,
to display their finery in church. In older lands, half a world
away, peasants brought into their houses the fronds of young
trees to savor the promise of spring as the buds burst in the
warmth.

> *Christ is risen.*
> *He is risen indeed.*

As for the members of the Church of the Earth they stood on the hillside watching the eastern horizon while the multitudes in the man-swarms snored, oblivious of the sun. The city dwellers had never seen it rise and had no wish to do so. But the true Whole-Earthers had watched it often. It was indeed an ancient ceremony. Had not Akhenaten of Egypt composed his hymn to the sun centuries before Christianity?

> Beautiful is thine arising on the horizon of heaven
> O Aten, giver of life.

And the Hopi Indians on their mesas welcomed him daily. Who could be so dead in spirit as to fail to greet our father Sun as he rises and the darkness is dispersed?

The time, Pacific standard, was 6:10 A.M. There was a burst of radiance on a band of low clouds and there he was, Sol, the star of the show, slowly exposed by the rolling of the planet. The Whole-Earthers watched him. He glowed, pulsated, sang. His power was unbelievable. As his disc expanded, one could no longer look him in the eye. Who takes the trouble to watch the rising sun? Who feels the thrill of that moment when he first appears over the rolling edge of spaceship Earth? Of all these billions who depend on his light, who rises to honor him? A few poor Indians. A few Whole-Earthers on Easter Sunday.

Not that Sol cared. He was too far off, too vast and quite impersonal, sending his rays on the just and on the unjust, illuminating forest, field, ocean, and the city dump with equal power. He shone on the spinning earth as indifferently as he illuminated the other planets, the cloud-mantled Venus and airless Mars, the remote and frozen masses of Saturn and Jupiter. Though Sol was indeed the father of life on earth, providing with its energy every organism that moved, he was a distant, totally indifferent father whose huge outpourings radiated into space and were, for the most part, utterly wasted.

Meanwhile the planet rolled and the Whole-Earthers

watched from the hillside, dispersing later not to have breakfast (for the fast would continue till noon) but to work on the new building or in the garden. At noon they assembled to exchange eggs, symbols of fertility. They had painted the eggs in various ways, some traditional, some original. The cross, symbol of death, was largely absent. Easter was reverting to what it had been before the Christians borrowed it, a pagan festival, a celebration of renewal, of a new cycle of growth and birth and life.

There were only nine Whole-Earthers at that Easter ceremony. This was not the total membership of the core group. Six were away studying at the Academy, a center for the training of aspirants, courageous enough to follow the *Path of Accelerated Completion*. The Academy was in England, housed in one of those monstrous stately homes, which, like fossilized remains from a previous epoch, clutter the English countryside. This particular one had forty-four bedrooms and sixty thousand square feet of floor space. It was the scene of passionate activity, for the work was there led by the last Magus. He attracted the more romantic segment of American youth who had gone there in swarms, fixing up the stately home (the plumbing of which was inadequate as it usually is in stately homes), reestablishing the walled gardens (waist deep in nettles), digging a rose garden and unearthing in the process the bones of some monks (the place had formerly been a monastery).

Compared with the Academy, the Church of the Earth was a small show, a family affair. The Gardener preferred it that way. He was not in the same league with the last Magus and could not teach large numbers of students. Large groups tended to fall apart and the close teacher-pupil relationship could not be established. A Zen Roshi traditionally had no more than six. Even Jesus had only twelve, and one of those was a traitor.

Oh those traitors! The Gardener, peeling a painted egg, reflected on the saying of Jesus at the Last Supper. "And none of them have I lost save the son of perdition, that the scripture might be fulfilled." He himself could certainly make no such claim. He had lost almost everyone. The room was crowded with ghosts of those that started and had not continued. He had said many times that it was better not to begin than to start on the way and then stop. "If you want to sleep, sleep soundly. If you want to awaken, it will take all your strength, all your will. Halfhearted attempts are worse than useless. You merely spoil your sleep without getting any benefit."

But how could one tell who would persist, who would drop out? Even the disciples had gone to sleep at the critical moment in the garden of Gethsemane. Three times Jesus had awakened them but finally gave up the task. "Sleep on now and take your rest. Behold he is at hand that shall betray me."

A thankless task trying to awaken the sleepers. The Buddha, after the enlightenment at Bodh-gaya, had at first considered the task not worth undertaking.

*Of what use to reveal to men that which I have discovered at the price of laborious efforts? Why should I do so?*

*This doctrine cannot be understood by those filled with desire and hatred. It is mysterious, deep; hidden from the vulgar mind. If I proclaim it and men are unable to understand it, the only result will be fatigue and annoyance for me.*

And yet the Buddha had preached and Jesus had gone to his death to prove—what? That man could awaken? That he did not have to be a slave to his illusions, that he could know the truth and the truth would set him free? But all man's history had shown that he could not learn the lesson. He was powerless, as powerless now as ever before, doomed to die like a poisoned rat in a hole, killed by the products of his own technology.

Why then had Jesus, who was presumably an enlightened being, allowed himself to be crucified by a gang of frauds and fools who were obviously incapable of learning anything? Why should he choose to die for such miserable puppets? Why should he think that his death would make any difference?

"I would give a lot," said the Gardener, "to know what really happened on that first Easter."

The crucifixion of an obscure Galilean carpenter had turned into the most publicized execution in human history. For two thousand years all sorts of people had puzzled over the event, and still it made no sense, no sense at all. Was the whole thing planned in advance, a sort of grim psychodrama, performed with real scourges, real nails, real agony and death? But what did the drama accomplish? It brought to a premature end the teaching of the Master. It incited the lowest passions both in the Jewish leaders and in the mob. It showed up the disciples as a bunch of turncoats and cowards. It inflicted the cross on the Christian church, a disgusting and shameful symbol, an instrument of death. The only person who benefited by the performance was the robber Barabbas.

And what about all that nonsense about the rising from the tomb! How could anyone in his right senses suppose that a corpse, well and truly dead and buried and wrapped moreover in linen, could somehow walk out of the cave in which it had been laid? The whole event, apparently, rested on the word of Mary Magdalen, an obvious schizophrenic out of whom Jesus had driven seven devils. She had evidently hallucinated the whole scene. Yet this delusion of a mentally unbalanced woman had been accepted by millions of believers for twenty centuries. Accepted also was the equally fantastic notion that the reanimated corpse, powered by some mysterious device, took off for the stratosphere. Men had believed this so strongly that they would gladly roast alive any of their fellows who dared question the myth.

Credulity and suggestibility, into what absurdities can you lead your victims!

But behind the fantastic tales of empty sepulcher and airborne, revitalized corpses lay shadowy concepts that were harder to dismiss. There was, for example, the *tulpa* theory. It was suggested and quite seriously believed in some circles, that Jesus, as a high initiate, had the power to generate a phantom body. Such phantom bodies, known in Tibet as *tulpas*, could be materialized by any competent magician and could be given enough substance to appear real to those among whom they were projected. According to this theory, it was a phantom that was crucified and a phantom that later dispersed, leaving no trace behind. The real Jesus had withdrawn, his mission accomplished, and returned to the Brotherhood in Egypt from which he had been sent out in the first place to warn the Jews of dangers to come.

Another theory held that the whole crucifixion story had been part of a secret drama not performed in real life, part of a mystery play designed to teach the disciples some basic truths about death and resurrection. Such dramas played a part in many ancient mystery religions. It was a recurrent source of amazement to man that the dried-up, seemingly dead seed that he buried in the ground instead of rotting, as did a human corpse, mysteriously rose again in a different form and lived a new life. Was it not reasonable to suppose that that which could happen to a seed could happen to a man, that man could rise again, not in the body of flesh which demonstrably rotted in the earth, but in some sort of higher body? It was, however, part of the mystery teaching that man did not possess this higher body but that he had to create it by intentional efforts under the guidance of an initiate. All the true initiations, as well as the secret teachings of Jesus, related to the formation of this second body, which might indeed survive death because it existed outside space and outside time.

Well, it was every man's right to select for himself the myth by which he would regulate his life provided he did not do violence in the process to established physical and biological laws. The Christian myth of the revitalization of the corpse of Jesus and its subsequent ascent into the upper atmosphere did violence to both. But the theory of the second body was more subtle. It was the sort of guess an intelligent man might accept as a working hypothesis. It made the life game more interesting, added a new dimension. The Gardener, though a skeptic and a scoffer, had a weakness for the theory. He taught it to his fellow workers in the creative community, warning them, as he did so, that none could prove it except by actually generating the second body and in it entering the after-death state.

As for Easter, when one had disposed of the bunnies and the eggs (fertility symbols) and the revitalized corpses floating into the stratosphere (a schizophrenic's delusions), one was left with a mystery that made sense only if one accepted the two-body theory.

Or one could simply take Easter as a joy feast, a celebration of the return of light and warmth, a time for seed sowing in anticipation of future harvests. A seed, seemingly so dry and dead, was a mystery in itself. The seed was a baby plant, wrapped up with its lunch and put to sleep as if by an enchanter. It could sleep for years. Then at the touch of moisture it would revive and rise from the tomb and start life all over again. Surely a stupendous invention by great nature that had devised this form of suspended animation to enable plants to survive the winter's cold. As for man, he envied the seed, and strove to emulate it, even going so far as to have his corpse frozen in liquid nitrogen in the hope that in the future, a more advanced biology would find a way to thaw it and restore it to life. Cryogenics in the service of the resurrection!

Idle reflections! It mattered little what became of the body and equally little what became of the soul. How pleasant it was to turn from the tangled myths of the Christians to the secret teachings of the masters. And the secret was so simple. *There was no self.* The separate ego was an illusion, a product of the state of waking sleep. What was death? Death was waking sleep, the state of living in lies, believing in phantoms of which the personal ego was the most persistent. And what was resurrection? It was nothing other than awakening, the awakening which came to one who had realized his utter nothingness, the unimportance of all his hopes, his dreams, his fears. Such a one had gone beyond the beyond. He was troubled neither by fear of death nor by longings for rebirth. Already in life he had experienced the egoless state and realized that all component things are transient. Having reached this point he needed to go no further.

# XXVIII

## That Date with Death

Fellow Whole-Earthers!

Among the snags and pitfalls that occur on the Way is the Thanatos Catch, which runs more or less as follows:

Why make efforts when death takes all in the end?

This trap is quite tricky. It doesn't bother the Fool very much because he is too stupid to realize that he must die. The Fool lives in dreams. He is not aware of the inevitability of his own death.

But if a man begins to awaken, even a little, he begins to realize that he has only two possessions, a certain supply of energy renewed from day to day and a certain amount of time. He does not even know how much time he has. He may die tomorrow. This realization can easily bring a certain despondency. Why make efforts? Why struggle to attain higher states of consciousness? The inevitability of death makes all games seem futile. Even the Master Game.

This is the Thanatos Catch, also known as tripping over one's own skull.

How does one avoid it?

The first and most obvious method is to avail oneself of the limited claim to personal immortality available to us all. Hand on your genes. Have a child. To each man and each woman it is permitted, even in these days of the population explosion, to replace himself and herself. Why should I care about death?

I have children and now grandchildren. The play goes on. The genetic code has been transmitted.

> And nothing 'gainst Time's scythe can make defense
> Save breed, to brave him when he takes thee hence.

More is needed, however. The spiritual paralysis induced by the Thanatos Catch needs more than the sight of one's children to cure it. So the real solution has to be sought elsewhere. This solution is known and has been known for centuries. It was handed on in the initiation ceremonies of the mysteries of Orpheus, it was part of the inner religion of the Celts and the Egyptians, the early Christians knew it and the later Christians lost it. The Tibetans embodied it in the Chöd rite. It was described in the *Upanishads*, in *The Mathnawi*, and by the Yaqui *brujo* whom Castaneda calls don Juan and the wise old medicine man known to the West as C. G. Jung. When so many testify from so many cultures and centuries, who can doubt that their testimony is true?

It has to be.

So what is the secret? It is simple. Make friends with Death. He knows the answers.

Yes, Death knows the answers. The difficult part is to find him, to enter his kingdom, to make the descent into the underworld, to learn the secrets of death and then return. So Nachiketas descended, asking of Death the great question and insisting on an answer. He was only a boy but he knew what he wanted.

> Surely there is no other teacher like you, O Death.
>                                   KATHA UPANISHAD

So there is this descent to be made, this death before death. In the mandala of the Four Spirits, the triad to the north is Azrael's, the angel of death. This is the place of winter, the fourth house of the sun. This is the house of Death. To this house the traveler must find his way. It is no easy journey.

How does one travel?

We can get a tip from don Juan, the Yaqui *brujo*.

> *Death was nothing all the time. Nothing. It was a little dot lost in the sheets of your notebook. And yet it would enter inside you with uncontrollable force and extend you over the sky and earth and beyond. And you would be like a fog of tiny crystals moving, moving away.*
>
> *Death enters through the belly. . . . Right through the gap of the will. That area is the most important and sensitive part of man. It is the area of the will and also the area through which all of us die. I know it because my ally has guided me to that stage. A sorcerer tunes his will by letting his death overtake him, and when he is flat and begins to expand, his impeccable will takes over and assembles the fog into one person again.*
>
> CARLOS CASTANEDA, *A Separate Reality*

In short, a man of knowledge plays with his death. He and Death are friends. There is nothing in the least bit gloomy or morbid about it. Nor is it a stupid gamble, like Russian roulette. The warrior plays with Death because it is necessary. He must rid himself of fear and meet Death. Only in this way can he be liberated. And only in this way can he learn.

He can learn a great deal from Death because Death has control of the Archives. You have read of these Archives in *Journey to the East*. Hermann Hesse did not say that the Archives were controlled by Death. Perhaps he thought it unnecessary. It is nonetheless true that to enter the Archives one must pass through the house of Death. For the Archives are the record of the dead, of all those who have lived in a manner worthy of a warrior, and who were capable of dying an honorable death. These left a trace with which others can make contact. The trace is in the psychosphere and lies outside of time.

> *The soul, the anima, establishes the relationship to the unconscious. In a certain sense there is also a relationship to the collectivity of the dead; for the unconscious corresponds to the mythic land of the dead, the land of the ancestors. If, therefore, one has a fantasy of the soul vanishing, this means that it has withdrawn into the unconscious or into the land of the dead.*
>
> C. G. JUNG, *Memories, Dreams and Reflections*

This "loss of soul" which Jung describes may happen accidentally to certain people. The warrior, however, does not lose his soul by accident. He projects it intentionally into the realm of the dead.

To do this he must master an art sometimes called "astral projection," sometimes "out of the body experience," and use it to enter the house of Death. There are various ways of doing this. The most dramatic is the Red Feast, part of the Chöd Rite.

In the Red Feast the practitioner begins by projecting his will out of his body into that of a female deity (*vajra yogini*) armed with a sword. Remaining separated from his physical body he now, in his astral projection, hacks his body to pieces. The bowels gush out, blood flows in streams. A host of hungry ghouls, summoned by the officiant, swarm round and devour the body. The officiant, deep in meditation, watches his body being eaten.

All this shows the Tibetan liking for blood and guts, a taste which the Westerner may not share. But, if performed in the right surroundings, *chöd* can be quite a hair-raising experience even for one who has no faith in the existence of flesh-eating demons. Even an educated Westerner may be surprised at the shapes which emerge from the unconscious when this rite is performed in lonely places, mountains or deserts, far from human habitation. As for the Tibetans . . .

> *What strange visions must the sons of these haunted wilds behold, these novices brought up in superstition, sent by their spiritual fathers through the night all alone, their imagination excited by the maddening rites. How many times, in the storm sweeping across the high table lands, they must hear their challenge answered and shudder with terror in their tiny tent, miles and miles away from all human beings. I very well understood the fear experienced by some celebrants of* chöd.
>
> ALEXANDRA DAVID-NEEL, *Magic and Mystery in Tibet*

More effective, if less flamboyant, than the Red Feast is the Black Feast which is also a part of *chöd*. It involves a form of meditation which is quite widespread, being used throughout Buddhist countries and even by such groups as the Eskimo shamans. In this meditation the body is contemplated as if from the outside and seen to decay by a process akin to that which takes place after death.

The flesh decomposes, leaving only a heap of bones. Finally even the bones dissolve into dust.

One who watches in this way the disintegration of his physical vehicle will gradually become accustomed to the process of death and lose all fear of that process.

In all these exercises the difficulty lies in moving the center of consciousness out of the physical body and becoming aware of that body as if from outside. This power to move out, this "spirit walking," is an accomplishment that can be mastered by special effort. The first stage of the process involves placing the seat of consciousness in what the Japanese call the *hara*, which is a point two inches below the navel (or in some, two inches above) and corresponds to what don Juan calls the gap. It is from this point that man can send out a tendril or feeler, a certain line of force, somewhat like the lines of force of a magnetic field. This line or thread is described by all those who are endowed naturally with a capacity for what is called astral projection.

The projection takes place from the *hara* and may take a definite form, sometimes human, sometimes animal. The widespread belief that a sorcerer can change himself into an animal is based on this "materialization" of the second body. Carlos Castaneda, for example, was instructed by his teacher, don Juan, to project his second body in the form of a crow. This projection as a bird is common among shamans. Birds can fly, and one of the characteristics of this form of projection is rapid travel that *feels* like flight. The Tibetan yogi, Milarepa, describes the same phenomenon.

Once the power of projecting the second body has been attained, the student is in a position to enter the house of Death, if he can find it. Some danger exists of becoming lost in the world out there. During these journeyings the physical body sinks into a rather deep state of trance, breathing becomes hardly noticeable, temperature drops. There is an intentionally induced catalepsy. The second body is to some extent freed from the first. So one has freedom in this state to travel widely. But it is not easy to find the entrance to the house of Death and thus gain access to the Archives. One may just drift around like a leaf in the wind.

> *There is a place where the two worlds overlap. The crack is there. It opens and closes like a door in the wind. To get there a man must exercise his will. He must, I should say, develop an indomitable desire for it, a single-minded dedication. But he must do it without the help of any power or any man.*
>
> CARLOS CASTANEDA, *The Teachings of Don Juan*

You may ask, at this point, whether the psychedelic drugs which don Juan made use of, either the mixture he called the "little smoke" or the preparation of Datura, the devil's weed, can help a man on these journeys. The answer is, only if he knows what he is doing. The drugs can liberate in one who takes them certain energies, but he cannot direct those energies unless he has developed considerable power. Moreover, until he learns how to get back, he may need help.

> *I asked don Juan what he thought of the idea of giving the smoke to anyone who wanted the experience.*
> *He indignantly replied that to give the smoke to anyone would be just the same as killing him, for he would have no one to guide him. . . . He said I was there, alive and talking to him, because he had brought me back. He had restored my body. Without him I would never have awakened.*

The random, disorganized drug trips that people indulge in today are not likely to lead to anything much, and may damage the body, sometimes irreparably. Meaningful travels in the second body can be embarked on without drugs. It takes longer and is more difficult to do it this way, but it is more reliable and less dangerous. The drugs can be safely used only for specific purposes by one who knows what he is doing and why he is doing it, who has properly prepared himself beforehand and who has at hand one who knows how to bring him back in case he gets lost.

Understand clearly, he who has made these journeys, who has passed through the crack between the worlds, entered the house of Death, studied the Archives, he alone has accomplished his task. He alone is an initiate, a Man of Knowledge. No one, nothing, can take this knowledge from him. He has attained a different level of being. He has died and returned. Now he hears at all times the waves of the world, waves that

268 THE HOUSE OF DEATH

are alternating phases of life and death. The wave of life reaches its crest, breaks, sweeps up the beach, returns whence it came, vanishes into the ocean. Every life is such a wave. Our own is no exception. One who has been in the house of Death knows the wave of his own life, can feel it crest and break, sweep up the beach and vanish. There is nothing to fear. Nothing to lament about. Out of the ocean it arose and back into the ocean it returns. The separate self vanishes, reabsorbed into the whole.

> *I died a mineral and became a plant.*
> *I died a plant and rose an animal.*
> *I died an animal and I was a man.*
> *Why should I fear? When was I less by dying?*
> *Yet once more I shall die as man, to soar*
> *with blessed angels; even from angelhood*
> *I must pass on. All except God perishes.*
> *When I have sacrificed my angel soul,*
> *I shall become that which no mind conceived.*
> *O, let me not exist! for nonexistence*
> *Proclaims: "To Him we shall return."*
> RUMI: *The Mathnawi*

So how does he die who has reached this realization?

He dies as he has lived, intentionally and with awareness. He knows when his time has come. He journeys to the crack between the worlds, a journey he has made many times before and from which he has always returned to his first body. Only this time he does not return.

# XXIX

## _Alfie the Toff_

Alfie the Toff was a cat. He was born, one of a litter of four, under the old part of the Gardener's house, the part which had gaps in its foundations under which mother cats could raise families in comparative safety. The cats on the mountain were mostly feral. Their population fluctuated wildly. One year the mountain would be crawling with cats. The next it would be practically catless. Periodic plagues decimated the cat population, as no doubt they decimated all the other wild animal populations on the mountain. Skunks, squirrels, coons, robins, bluejays all fluctuated in numbers. Only the deer seemed able to hold their numbers steady. Indeed they seemed to grow more and more numerous.

As for Alfie, he was sole survivor of the litter. One kitten died of unknown causes. Alfie's two sisters were discreetly disposed of to avert a local population explosion. Alfie became part of the family.

He was an aristocratic marmalade cat with a white shirt front that he kept meticulously clean. In his young days he hunted moles, gophers, and birds, but later, finding himself in the position of a gentleman of leisure, he gave up the chase for the pleasures of contemplation. He was gentle to the point of cowardice. Never did he fight with stray cats that wandered into his territory. Challenged by such a one he would quietly retire. At the sight of a dog he would climb the nearest tree.

He was something of a gourmet. He disdained the highly

advertised products of the pet food industry. The heads and backbones of the fish which the Gardener caught were carefully steamed, the flesh removed from the bones and served to Alfie with the stock, a sort of bouillabaisse. He enjoyed a dish of green beans and was especially partial to fresh corn on the cob. He would hold down the cob with one paw while delicately extracting the kernels with his teeth, then sit and clean his shirt front which had become somewhat beslobbered by this manner of feeding.

He became, in middle life, a pampered cat, a fat cat. At times the pleasure of eating seemed to dominate his life. One Christmas when the family sacrificed the principles of true Whole-Earthers and indulged in a store-bought turkey, it became a matter of scientific interest to the Gardener to see if Alfie would ever stop eating. No doubt about it, turkey was ambrosia to Alfie. He stuffed and stuffed, gulping the greasy morsels, reveling in the dripping. He grew so fat that winter that he resembled a Shmoo. He devoted his time entirely to sleeping and eating.

But in February, when the pussywillow flowered, he was out and around, working off his fat in an orgy of sexual activity. All the cats on the mountain were fucking simultaneously and the woods resounded at night with yowps and yowls. Alfie was up all night seeking a mate with plaintive cries. His winter-accumulated fat melted from his bones. He became first slender, then thin. Then he caught distemper, despite inoculations, and became downright skinny. Then a tick was carelessly removed from his ear and the head burrowed in, producing a pus-filled swelling. Alfie made his second visit to the vet and was operated on without anesthetic. He healed nicely.

He was still really in the prime of life when the great plague struck. It was not distemper this time but a virulent form of cat dysentery. Alfie's bowels turned to water. He was taken to the vet, kept there for seven days in the cat hospital, obviously miserable, dosed on antibiotics. Back home he seemed to improve for a while but then became ill again. There was agitation on the part of the family to take him back to the vet but the Gardener vetoed the move.

"Leave Alfie in peace."

The Gardener had a loathing for hospitals and a deep distrust for the medical profession. It extended even to veterinarians. If Alfie the Toff was going to die, let him die in the surroundings he knew instead of in exile, caged in an animal hospital.

It gradually became apparent that Alfie really was dying. He was offered the tastiest morsels, raw ground beef, fresh fish, liver. He could not seem to digest anything. He lay in the sun up in the vineyard meditating. His once immaculate shirt front was stained and matted with burrs. His lusterless coat sagged over his bones. He was too weak or too indifferent to groom himself.

But he died with dignity and without complaints. The Gardener, watching him, marveled at his calm. Hemingway, in one of his war novels, had said, concerning the death of soldiers, "They died like animals," implying that this was a sorry way to die. But the Gardener, watching the dying Alfie, reflected that animals know how to die very well. It was the humans who had lost the art. Moaning and fussing, hemmed in by nurses, doctors, intravenous drips, oxygen tents, pathetically clinging to a worn-out body, they made a miserable spectacle. Alfie the Toff, philosophically resting beneath the vine, his paws tucked under him, enjoying his last few days in the sun, was a far nobler beast than those lamentable humans. He was, in fact, so considerate and thoughtful that, right at the end, when almost too weak to walk, he set off somewhere or other and died quite alone, thus sparing the family some grief and the labor of burying his emaciated corpse, for, though they searched, they never found his body.

"A worthy beast," said the Gardener. "Alfie has given us a lesson in the art of dying."

So impressed was he by Alfie's example that he began forthwith to draft his Declaration of the Right to a Dignified Death. He had planned his death well in advance. His well-worn, battered kayak would serve as his coffin. In it he would make his last voyage as had William Willis in his tiny boat *The Little One*. They had found *The Little One* tossing on the Atlantic with Willis's passport on board but no Willis. William Willis had known how to die.

But the last voyage was still a long way off. The Gardener, who had seen a projection of his own life while in a trance, knew that, barring accidents, he would remain in his present planetary body until it was eighty-six years old, which meant he would make his last voyage in the year 1999. Eighty-six was no great age. A properly cared-for, yogically disciplined body would last that long or longer in perfectly good shape. One could easily live to be a hundred if one so willed, but eighty-six was enough. By that time he would have seen as much of the show as one wanted.

There was, however, always the possibility of an accident, an accident which could result in one's being incarcerated in one of those dreary human repair shops where professional fixit men take perverse pride in what they call "cheating death" without any regard for the wishes of those whose death they are cheating.

So the Gardener wrote his name and his address on a clean sheet of paper and assured all those who might be concerned that he was of sound mind.

"Let those who may be concerned understand this. I have now lived for nearly sixty years. My affairs are in order. My children are grown. My debts are paid. My sole desire now is to keep my independence, which includes the right to die without being pestered by doctors and nurses, however well intentioned.

"I therefore state that, should I suffer from some physical accident or impairment expected to render me incapable of independent existence, I decline to receive any treatment or sustenance designed to prolong my life. If I am in great pain I would appreciate receiving such drugs as are needed to relieve it. If I am no longer in control of my physical vehicle, permit me at least a quiet exit and do not spend time and money in trying to repair a worn-out machine which its owner no longer needs.

"Thank you."

# APPENDIX

# Helpful Hints on Building
# a Rural Community

The building of a creative community calls for two things, a matrix and leadership. A matrix can be provided by some sort of religious belief or by some aim held in common by members of the community. Essentially the matrix provides members of the community with a game worth playing. It has to be some creative game or the community will not hold together. One could hardly form a community to play the Fame Game or the Money Game. Both are essentially selfish games and cannot form a basis for communal activities.

The Church of the Earth matrix is naturally rural. It involves tending the earth, sowing, harvesting, weeding, composting shit, watching things grow, gathering food from the ocean, listening to the rain and the wind, loving the sun, the giver of life. There are dozens of rural communes in the United States, some stable, some short-lived. Whether they are stable or short-lived depends on the practicality of those who run them, the quality of leadership, and the amount of soul-glue. Soul-glue is the mysterious stuff that holds people together, opposing the fission force that sends them spinning off in opposite directions. This the *kali juga*, the age of betrayal. Husbands betray wives, wives husbands, both betray the children. Nothing is sacred, not even the bond that holds man to the land, though his very life depends on the bond. So members of a commune must know how to generate soul-glue or the whole enterprise will fragment, shattered by the divisive spirit of the age.

This appendix offers a few practical suggestions to groups

whose members want to play their life game in the matrix of a rural community. More detailed information will be offered in a forthcoming book: *Echo-Tech: The Whole-Earther's Guide to the Alternate Society.*

*Land.* A small plot of fertile land is better than a large plot of infertile land. A really fertile two-acre garden can provide most of the food requirements of a group of ten (five couples with children) as far as vegetables are concerned. One can even afford to use part of it for a small crop of wheat (about 100 by 100 feet). If you want to estimate the fertility of a piece of ground, look at the weeds. If the weeds grow well, the crops will grow well. If you are forced to buy poor soil, then build it up, a small area a time, by growing legume cover crops and plowing them under and adding all the compost and manure you can get. It takes four to five years to build up poor land in this way. Hilly land will present problems with soil erosion, bottom land problems with drainage and flooding. In dry areas (the southwest) the *quality* of water may be as important as the quantity of water. Some water is so heavily loaded with alkali as to be worthless for irrigation.

*Plants.* Food plants can be divided into groups. The full providers are those that offer a complete fuel for the man-machine. Because protein is essential both for growth and maintenance the protein producers should be given a place of honor. These are the members of the legume family, both peas and beans. Maize and wheat are protein plants but they also contain much starch. The vegetable proteins tend to be low in the amino acid lysine. Special high lysine strains of maize are now available.

The starch providers, potatoes, squash, carrots, onions, offer bulk, a good source of energy and, in the case of carrots and yellow squash, a source of carotene, precursor of vitamin A. They are not complete foods but are good supplements.

The leafy vegetables, chard, cabbage, lettuce, spinach, etc., are excellent sources of vitamins and various minerals if cooked in a minimum of water. Chard deserves special praise, being easy to grow, drought-resistant, and prolific. A chard patch can be cut again and again. When too tough for the humans it can be fed to the goats.

Of fruits the easiest to grow and store are apples. If properly cultivated, pruned, and fed, the trees can be kept relatively disease-free without spraying.

*Animals.* If you want milk, your best friend may be the goat. It is hardier than the cow and less expensive. Two Saanans here provide all the milk needed by three families. Chickens and rabbits are not worth raising if you have to buy food for them. Let them run around and find their own.

Fish can be raised in ponds. This form of aquaculture has been practiced for centuries in China, using carp. It is also possible to culture catfish. The pond has to be kept at a certain level of fertility as does the soil, for the starting point of the food chain is always the plant.

Any commune within easy reach of the ocean should avail itself of this source of animal protein. In 1971 the two fishermen in this group harvested a total of 1,052 pounds of fish from the rocky reefs off the coast in addition to quantities of mussels, the supply of which is virtually unlimited (save only during the winter months in California). Clams, abalone, and edible seaweed are also available. (On this subject see Euell Gibbons' *Stalking the Blue-Eyed Scallop.*)

If you have pasture, it makes sense to convert grass into animal protein. Again it make more sense to cultivate and improve a small acreage of pasture than have the animals work themselves to the bone searching for a few dry stalks in a square mile of wilderness. Pasture improvement is almost always possible by plowing natural pastures and reseeding with an appropriate mixture of grass and clover.

Remember, birds and beasts are a bond. They must be fed, watered, cows milked, eggs collected. Fish, however, can take care of themselves, and one who does not wish to be tied down, yet craves animal protein, should consider the fishpond if he cannot reach the ocean.

*Money.* If you don't intend to emulate Robinson Crusoe you will need money. Land taxes, mortgage payments, cars, appliances, doctor's bills, dentist's bills—they can be escaped only by finding a desert island. If you can find such an island and some people to share it with you and if you can include in the group a doctor and a dentist, you might manage without money. The Pitcairn Islanders seem to have done it. Otherwise, of course, someone must go out and get a job or the members of the commune must make something they can sell. How to handle the money? Shall it all be pooled and used as needed? The Bruderhof has adopted this method. It works for them. Synanon likewise.

If all monies are pooled, there will be problems. Some tend to take without giving, others to give without taking. In the end the group either develops a collective conscience and throws out the freeloaders or a leader emerges strong enough to halt the abuses. Functioning as a leader of a commune is certainly a thankless task, but unless a leader does emerge, the strains developed over money, sex, and work are likely to cause a breakdown of the group. Freeloaders, those who take without giving, are the curse of all communes and until they are thrown out no really creative work is possible.